Tea

by Lisa McDonald and Jill Rheinheimer

for **dummies**®
A Wiley Brand

Tea For Dummies®

Published by: **John Wiley & Sons, Inc.,** 111 River Street, Hoboken, NJ 07030-5774, www.wiley.com

Copyright © 2023 by John Wiley & Sons, Inc., Hoboken, New Jersey

Media and software compilation copyright © 2023 by John Wiley & Sons, Inc. All rights reserved.

Published simultaneously in Canada

For general information on our other products and services, please contact our Customer Care Department within the U.S. at 877-762-2974, outside the U.S. at 317-572-3993, or fax 317-572-4002. For technical support, please visit https://hub.wiley.com/community/support/dummies.

Wiley publishes in a variety of print and electronic formats and by print-on-demand. Some material included with standard print versions of this book may not be included in e-books or in print-on-demand. If this book refers to media such as a CD or DVD that is not included in the version you purchased, you may download this material at http://booksupport.wiley.com. For more information about Wiley products, visit www.wiley.com.

Library of Congress Control Number: 2023930241

ISBN 978-1-119-98625-6 (pbk); ISBN 978-1-119-98627-0 (ebk); ISBN 978-1-119-98626-3 (ebk)

SKY10043541_022323

Contents at a Glance

Introduction 1

Part 1: Getting Started with Tea 5
CHAPTER 1: It's Time for Tea 7
CHAPTER 2: Tea for You, Tea for Me 13
CHAPTER 3: From Garden to Cup 25

Part 2: Talking about Different Types of Tea 39
CHAPTER 4: Black Tea 41
CHAPTER 5: Green Tea 53
CHAPTER 6: Oolong (Wulong) Tea 63
CHAPTER 7: White Tea 69
CHAPTER 8: Other Teas 75
CHAPTER 9: Herbal Teas 83
CHAPTER 10: Drinking Tea Like an Expert 91

Part 3: Getting Curious about Caffeine 113
CHAPTER 11: Caffeine: Tempest in a Teacup? 115
CHAPTER 12: Less Is Not Always More — Decaffeinated Tea 133

Part 4: Spilling the Tea about Health Benefits 139
CHAPTER 13: Tea and Its Powerful Antioxidants 141
CHAPTER 14: Investigating the Health Benefits of Tea 149
CHAPTER 15: Investigating the Health Benefits of Herbal Tea 167

Part 5: My Cup of Tea — Around the World 183
CHAPTER 16: Exploring Tea-Producing Regions of the World 185
CHAPTER 17: Embracing Age-Old Traditions and Ceremonies 195
CHAPTER 18: Insight into the Tea Industry 207

Part 6: Let's Have Tea — In the Kitchen, at the Bar 217
CHAPTER 19: Cooking and Baking with Tea 219
CHAPTER 20: Tea and Food Pairing 249
CHAPTER 21: Tea Mixology 257

Part 7: The Part of Tens...................................285
CHAPTER 22: Ten Plus Things to Do with Tea That You Don't Like..............287
CHAPTER 23: More Than Ten Myths about Tea...............................291

Glossary..297

Index...305

Table of Contents

INTRODUCTION 1

About This Book... 1

Foolish Assumptions... 2

Icons Used in This Book 3

Beyond the Book.. 3

Where to Go from Here 3

PART 1: GETTING STARTED WITH TEA 5

CHAPTER 1: **It's Time for Tea** 7

Understanding the Popularity of Tea 8

Meeting tea drinkers the world over 8

Seeing why tea is so popular 8

Discovering some benefits of tea 9

Begin Your Tea Journey Here.................................... 9

Tea knows no age 9

Teas to try first... 10

Where to buy your tea 11

How much tea to buy 12

Storing your tea leaves...................................... 12

CHAPTER 2: **Tea for You, Tea for Me** 13

Brewing the Perfect Cup of Tea................................ 14

Basic equipment 14

Making a cup of hot tea!.................................... 16

Making iced tea 22

One Lump or Two: Discovering Other Ways to Enjoy Tea.......... 23

Milk and Sugar 23

Lemon... 23

Tea Lattes 24

Carbonated.. 24

Trends and Fads 24

CHAPTER 3: **From Garden to Cup**............................. 25

The Tea Plant, Where It All Begins 25

Varieties 26

Environment, or terroir..................................... 27

Gardens.. 27

Harvesting... 29

Discovering How Leaves Become Tea 30
   Processing steps 30
   Types of tea produced 32
The Often-Confusing Terminology of Tea 33
   The "orange" of orange pekoe. 33
   Orthodox versus CTC 34
   SFTGFOP 35
   The flush 35
   Sparrow beak. 36
   Single estate 36
Understanding How Teas Are Flavored 36
   Blending 36
   Oils and extracts 37
   Scented teas. 38

PART 2: TALKING ABOUT DIFFERENT TYPES OF TEA 39

CHAPTER 4: **Black Tea** 41
Taking a Closer Look at Black Tea. 41
   Considering the tea varieties. 41
   How black tea is made 42
   Flavor profiles of black tea. 42
Searching Far and Wide for Black Tea 43
   China 43
   India. 46
   Sri Lanka: Ceylon tea. 47
   Japan 48
   Wild-grown 48
   Classic blends. 48

CHAPTER 5: **Green Tea** 53
Taking a Closer Look at Green Tea. 53
   How green tea is made. 54
   Flavor profiles of green tea 54
   The difference between Chinese and Japanese green teas 55
Looking at Chinese Green Teas. 55
   Biluochun (green snail, bi lo chun, Dongting biluochun). 55
   Gunpowder. 56
   Huangshan maofeng (Yellow Mountain fur peak) 57
   Jasmine and other scented teas 57
   Lung ching (dragon well, long jing) 57
   Palace needle (ocean green needle). 57

Discovering Japanese Green Teas. 58
    Bancha 58
    Genmaicha and matcha genmaicha. 58
    Gyokuro (jade dew). 58
    Hojicha (houjicha) 59
    Kamairicha (tamaryokucha). 60
    Kukicha (twig tea, stem tea) 60
    Matcha and tencha 60
    Sencha and Kabusecha. 62
Finding Green Teas from Other Countries 62

CHAPTER 6: **Oolong (Wulong) Tea**. 63
Taking a Closer Look at Oolong Tea 63
    How oolong tea is made. 64
    Flavor profiles of oolong tea 65
Discovering the Varieties of Oolong Teas 66
    Dan cong (guangdong, phoenix). .66
    Dong ding (tung ting) 66
    Dongfang meiren (oriental beauty). 66
    High mountain. 67
    Jun chiyabari. 67
    Taifu. 68
    Tieguanyin (iron goddess of mercy, iron Buddha, ti kuan yin) 68
    Wuyi rock tea (da hong pao) 68

CHAPTER 7: **White Tea** 69
Taking a Closer Look at White Tea 69
    How white tea is made. 69
    Flavor profiles of white tea. 70
Discovering the Different White Teas. 71
    China 71
    Other white tea producers. 72

CHAPTER 8: **Other Teas** 75
Exploring Fermented Teas. 75
    Pu-erh tea. 75
    Yellow tea 77
Getting Chilly with Frost and Frozen Teas 78
    Nilgiri frost tea. 78
    Frozen black tea. 78
Discovering Additional Rarities 79
    GABA teas. 79
    Milk or milky oolong 80

Old tree bancha 80
Flowering or blooming tea 80
Purple tea 81

CHAPTER 9: **Herbal Teas** 83
Why Are Herbal Teas Called "Tea" When They're Not Tea? 83
Herbal Does Not Mean Caffeine Free 84
Guayusa 84
Guarana 84
Mate (yerba mate, maté) 84
Herbal Teas That Won't Keep You Up at Night 85
Rooibos 85
Honeybush (mountain tea, cape tea) 85
Fruit teas 86
Ayurvedic teas 86
All the rest 87

CHAPTER 10: **Drinking Tea Like an Expert** 91
Tasting — By the Experts 92
Tea professionals 92
Words the experts use 93
How experts taste tea 94
Tasting — And Figuring Out How to Describe What You Taste 97
It's simple: Look, smell, and taste 98
Coming up with the (right?) words 98
Accessories: Going Down the Rabbit Hole 100
So, you want to buy a teapot 100
And maybe some teacups 105
Other convenient accessories 108

PART 3: GETTING CURIOUS ABOUT CAFFEINE 113

CHAPTER 11: **Caffeine: Tempest in a Teacup?** 115
The Ins and Outs (or Ups and Downs) of Caffeine 116
Caffeine, a Stone Age drug? 116
What caffeine is 116
How caffeine works 117
The benefits of caffeine 118
The drawbacks of caffeine 119
The Magic of Caffeine plus L-theanine, the Calming Factor 121
Determining How Much Caffeine Is in Your Cup (Hint: It's
Complicated) 122
First, the tea plant itself 122
Second, how the tea is processed 123

Third, the caffeine-to-theanine ratio. 123
Fourth, how you brew and drink your tea .124
Misconceptions and Myths about Caffeine in Tea 126
Caffeine is bad for you 126
You can avoid the caffeine by throwing out the
first steep or "washing out" the caffeine 128
Caffeine is separate from flavor 129
Certain teas have less caffeine than other teas 130

CHAPTER 12: **Less Is Not Always More — Decaffeinated Tea** 133
Removing Caffeine from Tea Leaves 134
Decaffeinating methods 134
Putting the caffeine to other uses. 136
The Problems with Decaffeinating Tea 136
Degradation of tea leaves 136
Cost 137
Demand 138
Decaffeinated does not mean caffeine free 138

**PART 4: SPILLING THE TEA ABOUT
HEALTH BENEFITS** 139

CHAPTER 13: **Tea and Its Powerful Antioxidants** 141
Polyphenols and Why They Matter. 142
Green Tea and Its Polyphenols 143
Black Tea, with Polyphenol Conversion 144
The Best Tea to Drink 146
The benefits of green tea 146
The benefits of black tea 146
Does it matter which tea you drink? 147

CHAPTER 14: **Investigating the Health Benefits of Tea** 149
Seeking the Truth behind Health Claims .150
Health benefits versus health claims 150
The reliability of the research 152
Real-world applications versus observational and
laboratory studies 153
Looking at the Potential Role of Tea in Illness and Disease 156
Disease 157
Immune system and infection. 160
Neurological 160
Pain 161
Topical treatment 161
Weight control 162

Aging Well, with a Nod to Tea 162
    Cognition and dementia..163
    Motor function and muscle strength 163
    Life span 164
Stay Calm and Drink Tea: Relieving Stress.....................164
Tea for Two: Enhancing Your Social Life 166

**CHAPTER 15: Investigating the Health Benefits
of Herbal Tea** 167
Seeking the Truth behind Health Claims 168
    Health benefits versus health claims 168
    The reliability of the research 169
    Real-world applications versus observational
    and laboratory studies 170
    Bioavailability complicates things 171
Evaluating Common Herbal Teas 172
    Some that show promise 172
    The jury is still out 177
    The many misconceptions around turmeric...........180
    The problem with claims about herbal blends 181
But if It Works for You, Then It Works 182

PART 5: MY CUP OF TEA — AROUND THE WORLD........183

CHAPTER 16: Exploring Tea-Producing Regions of the World....185
Looking at Where Tea Is Grown 185
Asia 187
    China...187
    India..188
    Indonesia 189
    Japan 189
    Nepal 190
    South Korea 191
    Sri Lanka 191
    Taiwan..191
    Turkey 192
    Vietnam..192
Europe..192
Africa 193
South Pacific...193
The Americas 193
    United States 194
    South America 194

CHAPTER 17: **Embracing Age-Old Traditions and Ceremonies** 195

    Heading to China, Where It All Began.........................196
        Tea ceremony...196
        The gaiwan 197
    Investigating India 198
    Examining Tea Traditions Around the World 199
        Japan 199
        Korea...199
        Britain (and the art of having tea)...................200
        The Himalayas 202
        Morocco 202
        Germany..202
        Ireland...203
        Turkey 203
        Russia 204
        United States 204
        South America 205

CHAPTER 18: **Insight into the Tea Industry** 207

    Looking at the Lives of Tea Workers..........................208
        Living and working conditions/wages 208
        The dangers of chemical exposure....................209
    Reviewing Tea Certifications 210
    Looking at Tea Purity and Quality.............................211
        Purity...211
        Quality...212
    Developing New Cultivars 212
    Fingerprinting Tea...213
    Traveling from the Garden to You 213
    Noting the Environmental Impact of Tea.....................213
        Repurposing spent tea leaves 214
        Impact of climate change............................214
    Contemplating the Future of Tea 215

PART 6: LET'S HAVE TEA — IN THE KITCHEN, AT THE BAR..217

CHAPTER 19: **Cooking and Baking with Tea** 219

    Tea as a Spice..219
    Tea as a Dry Ingredient...220
    Tea as an Infusion 221

Recipes: Snacks 223
Recipes: Mains 226
Recipes: Sides. 235
Recipes: Desserts. 243

CHAPTER 20: **Tea and Food Pairing** 249
Noting the Similarities to Wine 249
Getting Scientific: How Our Senses Come into Play. 250
Using a tasting wheel 250
Thinking about the tongue. 252
Perfectly Pairing Tea with Food. 254
Matching tea with different foods. .254
Putting together a menu 255

CHAPTER 21: **Tea Mixology** 257
Deconstructing Cocktails 259
Essential cocktail ingredients. 259
Extraction chemistry 260
Putting Tea into Cocktails. 262
Choosing the method 262
Types of tea infusions 264
Recipes for Tea Syrups, Infusions, Tinctures, and Bitters 265
Tea Cocktail Recipes 277

PART 7: THE PART OF TENS 285

CHAPTER 22: **Ten Plus Things to Do with Tea That You Don't Like** 287
Try to Brew It Differently 287
Embellish It. 288
Chill It. 288
Combine It with Something Else 288
Combine It with Something Alcoholic. 288
Use It as a Spice 289
Get Crafty with It 289
Put It to Work Around the House 289
Put It to Work for You 290
Offer It on Social Media 290
Gift It 290

CHAPTER 23: **More Than Ten Myths about Tea** 291

　　　Price Equals Quality 291

　　　Rinse the Tea Leaves 292

　　　You Can Wash Caffeine Out 292

　　　Tea Has More Caffeine than Coffee 293

　　　Never Rinse the Teapot 293

　　　Experts Always Know What They're Tasting 293

　　　Green Tea Is the Healthiest 293

　　　Earl Grey Origin Story 294

　　　Tea Is Bitter 294

　　　Tea Expires 295

　　　Pinky Should Be Raised 295

　　　The Brits Drink the Most Tea 296

GLOSSARY 297

INDEX 305

Introduction

The second-most consumed beverage in the world is tea. That's right, tea! Only water is consumed more, yet you probably don't know a lot about this amazing beverage. For most of us, tea is something that we order at a restaurant, grab in a can or bottle, drink at a fancy hotel, or maybe make at home for ourselves and friends.

However, in some cultures, tea is a livelihood and has been an integral part of daily life for hundreds of years. Tea is as nuanced as wine — if not more so — due to leaf variety, production methods, brewing, and serving styles.

The world of tea can be overwhelming with talk about which flush a tea is, or whether it is high-grown or low-grown, or even whether it is a green, black, white, oolong, or other type of tea. Every day, new varieties of the tea plant are cultivated and new production methods are developed, but, in the end, it all starts with one leaf from one plant — the *Camellia sinensis*.

Some "tea snobs" will judge your tea selection, brewing methodologies, whether you add milk or sugar, and even your water source and type of cup you are using — but tea needn't be so intimidating. It is actually as simple as finding what you like the most and making it the way you prefer it.

About This Book

Tea For Dummies covers all things tea — from garden to cup. Tea has been the center of trade, culture, and even politics for centuries and is still evolving to fit into our ever-changing world. We explore many of these aspects, including the following:

>> **Your many tea options.** When writing about tea, we are primarily referring to the *Camellia sinensis* plant, which is used to produce black, green, oolong, white, and a few other teas. However, we also help you gain more insight into the world of herbal teas.

>> **Brewing the perfect cup of tea.** With our step-by-step guide, your next cup of tea will be brewed to perfection!

>> **Caffeine.** It seems like everyone has an opinion about it. We explore its benefits, how it works with tea's unique amino acid L-theanine to your advantage, and why it's impossible to figure out just how much is in your teacup.

>> **Health benefits.** Tea's potential for our health is incredible, but where does the science stand? We review the research for both tea and herbal teas and disentangle health claims from demonstrated health benefits.

>> **Tea around the world.** We take you to the major tea-producing countries, and we highlight some of the rich traditions that have developed around tea. In addition, we examine the tea industry and consider the future of tea.

>> **Tea as an ingredient.** Dive even deeper into tea by learning how to use it in your cocktails, cooking, and baking. We supply both general guidelines and plenty of recipes.

In this book, we want to share our knowledge to help you better understand and appreciate our favorite beverage. Most importantly, we hope to guide you in your tea journey as we follow that single leaf, grown and picked far from your home, to the perfectly brewed cup you hold in your hands — and teach you about everything in-between.

Foolish Assumptions

We assume that you're exploring this book for one or more of these reasons:

>> You don't know much about tea, but you are thirsting to learn.

>> You want to learn how to select teas that you will like and then perfectly brew them.

>> You do know something about tea, perhaps more than most people, but you want to build upon that knowledge and immerse yourself in the world of tea.

>> You know a lot about tea, but you want to continue on your tea journey because you know that tea exploration never ends — there is always more to learn and oh-so-many teas to try!

Icons Used in This Book

The pictures in the margins of this book are called icons, and they point out different types of information.

TIP

This icon points out tidbits of insight or advice that will enhance your tea experience.

REMEMBER

We mark the important info with this symbol, the things that we want you to keep in mind as you explore tea. In fact, you can read *only* these sections, and you'll be good — although we hope that you read the rest of the book as well!

TECHNICAL STUFF

Science-y stuff is part of tea. However, if the more technical aspects aren't *your* cup of tea, you can safely skip paragraphs marked with this icon. You can always go back and read them later. Or not. You may want to just get down to brewing your favorite leaves.

WARNING

Occasionally, we use this symbol to alert you to potential hazards. It doesn't appear very often because having a cup of tea isn't considered high-risk, unless you drink it scalding hot, perhaps. In which case, we'd also add a tip, such as suggesting you let it cool down a bit.

Beyond the Book

For a handy reference guide, see our online Cheat Sheet. To access it, search for "Tea for Dummies Cheat Sheet" at www.dummies.com. This guide gives you some basics about tea and how to brew it. It also provides a few fun facts that you can share with your friends at your next tea party, as well as some tips on how to use tea as more than just a drink.

Where to Go from Here

This book is arranged so that you can quickly and easily find exactly what you're looking for. The tea world is enormous, so this reference guide will help you navigate its complexities with ease.

If you're new to tea, we suggest you start at Chapter 1 for an overview and to learn why tea is so valued. However, if you want to jump right in and begin brewing your loose leaves, go directly to Chapter 2. For a closer look at the various kinds of tea available, turn to Part 2.

When you're ready for a deeper dive into the tea world, peruse Parts 3 through 5. Whether you're interested in the science behind caffeine and tea's health benefits, want to explore global tea traditions, or have questions about the tea industry, there are chapters for you. And, to expand your culinary and mixology skills, check out Part 6, where you'll find general guidelines and information plus lots of terrific recipes.

Let's get brewing!

1

Getting Started with Tea

Figure out which teas to try first and then pick up a few tips on where to buy your tea, how much to buy, and how to keep it fresh.

Uncover the essentials to brewing the perfect cup of tea, including equipment, brewing steps, and your water.

Find out about the tea plant and learn how those leaves become tea. Decipher tea terminology, which can be confusing and even off-putting. Also, explore the many ways that tea can be flavored.

Chapter **1**

It's Time for Tea

Did you know that tea is the second-most consumed beverage in the world? Most think of coffee or even beer before tea, but they are wrong. Tea is second only to water.

Throughout history, tea has played an important role in politics, economics, and society. Whether picked up in a gas station cooler or sipped in a fancy tearoom with friends, this drink's steeped in complexity. So, let's take a closer look at what has become one of the fastest-growing industries as well as the second-most popular drink around the globe.

In this chapter, we consider just what makes tea so enduring and loved. Is it just its flavor, or is there more to it? We briefly look at the benefits of drinking tea, and then we head into a few practical issues to get you started on your journey into the world of tea. About a gazillion teas are out there, but we offer some recommendations for where to begin, and then we supply a handy guide for how many cups of tea you can expect out of a bag of leaves. Finally, we offer a few tips on how to best store your leaves. Oh, and we do want to welcome you to the communi-tea!

Understanding the Popularity of Tea

It is safe to say that nations were built and economies were structured on tea. Today, nearly 4 *billion* cups of tea are enjoyed every day! That's more than 165 *million* cups an *hour*! Imagine how many leaves are picked daily to bring you this amazing elixir.

Meeting tea drinkers the world over

In the United States, tea is mostly consumed cold and quickly, but it is still an important part of our culture. Whether at a backyard barbeque, given to us for a sore throat or upset tummy, or served at a fancy tea party, we all have had a cup at some point in our lives — for some of us, multiple cups a day.

In many places in the world, tea is so woven into the culture that businesses and homes must welcome you with a cup of tea, while in other countries serving tea is a ceremony with deep traditions and meanings. People on every continent have made tea their own.

So, whether you're guzzling a refreshing iced tea while driving to your kid's soccer game, or someone across the ocean is getting all dressed up for a special tea party, or another person is attending a traditional tea ceremony, we are all enjoying the same drink.

Seeing why tea is so popular

Just why is tea so popular? For one, the world of tea is incredibly diverse. Although "tea" may conjure up an iced black tea, you can find tea to suit any taste. Bold or subtle, toasty or vegetal, bitter or sweet, smoky, fruity, floral, simple or complex, you get the picture. Some teas explode with flavor when iced, and others brace your spirits on a bone-chilling rainy night. Some pair amazingly well with food, whereas others are meant for thoughtful sipping.

Further, tea gives you what's often called a "calm alertness." Unlike the caffeine in coffee, which hits you quickly and sometimes hard, that same caffeine in tea is tempered by an amino acid that's unique to tea. In a cup of tea, you get the best of both worlds: that alertness of caffeine, coupled with a calm and relaxing focus.

On a deeper level, having tea together binds us socially. A boisterous night over tea cocktails fosters camaraderie among friends; a solemn tea ceremony may ground us. We offer comfort and support when we pour a cup of tea for a grieving friend. Simply holding a steaming cup of tea promotes well-being. When someone asks you if you want a cup of tea, they're extending hospitality and kindness at the very least. If someone you love asks you that same question, you know that cup symbolizes empathy, connectedness, and love.

Discovering some benefits of tea

REMEMBER

There's a lot of media coverage these days about the health benefits of tea and why you should drink it. Although tea is a healthy alternative to high caloric drinks like soda or pop, it isn't a cure-all. Yes, tea can be an important part of a healthy diet and may indeed offer some benefits, but tangible physical effects are only now being defined and understood. However, preliminary results are exciting as we learn, for instance, how tea positively impacts our frame of mind, including outlook, mood, and our perception of others. There's hope that tea helps preserve cognition. In fact, so much research is being done that we dive deeper into the science in Chapters 13 and 14.

If you're an herbal tea fan, don't worry. We have you covered as well, with Chapter 15 devoted to current research on herbal teas.

Begin Your Tea Journey Here

Tea. It's as simple as boiling water, pouring it over leaves, taking a couple minutes to relax, and straining out the leaves. One cup of the perfect tea can hook you for a lifetime.

Tea knows no age

When I (Lisa) opened TeaHaus, my older son was two years old and my younger one was three days old — yes, I know, I'm crazy. They have both been drinking tea since, well, forever. I can remember giving my baby a little cooled ginger rooibos when his tummy was upset, and my older son would be so excited to get his favorite fruit tea in his sippy cup. On the other hand, my husband was forty-five before he started really enjoying tea. He remembers having it as a kid but only when he wasn't feeling well or when his grandma was visiting.

Meanwhile, Jill has finally gotten her decades-long-coffee-drinker husband into tea. Granted, he drinks only two black teas, one fruity black tea, and absolutely no green teas, but he *really* likes those three teas.

REMEMBER

Tea can be enjoyed by anyone at any age. Sure, some teas are better suited for kids (caffeine free), and sometimes it takes finding the one that you personally love, but tea is to be had by all.

Teas to try first

If you are trying to get into tea, you'll probably want to hold off on some teas. Lapsang souchong, Japanese green teas like sencha or matcha, and white teas may not be what you are expecting. You may want to ease into these teas after you're more accustomed to tea and its various flavors.

So then, where *do* you begin?

For many, their journey into the world of tea starts with something more familiar, like earl grey or a teabag from a box. Although teabags have gotten better throughout the years, they will never be what tea is meant to be. In this book, we focus on loose-leaf tea.

At our store, we have seven different versions of loose-leaf earl grey, one of which is our number-one-selling tea. In fact, three of our best-selling teas come from our earl grey collection, and they generally rank within the top ten teas every year, which speaks to their enduring popularity. Once you have a cup of high-quality loose-leaf earl grey, you will never teabag again.

Another commonly known tea is chai. This spiced and often sweetened tea is a popular starting point in coffee shops and cafes. Fruity flavored teas are another great entry tea, especially iced. Even as a tea sommelier, I never judge if someone's favorite is a pineapple-mango tea or a sweetened caramel tea. I like to look at these teas as gateway teas. You should always drink what you enjoy the most and then branch out every so often. You might find a new favorite.

Things to consider when picking a black tea is how strong and bold you want it, how much astringency (that dry feeling in your mouth) you want, whether you prefer a tea that is simply strong versus something that has layers of flavor, and whether you like earthy or smoky notes.

For a less intense black tea, there are plenty of options. Ceylon teas are full-bodied and brisk, but not overly so, and they have just the right amount of astringency. They are what many people think of when they envision black tea. Ceylon is great iced and works well with lemon, sugar, milk, and so on. Assam teas pair particularly well with food, so they can be nice with a snack or meal, and they hold up to a little cream and sugar.

If, however, you want a strong tea, breakfast teas are a good match — and you have a lot to choose from: Irish, Scottish, English, Russian, and East Frisian blends, among others. Every tea blender will use a different ratio of teas, so you may find that you prefer some breakfast blends over others. Yet, all of them are robust enough to stand up to milk and sugar. Just take care in brewing these teas so that they don't become bitter.

For coffee lovers who are used to deep and complex flavors, consider an Assam from India or the many pu-erh and Yunnan teas from China. Some wild-grown teas would also make this list. Although these aren't in-your-face bold like the breakfast blends, they are intriguingly full-bodied and multilayered in flavor.

TIP

Note that teas that have been processed by the cut-tear-curl (CTC) process (these teas are in tiny bits) will release caffeine more quickly than teas composed of intact or largely intact leaves, especially if those leaves have been tightly rolled. However, this isn't to say that you will get more caffeine overall. The caffeine issue is complicated, and we suggest you go to Chapter 11 for a comprehensive look at how it operates in tea.

To start your green tea journey, Chinese green teas are more common and recognizable, so they are often our first recommendation. Japanese teas tend to be grassier or "seaweed"-like in flavor, so, for some, it takes a bit getting used to. Often, people's first experience with green tea is with a sweet matcha latte in a coffee shop or the tea served at their favorite Asian restaurant. Green tea is as nuanced as black tea, but it may take a bit more time to find your favorite.

Oolong, pu-erh, some white teas, and other tea types can also be great first-time teas as well, but we often recommend starting with the basics when first *steeping* into the world of tea.

REMEMBER

If you caught Lisa's reference to rooibos in the "Tea knows no age" section, sharp eyes! In this book, we include both tea —made from the tea plant — and herbal tea. Rooibos is a type of herbal tea, as are fruit teas (check out Chapter 9).

If you aren't sure you're ready for tea, but want a healthy or caffeine-free beverage, we suggest you start with some of the many herbal teas available. Fruit teas, which consist of fruit and other herbals, are a terrific substitute for high-calorie juice. You can find just about any fruit you want, and they are usually fantastic iced. Low in sugar but filled with flavor, these are wonderful for everyone in the family. Kids generally love fruit teas!

Rooibos and honeybush blends are also both kid- and adult-friendly options. You can readily find fruity, floral, earthy, or other blends, so you're sure to find something you enjoy, and they are naturally caffeine free.

Where to buy your tea

REMEMBER

When shopping for tea, it is important to know how and where the store sources their teas. You needn't know the exact gardens or time of day your tea was harvested, but it is important to know that the tea store sources teas from gardens that go above and beyond to ensure the highest quality.

This is not to say that grabbing a teabag tea in the hotel lobby is a no-no, but buying quality loose tea is worth the extra penny. Plus, not all high-quality loose-leaf teas are expensive. A very high-quality loose-leaf breakfast blend may not cost much more per gram than a box of teabags at the grocery store. Single-estate, handpicked, and rare teas from small gardens may seem a bit pricey, but keep in mind that a 50-gram bag of tea can make 15 to 20 cups, and some teas can be brewed several times. A $30 bag of tea that can yield 20 cups makes the per-cup price only about $1.50, which is well under the cost of a hot drink at most cafes or restaurants.

How much tea to buy

REMEMBER

Tea may be sold by the ounce or gram. Most teas require about 3 grams (0.1 ounce) of leaves to make an 8-ounce cup, giving you the following general guidelines:

>> 50 grams (1.8 ounces) of leaves yields 15 to 20 cups of tea

>> 100 grams (3.5 ounces) of leaves yields 30 to 40 cups of tea

>> 200 grams (7 ounces) of leaves yields 60 to 80 cups of tea

>> 500 grams (17.6 ounces) of leaves yields 150 to 200 cups of tea

TIP

Remember that many leaves can be brewed a second time (or more), which doubles the number of cups you get!

Storing your tea leaves

REMEMBER

It is important that your tea is stored in an area free of moisture, strong odors, and light. For this reason, we recommend that you do not use glass jars. Although it is so tempting to stock up on teas when you go to a beautiful tea and spice store that has rows and rows of jars filled with teas and spices, remember that the teas (or spices) probably won't be of great quality because of how they were stored and displayed.

TIP

Metal tins are good if they have a tight seal but be aware that tins will absorb aroma so keep similar teas in each tin (for instance, if you've stored a smoky tea in a tin, keep that tin for smoky teas, or if you have an earl grey tin, keep it an earl grey tin).

So, now that we have your interest, let's steep ourselves with more knowledge about the amazing beverage known as tea!

Chapter **2**

Tea for You, Tea for Me

While growing up, I (Lisa) drank a lot of tea. When I was cold, Mom made a cup of tea. When I was sick, Mom made a cup of tea. When we had people over, Mom made a pot of tea. You get the point — we drank a lot of tea. The funny thing is, it was always the same. Always. It was a small teabag filled with the same black powder-like tea, brewed for the same amount of time, and almost always served in the same cup. It wasn't until I got older that I realized there was a lot more to tea than the cup my mom made me.

When I started seeking out better-quality tea and different types of tea, it was all a little intimidating. I was told I needed a special kettle. Some said a tea ball was necessary while others said to never use one. I was told I needed a specific type of filter, a Japanese kyusu, a Chinese gaiwan, a clay pot, a porcelain pot, a glass pot, and so on. It was starting to look like an expensive hobby.

But then I vacationed in Egypt. There, I walked into a woman's humble kitchen where she was boiling water in a pan over a fire. She poured the water over some leaves she had put in a glass with her fingers, and she handed it to me. It was one of the best cups of tea I have ever had. She didn't use any special brewing equipment or fancy serving ware, just a pan and a cup. Don't get me wrong — there are some amazing ways to make and serve tea from all parts of the world, which we discuss in Chapters 10 and 17. But here, let's focus on the essentials.

In this chapter, we go over the basic equipment that you need to brew a cup of tea, and then we show you how to make terrific tea. We discuss several ways to make iced tea, and we look at some additional ways to enjoy tea.

Brewing the Perfect Cup of Tea

No matter what you've heard, brewing loose tea is easy. It requires only a few pieces of equipment that you likely already own, and then you simply brew your leaves. With our tips, you can brew any tea and get terrific results. Of course, you'll want to experiment a bit for your personal preference, but that's part of the fun!

Basic equipment

REMEMBER

This is all you need to brew tea:

>> Something to heat water

>> A cup or mug

>> A brew basket or strainer of some sort

That's it! But here's a closer look at each of these, along with a few suggestions.

Ways to heat water

Some pretty fancy water kettles are out there these days. Even we are drawn toward the ones with all the buttons, temperature controls, automations, and stellar designs. At TeaHaus, we have three water dispensers that offer a constant supply of filtered water, each set at a specific temperature. However, at home, I have a simple glass electric kettle.

TIP

If you'd rather not have an electric kettle that takes up space on your countertop, you can easily heat water in a pan on your stove (keep reading to learn how to visually gauge water temperature), although a whistling kettle is nice. It lets you know when your water is boiling and reminds you to turn the stove off, a good safety feature. Any style of whistling kettle will do but stay away from cheap aluminum or thin stainless steel. It is worth the few extra dollars to get a sturdier kettle.

WARNING

We recommend that you never use a microwave oven to heat your water. The water heats unevenly, you can't control the temperature with any accuracy, and you can easily burn yourself with superheated water.

Cup or mug

Much debate is ongoing about whether a cup should be glass or porcelain or clay or some other material. Although the array of cup choices adds to the drinking experience (see Chapter 10), in this chapter we're keeping it simple, so go with a cup or mug of your choosing. I prefer white porcelain or glass because I like to see the color of my tea, but everyone has that favorite mug or cup.

Strainer

If we are making a cup of tea for ourselves, we like to use a tea brewing basket that we can set directly into a mug or cup. However, a small kitchen strainer will also get the job done. (See Chapter 10 for more information about brewing baskets and filters.)

TIP

We don't recommend the classic tea balls for most loose-leaf teas because the leaves need room to expand. For example, Figure 2-1 shows how oolong tea leaves unfurl into intact leaves and leaf sets that would be tightly packed into a tea ball. However, these balls are often adequate for small-leaf teas or CTC (cut-tear-curl; see Chapter 4) teas like a classic English breakfast. In Figure 2-1, you can also see that the breakfast tea leaves expanded only a little bit during brewing.

Classic English Breakfast

Sumatra Oolong
Iron Goddess of Mercy

FIGURE 2-1:
English breakfast tea leaves don't expand significantly during brewing (top), unlike the intact leaves and leaf sets of an oolong (bottom).

Photo by Lisa McDonald

Making a cup of hot tea!

When you have your basic brewing equipment, all you need are tea leaves and water. Here's an easy guide to making a terrific cup of tea.

Measuring your tea leaves

Most teabags are perfectly portioned for an eight- to twelve-ounce cuppa, but it gets a bit tricky with loose-leaf tea. Many directions say you should use a teaspoon or a heaping teaspoon of tea leaves, but this isn't always the best form of measurement for the perfect cup.

The problem is that tea leaves vary from tea to tea, sometimes dramatically. Therefore, measuring tea by weight is more accurate than measuring tea using a teaspoon. You generally need about three grams of tea for an eight- to twelve-ounce cup, so when we train new employees to brew tea at TeaHaus, we have them use a gram scale for the first few weeks. After they get a feel for what three grams of various teas look like, they can start to use an eyeball estimate, along with a teaspoon, when brewing tea for customers. If a customer likes a stronger or weaker tea, we don't adjust the brew time or the recommended temperature. Instead, we adjust the amount of tea used.

TIP

If you don't have a gram scale, start by using a teaspoon but remember that you'll need to adjust for the tea. Figure 2-2 shows an example of how three grams of tea can look drastically different. Three grams of CTC tea (left side of photo) are easily measured by a teaspoon. However, some whole-leaf teas, especially those that are very fluffy, like the tea on the right side of the photo, require more tea by volume. For these teas, if your directions say to use a "heaping teaspoon," you may find that the leaves are so difficult to measure with a teaspoon (they are large, unwieldy, and don't stay nicely on the spoon!) that realistically you may need a mega-heaping teaspoon or two heaping teaspoons.

REMEMBER

Keep in mind that no exact science dictates how much tea to use, and personal preference should help you decide how strong you like your tea — and, thus, how much tea to use.

Heating your water

Whether you have a stove top kettle or a simple electric one, we have a few recommendations. At home, we really like an electric kettle. We especially like the glass ones because we can see the bubbles form, which indicates the approximate temperature of the water. You can easily teach yourself how to visually gauge the water temperature (this also works well if you're heating your water in a pan on the stove):

FIGURE 2-2:
Comparison of 3 grams of O'Sullivan's favorite, a CTC Irish breakfast tea, and 3 grams of South India havukal, a whole-leaf white tea.

Photo by Lisa McDonald

>> **Shrimp eyes.** When tiny bubbles (shrimp eyes) start to form on the bottom of the kettle, the water is approximately 155 to 160°F.

>> **Crab eyes.** When the water starts to produce steam and the bubbles are bigger (crab eyes) but are still on the bottom, the temperature is around 175°F.

>> **Fish eyes.** When the bubbles (fish eyes) begin to release from the bottom, the temperature is around 180 to185°F.

>> **Pearl strands.** When the bubbles are more like a strand of pearls than eyes, the water is between 190° and 205°F.

>> **Boil.** Soon after, you have a rolling bubble, which is 212°F.

TIP

If your kettle isn't transparent and you can't see the bubbles, you can listen for the sound. You'll know when you're at the pearl stage because you will hear the low rumble of the pot as the bubbles begin to release. This is, of course, all made easier with a thermometer or a temperature-control kettle.

TIP

Note that if you live in an area with good water or if you are using filtered water, there is no reason to bring your water to a boil and then cool it to the correct brewing temperature.

WHAT KIND OF WATER IS BEST?

What's the best water to use to make tea? You should consider several things:

Filtration. At TeaHaus, we use a five-stage filtration system for our water. This isn't necessary, but good water is best to ensure great flavor. If your tap water is good, you don't need to filter it, but a simple water filter isn't a bad idea (even for coffee and other beverages).

Dissolved solids. If your water has too few dissolved solids, your tea will taste flat (which is why you shouldn't use distilled water). On the other hand, if your water has too many dissolved solids, they interfere with the tea's flavor. You want water that's somewhere between hard and soft.

pH level. A slightly alkaline pH is better than acidic water (pure water is neutral). Most tap water in the United States aims for a slightly alkaline level so this is unlikely to be an issue.

Standing water. If your water is on the hard side, you may not want to use water that's been sitting in your kettle. You're likely to have mineral buildup in your kettle; that will eventually seep into the standing water.

Already-boiled water. Boiling concentrates impurities, but if your tap water is safe, you can reboil your water (see next point).

Dissolved oxygen. You may hear that you should use only fresh, cold, oxygenated water. However, it's unlikely that oxygen affects your tea because there's little to no oxygen in hot water. Further, as your boiled water cools, it reoxygenates. Therefore, you can reboil water to make tea.

Brewing hot tea

At TeaHaus, we give our customers a little guide to brewing. The front of the post-card illustrates the brewing steps (Figure 2-3), and the back provides a simple guide for brewing time and temperature (Figure 2-4).

TIP

You'll see that most teas have a range of water temperatures, but less-oxidized green tea is always brewed at lower temperatures than fully oxidized black tea. White tea, the most delicate and minimally processed of leaves, must always be brewed at relatively low temperatures or else you damage the leaves, and your tea won't taste very good. Note, too, that if you brew tea for too long a time, it will become bitter. Herbal teas (this includes rooibos and fruit teas), on the other hand, can never be over-brewed.

FIGURE 2-3: Brewing guide.

Source: Illustration by TeaHaus

REMEMBER

Keep in mind that these recommendations are just starting points; you should always adjust the parameters to best fit your own preference.

To brew one cup of tea at a time using a cup-sized brewing basket (see Figure 2-5), follow these steps:

1. Place the basket into your cup.

2. Add about three grams of tea into the basket. (See "Measuring your tea leaves" section earlier.)

3. Pour hot water over the leaves and set a timer. At TeaHaus, we put our recommended brewing time and temperature on the package for each tea, but when in doubt, brewing for 2–5 minutes is going to be okay for most teas, depending on the tea and your tolerance for bitterness.

4. When the timer goes off, remove the basket, and your tea is ready to drink.

5. Shake out the leaves into your compost bin or trash and rinse out the remaining leaves — unless it's a tea that you want to rebrew later in the day. In that case, you can just let the leaves stay in the basket (no need to refrigerate).

Making the PERFECT cup of tea!

There's no better way to find your perfect cup than by experimenting.

However, a tea measuring spoon and a Finum brewing basket–*just like we use at TeaHaus*–can really help you out.

Then, simply adjust our brewing guidelines* to find your perfect cup of tea!

TEA	AMOUNT (per 8 oz)	WATER TEMP	BREW TIME
BLACK	1 tsp	194–212°F	2–5 min
OOLONG	1 tsp	176–212°F	2–3 min
GREEN	1 tsp	140–194°F	1–3 min
WHITE	2 tsp	158°F	1–2 min
ROOIBOS	1 tsp	212°F	5–10 min
FRUIT	2 tsp	212°F	5–10 min
HERBAL	2 tsp	212°F	5–10 min

*or consult the label on your TeaHaus tea for specific instructions

FIGURE 2-4: Brewing guide by tea type.

Source: Illustration by TeaHaus

TIP

Step 5 is where teabags are easier to use — even we will admit that. However, you can make your own teabags ahead of time. Just purchase paper filters or teabags for loose tea and spend a few minutes filling enough for the week, for example. Keep in mind, though, that the bag, much like the tea ball, will constrict some unfurling of the leaves, so larger-leaf teas are still best when brewed using a strainer or basket.

Here is an alternate way to make either a cup or a pot of tea. This method allows the leaves to really unfurl and move around freely, which gives you a better cup of tea (see Figure 2-6). Follow these steps:

1. Measure your tea leaves into any vessel that can withstand heat. (We recommend a glass vessel, such as a glass measuring cup.)

2. Pour your hot water over the leaves and set your timer.

3. When the timer goes off, strain the leaves through a brewing basket (or even a small kitchen strainer) into your teacup or tempered teapot.

4. If you plan to rebrew the tea, shake the leaves back into the brewing vessel; otherwise, shake them into your compost bin or trash.

FIGURE 2-5:
Steps for brewing with a basket filter.

Photo by Lisa McDonald

FIGURE 2-6:
Brewing a pot of tea using a basket filter.

Photo by Lisa McDonald

Hint: Tempering your pot helps to keep your tea hotter for longer. Just fill your pot with boiling water and then dump it out before filling it with tea. You can also use a tea warmer or tea cozy. We personally like tea warmers, which are small stands with a spot for a tea light candle; the warmer with lit candle is placed under the teapot. Yes, tea lights are actually for tea, not just for setting a romantic table.

People ask all the time if they can rebrew their leaves. With a brewing basket, it is quite simple. Just place the basket back in your cup and pour more water over it. If you've brewed your leaves loose in another vessel, simply add water again.

There are some teas that rebrew well and others that don't. We always recommend that people just try it. There is no real answer. Larger leaves often brew better the second time around since they unfurl more during the second brew, but, again, this is up to personal preference.

Making iced tea

People ask us all the time how to make iced tea. It is actually quite simple. If some friends come by for a surprise visit or you find yourself parched, this quick method is super easy. (We use this method at the store when people order any of our teas iced to drink in the cafe or take with them to-go and when we brew large quantities for events.)

For example, to make a small pitcher of iced tea, brew the tea exactly how you would if you were making it hot but with *half* the amount of water:

1. Measure out the tea leaves that you need for 32 ounces of tea (approximately 12 grams, or around 4–8 teaspoons, depending on the tea).

2. Add 16 ounces of water at the recommended temperature.

3. Brew for the recommended amount of time.

4. Pour the tea through a strainer into a 32-ounce pitcher that is filled with ice. Enough ice will melt in the concentrated hot tea to give you the perfect strength of ice-cold tea.

Alternately, if you want to do things ahead of time, make your tea at regular strength with all the usual parameters and just let it cool in the fridge.

Sun tea is brought up a lot by customers in the store. We personally are not fans. The number of bacteria that can grow quickly in a warm, moist environment is astounding; the sun tea method creates the perfect environment for bacteria breeding.

We do, however, recommend cold brewing tea sometimes, although it can be tricky to figure out the best brewing time. Some teas can be cold brewed for no more than 3–4 hours or they get too bitter; others can be left brewing in the refrigerator for days. This is something that is super easy to do, but you may need to experiment to find the perfect brew time to suit your taste.

TIP

Another fun thing to do with iced tea is to turn it into ice cubes. If you have some leftover tea or want to make some extra, pour the cooled tea into ice cube trays and stick them in the freezer. You can use these cubes in iced tea that you don't want diluted with melting ice, or even in your favorite cocktail.

One Lump or Two: Discovering Other Ways to Enjoy Tea

Although we might prefer certain teas all on their own, some teas are lovely with a little sweetener or citrus, or you can change them up with carbonation, for instance. Here are a few ideas to get you started.

Milk and Sugar

We will end the debate here and now! IT DOESN'T MATTER! What debate, you may ask? It's the perennial "Should I put the milk in my cup before the tea or after I pour the tea?" dilemma!

Some argue that it's best to add a little cream to the cup before the hot tea to avoid cracking the cup, while others say that you cannot see the color properly if the milk is added first. So again, it does not matter. When once asked this important question, the butler for the late Queen Elizabeth II of the United Kingdom said that the queen preferred to pour her tea first, then add cream. There — it's settled.

Personally, we don't use cream or sugar in any of our teas other than in a traditional masala chai or perhaps in a dessert tea that has chocolate or caramel pieces. That said, we don't judge. A teaspoon of sugar and a splash of milk or cream is a lovely way to make a cuppa.

Lemon

Lemon is another common request with a cup of tea. There is something magical about a tall, cold glass of a classic iced tea with a squeeze of lemon. Some even enjoy a touch of lemon in their hot tea. Acid from the lemon may change the color of your tea and add a little bite on the tongue but it won't make it more, or less, healthy as some claim.

Tea Lattes

People often come in and ask for a tea latte. This concept has been popularized by chain coffee shops and cafes. Some places will simply add a premade, often sweetened, tea syrup into steamed milk or milk alternative. At home, you can simply add a splash of milk to your tea and keep the calories down.

Carbonated

One of our favorite beverages to drink in the summer is carbonated iced tea! Because fruit teas keep well cold and don't get bitter with time, we like to keep strong brews of them in the fridge. Anytime we need a little refresher, we fizz up some water with a countertop carbonator or crack open a can of sparkling water to top off a glass of cold fruit tea.

Alternately, you can make concentrated tea-infused syrups. Keep them in your fridge and add them to carbonated water (or an inexpensive sparkling wine, such as prosecco). Here are two ways to make tea-infused syrups:

>> Syrup A: Add 12 grams (about 0.5 ounce) of fruit tea to 16 ounces of boiling water; allow to infuse for 15 minutes to overnight. Strain and cool completely.

>> Syrup B: Add loose tea to water heated to the appropriate temperature for that tea and allow to brew for 10 minutes (or do a 4-hour cold infusion). Strain the tea and add sugar. Bring to a boil, stirring, and then, at low heat, reduce syrup for approximately 20 minutes. Cool completely.

You can make syrups with all types of tea but be careful because some can get bitter. Fruit teas, on the other hand, don't get bitter, nor do they require added sugar. Head to Chapter 21 for some tea syrup recipes.

Trends and Fads

Trends come and go. Our store is in a college town, and when we walk around, we can count at least six bubble tea places in our city. This trend is sweeping the nation. Some places use real, freshly brewed tea, but many use powder mixes to make their bubble beverages. Either way, bubble tea — or even a coffee-chain matcha latte — can be fun.

Instant tea has always been around, but we have seen more in the form of cute shapes that you can simply pour hot water over. Powdered tea mixes are also popular because you can either just add them to a bottle of water, shake, and enjoy cold, or pour them into a cup of hot water and stir. We admit to not having tried many of these quick tea concepts. We are fairly old school when it comes to tea.

Chapter **3**

From Garden to Cup

Tea has been enjoyed around the globe for centuries and is now consumed in every part of the world. It's the second-most consumed beverage worldwide (water is first) — and is also an important economic and agricultural aspect of many countries. And, like any agricultural product, tea is dependent on climate, economics, and even politics. Any change in these many variables can change what is in your cup, so understanding where tea comes from will help you appreciate and enjoy every sip.

In this chapter, we talk about the amazing plant that gives us tea. How is it grown and harvested? And how do those leaves turn into the tea leaves that we put into our teacups? We then run through some of the terminology used to describe and rate tea. Although you truly do not need to know what these terms mean to fully enjoy your tea, you may be curious. (Really, does *anyone* specify "SFTGFOP" when they order a cup of tea?!) Finally, we discuss the ways in which tea can be blended and flavored.

The Tea Plant, Where It All Begins

All tea begins at the same place: with the *Camellia sinensis* plant. Two main varieties account for nearly all the tea produced. Tea gardens flourish in hot lowland areas as well as high in the mountains, and, therefore, harvesting methods must accommodate each garden's setting. Let's take a closer look at how tea is grown and harvested because what you taste in your cup reflects the plant's life before it was made into tea.

Varieties

The two main varieties of *Camellia sinensis*, a subtropical evergreen, are as follow:

>> *Camellia sinensis* var. *sinensis* is native to China. This variety has small leaves and is used primarily to produce green, white, and oolong teas.

>> *Camellia sinensis* var. *assamica* is native to Assam in India. This variety has large leaves and grows taller than the *sinensis* variety. It's used primarily to produce black tea.

REMEMBER

Note, however, that either variety can be used to make any type of tea!

More than 2,000 subspecies of *C. sinensis* exist. Some are indigenous to a locale, and others are the result of experimentation. These hybrids or cultivars may be developed for flavor, yield, adaptability, resilience to environmental stress, and so on. But they all derive from the original plants, beautifully illustrated in Köhler's *Medicinal Plants,* published in the late 1800s (Figure 3-1).

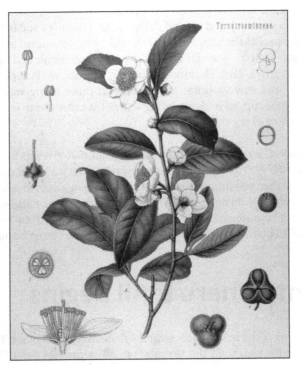

FIGURE 3-1: Botanical illustration of *Camellia sinensis* from Hermann Köhler's *Medicinal Plants.*

Franz Eugen Köhler / Wikimedia Commons / Public Domain

Environment, or terroir

Although the French word *terroir* derives from Latin *terra*, meaning "earth," it encompasses vastly more. A standard dictionary defines terroir as "the complete natural environment in which a particular wine is produced, including factors such as the soil, topography, and climate; the characteristic taste and flavor imparted to a wine by the environment in which it is produced." Substitute "tea" for "wine," and you know it's the terroir that gives each tea its character. Figure 3-2 illustrates the terroir in tea-growing Shiga Prefecture in Japan.

FIGURE 3-2: Landscape, Shiga Prefecture, Japan.

Photo by Lisa McDonald

Gardens

The place where tea is grown can be called a garden, an estate, a plantation, or just a small plot. TeaHaus even has a few tea plants in pots outside the store. Does this make it an estate? The words are interchangeable, so why not?

The tea plant doesn't self-pollinate so it must be grown from seeds (from cross pollination) or from cuttings (clones). Plants propagated from seeds grow at different rates and have different characteristics. Clones, on the other hand, ensure plant consistency and are, therefore, more popular nowadays. Garden owners continually look for new clones and varieties to keep up with the changing climate, trends, and global demand.

Gardens are as diverse as the teas we drink. They can be in the lowlands, in high mountains, or even at 204 North 4th Avenue in Ann Arbor, Michigan. At higher elevations, the plants grow more slowly and are exposed to higher levels of ultraviolet light, allowing the leaves to develop a more complex flavor. However, this is not to say that lower-grown teas are inferior — they simply have different characteristics.

Tea leaves can be harvested much of the year; the plants are regularly trimmed to encourage new growth and to help keep them manageable. The plants can grow to more than six feet in height, although they're normally kept at waist level for easier harvesting. In gardens that are not plucked year-round, the plants are pruned before winter dormancy. Most of the plants are less than fifty years old, although tea can still be produced from plants that have been around for hundreds of years.

In some regions, tea plants can withstand up to six feet of snow cover (see Figure 3-3), while in other areas, the temperature may never drop below that of a warm summer's day. In some gardens, sprinklers or fans that circulate warm air downward (see Figure 3-3) help protect the plants from frost. In other gardens, large trees are grown to help provide shade for garden workers.

Whether a garden is high or low, big or small, organic or conventional, the goal is to produce leaves that will eventually produce the ideal cup.

FIGURE 3-3: Snow cover (upper) and fans in tea garden (lower).

Published with permission from Mandokoro Tea Garden and Authentic Nippon LLC (upper); photo by Lisa McDonald (lower)

Harvesting

Because of the terroir of some gardens, the only effective way to harvest the leaves is to pick them by hand, as shown in Figure 3-4. The hand-picked leaves are gently tossed into baskets and carried back down the hillside to be withered and processed. (See the section, "Processing steps," later in this chapter.)

FIGURE 3-4: Harvesting by hand.

Photo by Lisa McDonald (upper left); published with permission from Mandokoro Tea Garden and Authentic Nippon LLC (upper right, below))

Mechanical harvesting is done by a portable harvesting machine held by two people or by a machine harvester that can be manned or automated. Plants that are grown in rows make this type of harvesting easy and more efficient, as Figure 3-5 illustrates.

FIGURE 3-5:
Mechanical
harvesting.

Published with permission from Takatomo Katagi, Katagi Koukaen (upper); photo by Lisa
McDonald (lower)

Discovering How Leaves Become Tea

Because any type of tea can be produced from any *Camellia sinensis* leaf, the processing steps are key to producing the unique and varied flavors in your cup.

Processing steps

Regardless of tea type, the process is basically the same, although the process may differ in how long the leaves are withered or wilted, how the leaves are oxidized, and how the leaves are dried. We discuss the processing steps in more detail in the following chapters, but essentially you make tea by

>> Picking

>> Withering/wilting

>> Processing (oxidation)

>> Drying

Small-scale production facilities may use small, low-tech, and sometimes outdated equipment (Figure 3-6), whereas large-scale operations may look like laboratories (Figure 3-7). Particularly fascinating may be the multistory nets in which the leaves are dried. But no matter what the scale, tea leaves are taken through the requisite processing steps and sorted (Figure 3-8).

FIGURE 3-6: Small-scale production facility.

Photos by Lisa McDonald

 FIGURE 3-7:
Large-scale
production
facility; photo on
lower left shows
drying nets.

Photos by Lisa McDonald

Types of tea produced

REMEMBER Black, green, oolong, white, pu-erh, and yellow tea all start with the same leaf. We
go into more detail about the different types of tea in the following chapters.

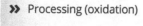 Processing (oxidation)

>> Drying

Small-scale production facilities may use small, low-tech, and sometimes out-dated equipment (Figure 3-6), whereas large-scale operations may look like laboratories (Figure 3-7). Particularly fascinating may be the multistory nets in which the leaves are dried. But no matter what the scale, tea leaves are taken through the requisite processing steps and sorted (Figure 3-8).

FIGURE 3-6:
Small-scale production facility.

Photos by Lisa McDonald

FIGURE 3-7:
Large-scale
production
facility; photo on
lower left shows
drying nets.

Types of tea produced

REMEMBER

Black, green, oolong, white, pu–erh, and yellow tea all start with the same leaf. We go into more detail about the different types of tea in the following chapters.

FIGURE 3-8:
Processing
and sorting
the leaves.

Photos by Lisa McDonald

The Often-Confusing Terminology of Tea

Similar to wine, fine cheeses, or any other food or drink, many terms are used to describe tea. We talk about tasting terminology more in Chapter 10, but here we discuss some classic terms often used to describe tea types.

The "orange" of orange pekoe

Ubiquitous on boxes of teabags, where did the "orange" of orange pekoe tea come from and what does it mean? Well, we can view it with multiple lenses:

>> **Position of leaf on tea plant.** "Orange pekoe" and "pekoe" refer to the leaf used, not the quality of the leaf (teabags often contain the lowest grades of orange pekoe). Counting down from the bud, the youngest leaves are

- 1st leaf: orange pekoe

- 2nd leaf: pekoe

- 3rd leaf: pekoe-souchong

- 4th leaf: souchong

- 5th leaf: congou

>> **Physical description of leaf.** The buds and underside of young tea leaves are covered with fine silvery-white hairs. According to the Oxford English Dictionary, "pekoe" means "white down" (Chinese, Amoy dialect). Although these hairs are retained on white tea, you won't see them on orange pekoe tea, which is usually a black tea.

>> **Historical references.** While "orange" could allude to the orange tinge of brewed black tea, it more likely refers to the Netherlands House of Orange. Founded in the 1500s by Willem I, Prince of Orange, the House of Orange–Nassau rose to power through military success and political leadership, but their savvy use of material culture reinforced their power. Artwork, and even clothing, featured oranges, the orange plant, and the color — all rife with meaning. Orange marmalade, orange liqueur, and other food became strategies. Even carrots were selectively propagated for those that were orange.

Their relationship with the Dutch East India Company led to trade supremacy over coveted items such as tea and porcelain. Did the Dutch East India Company, then, add "orange" to "pekoe" as a marketing strategy, or was this yet another way for the House of Orange–Nassau to bring "orange" to the fore?

Orthodox versus CTC

The difference between orthodox and CTC tea is whether the leaves are left intact or are cut during production.

>> **Orthodox tea.** The leaves are bruised by rolling, which damages the cell structure enough so that they oxidize in a slow, controlled manner. Repeated rolling allows the polyphenols to convert into their most complex forms, and the tea grows more mellow (see Chapter 13). This process takes time and expertise, but it results in teas with complexity and nuance. Note that tea leaves can break during this process, so "whole leaf" means that they remained intact, whereas the rest are called "broken."

>> **CTC tea.** The leaves are machine-chopped into uniform, small pieces during production, and, therefore, are called cut-tear-curl or crush-tear-curl (CTC) tea. This extreme damage quickly oxidizes the leaves, and flavor nuances don't

have time to develop. For that reason, lower-quality tea leaves are used for CTC teas. These teas are also faster and cheaper to produce.

SFTGFOP

Some tea names include seemingly random arrangements of letters, such as SFTGFOP. Such designations can sometimes be perceived as snooty and pretentious — and FTGFOP has occasionally been translated as meaning "Far Too Good for Ordinary People"! But this is *so* not true! These letters are merely initials for tea descriptors that tell you what types of tea leaves comprise your tea. They don't necessarily denote quality. Here is a breakdown of what each letter means:

» S: special (more rare)

» F: finest, fancy

» T: tippy (leaf tips)

» G: golden (young leaves)

» F: flowery (buds or leaf tips)

» O: orange

» P: pekoe

If "1" is tacked on the end, it's perhaps used more for marketing than holding real meaning. If "B" is included, the leaves are "broken"; otherwise, the tea is whole leaf. This grading system is used for tea produced in India.

TIP

The youngest (or most immature) leaves on a plant are the smallest in size. Thus, the more of these initials used to describe a tea, the higher the content of young leaves — so SFTGFOP means that the tea consists of the smallest leaves. If only OP is used, it simply means that the first leaf was harvested, but probably later in the season when it's more mature and larger.

The flush

REMEMBER

In Darjeeling and Assam, the "first flush" means the first harvest, which takes place in early spring when only the buds and immature leaves are plucked. This is at the beginning of the growing season, after winter's dormancy, so it's the first new growth.

REMEMBER

The "second flush" is the second harvesting of leaves, in later spring, followed by the summer's monsoon harvest and then the autumnal harvest. This term isn't used in regions where the leaves are harvested year-round and the plants never go into a winter dormancy.

Sparrow beak

A hand-plucked leaf set (bud and first two leaves) looks rather like a sparrow's beak and tongue. Therefore, following early spring's plucking of just the bud (*ujeon*), green tea in South Korea is classified by the size of the "beak":

>> Sparrow's small beak *(sejak),* plucked after April 20, bud and first leaf

>> Sparrow's medium beak *(joongjak),* plucked around May 20, young leaves

>> Sparrow's large beak *(daejak),* plucked around June 21, mature leaves

Single estate

Single-estate teas come from one tea garden or estate and aren't blended with any other tea. These teas are generally expensive and sometimes have limited production. Well-known examples include Darjeeling and Assam teas, whereas Jun Chiyabari in Nepal is a relatively new producer of single-estate, or single-origin, tea.

Understanding How Teas Are Flavored

Even a true tea sommelier sometimes wants a little fun in their cup. A mug of TeaHaus decaf caramel chai can sooth a sweet tooth on a cold winter's night, while a glass of refreshing iced strawberry mint lavender black tea is just what's needed on a summer's day. Flavored or aroma teas are a great way to try new flavors like lychee or cardamom, or you can stick to classics, like the popular earl grey. (Note that "aroma" is often used to describe teas that have additional ingredients.)

The following sections explain the most common ways to flavor teas.

Blending

REMEMBER

The word "blending" has multiple meanings when you're talking about tea. It can refer to a blend of various teas, either the same type of tea or different teas. For example, in Japan, it's important that the look and flavor of sencha remains consistent. Therefore, teas from multiple gardens are sent to a blending house where they're mixed to produce a final product that is similar to senchas from previous years. Sometimes tea from the previous year will even be added to the mix to ensure consistency. This is a tea-tea blend.

Breakfast teas are another example of a tea-tea blend. For these, various black teas are chosen for their unique contributions. For instance, Assam tea offers maltiness while keemun imparts a smoky note to the blend.

Another form of blending is to use various inclusions such as blossoms, herbs, or spices. Even things like toasted rice can be added, as in Japanese genmaicha. Figure 3-9 shows a black tea blend that includes fruit pieces and flower petals; an oolong blend with basil, lemon granules, and blossoms; a classic green tea blend, matcha genmaicha; and a scented tea sprinkled with jasmine flowers.

pineapple mango

lemon basil

matcha genmaicha

jasmine

FIGURE 3-9:
Black tea blend (top), oolong blend (second from top), green tea blend (third from top), and jasmine green tea (bottom).

Photos by Lisa McDonald and Jill Rheinheimer

Oils and extracts

REMEMBER

Whereas *oils* are extracted, *extracts* have been soaked in a liquid to isolate flavor. Both methods are effective for flavoring tea.

When you're talking oil and extracts, you should be familiar with a few terms. Natural, nature-identical, and artificial are types of flavorings used in the tea industry, but some governments regulate the words and how they're used more than others. For example, in the United States, nature-identical flavor is considered artificial and must be labeled as such — even though it is made from naturally occurring molecules that have been isolated by a chemist to synthesize the equivalent compound. The United States doesn't have a term for these compounds, so they fall under the same name as artificial flavorings that are *not* naturally occurring.

When oils or extracts are used to flavor tea, the leaves are often sprayed with flavor or flavor is poured over the leaves. Alternately, large quantities of leaves may be put into giant drums and slowly turned while oils or extracts are slowly added.

Scented teas

Flower-scented teas (jasmine, rose, magnolia, and osmanthus, among others) have been produced in China for centuries, with credit going to Zhu Quan (1378–1448) for the innovation. In the wet scenting process, moist and pliable tea leaves are exposed to fresh flowers or aromatic fruit (such as lychee or orange), usually by layering them. The moisture in the leaves serves as a carrier, enabling the leaves to absorb and retain both the aroma and flavor of the flowers or fruit.

The scenting process determines the grade of scented teas. (Note, however, that grade doesn't necessarily equate to quality, as we discuss in Chapter 23.) For example, jasmine tea is available in many grades. On the one end, lower-quality flowers and lower-grade tea leaves, harvested later in the season, may be layered only one time. For the better grades, however, the most desirable tea leaves are harvested early in the season, processed, and stored until summer's jasmine flowers bloom. The tea leaves are then layered with fresh flower buds that are in the prime of the season and are the most aromatic. The tea leaves and flowers are allowed to mingle for several hours, during which time the temperature rises, the flower buds open, and the moist tea leaves absorb the flower aroma and flavor. The flowers are then removed, and the tea leaves allowed to rest. This cycle of layering and resting is repeated multiple times. For the finest jasmine teas, the process may take weeks. Traditionally, the flowers are always removed, but today, fresh flowers may be sprinkled in for visual appeal (see Figure 3-9).

Be aware that not all jasmine (or other traditionally scented) teas are scented teas. Flowers may simply be added to tea leaves, the tea leaves may be sprayed with extract, or the tea may be artificially flavored. When flavored by these vastly cheaper and less labor-intensive methods, the leaves don't incorporate the essence of the flowers as they do in the scenting process.

2

Talking about Different Types of Tea

Discover how black tea is made and its common flavor profiles, and then familiarize yourself with the many black teas available, including some classic blends.

Unwrap the differences between Chinese and Japanese green tea — and the differences between the types of matcha you may encounter — and survey your green tea options.

Delve into the complicated production and multiple flavor profiles of oolong tea. Consider the meaning of its name, and take a look at representative oolongs.

Step into white tea, the least processed — and most subtle — type of tea.

Survey some of the less common teas, including fermented, flowering, frost, and purple teas.

Review the components of herbal teas, including a look at why these are called "tea" even though they don't come from the tea plant.

Come along with a tea sommelier to find out how experts taste tea, and then try your hand at it, using our Tea Tasting Notes guide. Plus, dive into the plethora of tea accessories out there — and decide if any of them are for you.

Chapter **4**

Black Tea

S ay "tea," and chances are good that people envision black tea, whether a sweetened iced tea or a teabag in a cup. This isn't surprising. In the United States, eighty-some percent of the tea consumed is black tea, and more than three-quarters of that is iced. We agree that iced tea goes great with a burger, and grabbing a ready-to-drink tea is convenient for road trips, but when you're at home and want a cup of tea? Well, you have so many choices! Black teas are available for every preference — from pleasantly light to in-your-face bold, with broodingly complex, intensely smoky, and malty also in the mix.

In this chapter, we look at how black tea is made, and we explore some black teas that are produced by the major tea-producing countries.

Taking a Closer Look at Black Tea

Let's see how that unpresuming green tea leaf turns into your favorite cuppa. (Please see Chapter 3 for an overview on tea terminology, much of it specific to black tea.)

Considering the tea varieties

One of the coolest things about the *Camellia sinensis* plant is that you can pick a leaf from any variety and then decide what kind of tea you want to produce. Of course, certain varieties may lend themselves better to certain teas because of growing conditions, climate, and even tradition. The *assamica* variety is most commonly used to make black tea — but never let the leaf in your hand dictate what tea is in your cup.

How black tea is made

Although the process for making tea is similar for all types of tea, tea leaves that are fully oxidized are considered black tea.

After tea leaves are harvested, they are first wilted (withered), and then are either broken, torn, crushed, or rolled (or a combination), which breaks down cell walls. This allows the cell contents to mix with oxygen, and the leaves oxidize, similar to an apple oxidizing, as shown in Figure 4-1. When the desired level of oxidation is achieved, the leaves need to be dried. Typically, black teas are dried with dry air heat.

FIGURE 4-1:
Stages of oxidation in apples.

Photo by Lisa McDonald

Each type of black tea has unique qualities, which come from the variety of *Camellia sinensis* used, the growing conditions, and the time that the production processes take. For example, a slow oxidation process is often used in China. This process allows more of the polyphenols to convert to thearubigins, making the tea mellow and complex (see Chapter 13). The time of the year when the leaves are picked and the length of the wilting step also play a role in what your brew will be.

Flavor profiles of black tea

REMEMBER

One of the most amazing things about tea is its diversity. A single leaf from a *Camellia sinensis* plant can yield a wide array of aromas, liquors, and flavors. Often, people describe black tea as being stronger than green or white tea, for example. Some would say it is more bitter or tannic in flavor. These generalities are often true, but great variation exists within the teas that are classified as black tea.

Searching Far and Wide for Black Tea

Although it may seem that black tea is just black tea, there are many types of black tea, produced in multiple countries. Each tea reflects its unique terroir (environment) and production techniques.

China

China has been producing black tea (*hong cha*) for some 400 years now! In China, black tea is called "red tea," which refers to the color of the liquor rather than the color of the dry leaves.

Gunpowder

Gunpowder tea was ideal for early trade with Europe and North America. During production, the tea leaves were hand-rolled into tight balls. Because little of the leaf was exposed to the environment, the tea better maintained its flavor and quality during the months-long sea voyages — and its resemblance to gunpowder pellets may have given the tea its name (see Figure 4-2).

FIGURE 4-2:
Gunpowder tea
from China.

Photo by Lisa McDonald

TIP

Today, gunpowder may be hand- or machine-rolled into its signature pearls or pellets (you may see either term used to describe this tea). The smaller the pellet, the younger the leaf and the higher the quality of the tea. When you brew gunpowder tea, you'll probably need to steep the leaves more than once before they fully unfurl.

REMEMBER

The flavor profile for a gunpowder is often described as woody and slightly smoky. It has a rich, deep flavor without a bitter finish. Some say the woodiness originally came from the barrels that the tea was kept in for the long journey across the ocean.

Keemun (qimen, qihong)

First produced in 1875, keemun remains on China's "famous teas" list (see Figure 4-3). The tea is grown in the Huangshan mountain range in Qimen County, Anhui Province, where the terroir heavily contributes to the tea's unique flavor. Because the mountainous, forested, and foggy environment also limits sunlight, keemun is high in theanine, an amino acid that imparts an umami flavor. The tea's rose fragrance is due to unusually high levels of the terpenoid alcohol geraniol and the essential oil myrcenal.

FIGURE 4-3:
Keemun tea
from China.

Photo by Lisa McDonald

REMEMBER

Like most Chinese black teas, keemun is often said to have a slight smokiness; it is dark and rich in flavor. Keemun brews a slightly more reddish hue than many of the other black teas.

Lapsang souchong

An intensely smoky black tea, lapsang souchong is produced in China's National Wuyi Mountain Nature Preservation Zone, traditionally using the native bohea variety of *C. sinensis* var. *sinensis* tea. After plucking, the leaves are dried over a smoky pine wood fire, which allows the leaves to absorb the smoke.

Both tea and pine variety are integral to the tea:

>> Leaves of the bohea variety absorb more pine smoke elements than other tea varieties can.

>> The native pine tree used for drying and smoking gives the tea its unique flavor due to its specific chemical makeup and its pyrolysis products generated by the heat.

Lapsang souchong is the granddaddy of all black teas. First produced in 1568, it reached Europe a few decades later.

TIP

If, perchance, you have some of this tea and you *just cannot* drink it, don't toss it! This is a terrific tea to incorporate into savory recipes or cocktails (see Chapters 19 and 21), which, by the way, is how we enjoy this smoky tea.

Yunnan

From the *assamica* variety of tea plants in China's Yunnan Province, these teas contain high levels of the terpene alcohol linalool, which contributes floral and spicy qualities. This also makes them more similar to Darjeeling teas, which also are high in linalool, than to other black teas from China.

REMEMBER

Yunnans are often more earthy or mushroom-y, with a slight sweet tobacco note. Much like the other Chinese black teas, they are full bodied and offer a bit more complexity than a classic keemun might. The production techniques for yunnan teas vary considerably and therefore each tea has specific unique qualities. Figure 4-4 shows one example of a yunnan tea.

FIGURE 4-4:
Yunnan tea
from China.

Photo by Lisa McDonald

India

The *assamica* variety that is most often used for black tea production is native to Assam and is now found in tea gardens throughout India.

Assam

Assam, in northeast India, is bisected by the Brahmaputra River. The unique environment — hot and humid — contributes to the tea's characteristic malty flavor. The first harvest, or the first flush, begins in February. The May-to-June second-flush harvest, however, yields the highest-grade Assam teas, characterized by a full-bodied, spicy, and malty flavor. Some gardens will also have an autumnal flush in October and November. (See Figure 4-5.)

TIP

The malty nature of Assam teas lends itself to food pairings — especially with sweets in the afternoon. Their full-bodied quality also tends to stand up to a bit of cream.

Darjeeling

Considered the Champagne of tea, Darjeeling tea has a geographical indication stamp, meaning it can be produced only in Darjeeling. The most esteemed (and often more expensive) are the first-flush teas, which comprise the emerging buds and leaves plucked after winter's dormancy. Darjeeling tea leaves are high in the terpene alcohol linalool that contributes floral and spicy notes.

>> **First flush.** The hand-plucked newly emerging leaves are delicate and often include the new bud (see Figure 4-5). They are described as crisp and have a slightly grassy aroma; they are a bit nutty, but more astringent; and they are slightly more delicate and fresher in flavor than the fuller-bodied second flush.

>> **Second flush.** The more mature leaves have a nuttier and slightly warmer note. They have gathered more nutrients from the plant and have a more robust flavor than the earlier picked leaves (first flush). They are still more characteristically astringent than an Assam but are not as delicate as the first flush.

TIP

We often explain the difference between the first and second flush by comparing them to a green banana and a riper banana. The greener banana has a crisper note and often leaves the palate dry whereas a ripe banana is nutty and sweet.

Assam

Darjeeling first flush

FIGURE 4-5:
Tea from Assam (upper) and Darjeeling (lower).

Photos by Lisa McDonald

Sri Lanka: Ceylon tea

Capitalized on by Sir Thomas Lipton, Ceylon teas embody "black tea" — for good reason! These full-bodied and brisk teas lend themselves to being iced, work well with anything you want to add to them (dairy, sweetener, citrus), and have just the right astringency. The altitude of the tea garden partly determines the tea's characteristics and quality:

>> **Low elevation.** Usually considered of lower quality than those produced at higher altitudes; these teas are strong and generally enjoyed with milk.

>> **Middle elevation.** Characterized by a rich flavor.

>> **High elevation.** Premium teas that are sweet, with floral notes.

REMEMBER

Note that we're talking only about loose tea. Although Ceylon black tea is in many a teabag, you don't get the flavors that you do when you brew loose tea.

TIP

When someone comes into the store and says they want a "normal" black tea, this is our go-to. It is often described as, "you know, a *tea* tea."

Japan

Most black teas are produced from *C. sinensis* var. *assamica* leaves. Japanese black tea, however, is made either from *C. sinensis* var. *sinensis* (which is usually used for green tea) or from a hybrid of the two varieties, such as the Benifuki (Benifokûki/Benifuuki) cultivar, developed in the mid-1900s. This results in a tea with a mild, sweet flavor and little astringency.

Because green tea remains predominant in Japan, not all farmers produce black tea, and not all that do produce it yearly. The discovery that the Benifuki cultivar contains a lot of methylated catechins, which have potential anti-allergic effects, sparked renewed interest in the cultivar, but mostly for green tea production.

TIP

Japanese black teas are often described as having a slightly more sweet, vegetal note — perfect for a lighter afternoon cup.

Wild-grown

Although tea is usually cultivated, it can grow wild, like the untended plants shown in Figure 4-6. The term "wild grown" is often used to raise the perceived value of a tea. "Wild" does seem to evoke something that seems unique or hard to come by, and, admittedly, many of us want to go a little wild every so often! This term, however, can be used for several types of teas, all of which may be considered "wild":

>> The plant is indigenous or native to an area and grows without cultivation.

>> The plant grows in forests.

>> The plant is minimally pruned.

REMEMBER

There is something to be said about wild-grown teas. They often seem more nuanced and are often described as having more layers of flavor and complexity than estate teas. You will most likely also taste the difference between batches more, since the growing conditions are not as controlled.

Classic blends

Various black teas are often combined to create breakfast blends. Alternately, bergamot oil or spices may be added to black tea leaves, but some of these blends still fall under classic black teas.

FIGURE 4-6:
Tea plants
growing wild
in Japan.

Photo by Lisa McDonald

Breakfast blends

TIP

Breakfast teas are robust and hearty — quickly releasing bold flavor along with a shot of caffeine. Due to their heartiness, they are usually had with milk and sugar. See Figure 4-7 for examples of English breakfast tea and a CTC Irish breakfast tea.

>> **English breakfast blends.** Breakfast tea was first marketed by Scottish tea master Mr. Drysdale, but the English quickly seized the idea, and English breakfast teas were born. They originally were designed to accompany the hearty breakfasts of late-1800s England, but it is said that Queen Anne wanted something a bit lighter to accommodate her classic breakfast. Because they depended on tea availability, the blends were flexible.

Today, English breakfast blends include teas from all over the world, although teas from India are still predominantly used. Yet, almost anything goes to achieve the perfect blend these days, with each blend dependent on the tea company that's blending it. English breakfast is normally the least bold of the breakfast blends.

>> **Irish breakfast blends.** Irish tea is strong enough to stand a fork in it.

Most Irish blends are heavy on the Assam leaf and have a more malty finish: think Guinness. Also, dairy is an important part of Irish life, so a strong cup — to be enjoyed with milk — is an Irish tradition. These blends are normally the strongest of the breakfast blends.

>> **Scottish breakfast blends.** Scottish blends are the least known of the breakfast blends and, like the others, can be made from any and all black teas. Chinese-style teas are often added, which may make the Scottish blends a bit woodier tasting.

>> **Russian breakfast blends.** Often, Russian-style blends use more Chinese black teas and are, therefore, a bit on the smokier side than their Western counterparts. The tea is often served with black cherry preserves or lemon; it is almost always served with sugar.

English breakfast

Irish breakfast

FIGURE 4-7: English breakfast (upper) and Irish breakfast (lower) blends.

Photos by Lisa McDonald

Earl grey

Earl grey is a blend of tea and bergamot oil, which is extracted from the peel of the bergamot orange. The first record of the blend seems to have been in 1824, when bergamot oil was used to improve low-quality tea. Today, earl grey is one of the most well-known and beloved teas out there.

Masala chai

In India, masala chai — a sweetened, spicy, milky tea — is a favorite. "Masala" refers to a blend of spices, and *chai* means "tea" (which is why it's not called "chai tea"). Chai can be many things, and there is no one recipe. You will find black-, green-, or black and green tea-based chai as well as various combinations of spices sans the tea leaves (see Figure 4-8).

TIP

Chai is traditionally sweetened, with a splash of dairy or dairy substitute. (We suggest sweetened condensed milk or a dollop of raw honey on a chilly day!)

chai spices

chai (black & green tea-based)

FIGURE 4-8:
Spices (upper) and chai (lower).

Photos by Jill Rheinheimer

Chapter **5**

Green Tea

I f you've had only black tea, your first foray into green teas should be fun! Green teas are vastly different from black teas, and Chinese green teas are wildly different from Japanese green teas. If this seems a tad daunting, keep reading; the differences are quickly explained, and you'll be able to make an educated guess about what you're most likely to enjoy. Yes, some green teas can give that seaweed-y vibe — but others are nutty or starchy or smoky. There's really a lot to like, and we provide a few tips to get you started!

In this chapter, we see how green tea is made, including the differences between Chinese and Japanese production methods, which impacts the characteristics of these teas. We highlight some of fundamental qualities of Chinese versus Japanese teas to help you figure out where to start if you're new to green tea. We then look at some of the most classic green tea styles made, including a rundown of what "matcha" means and how to differentiate between the options.

Taking a Closer Look at Green Tea

For general production methods as well as a look at tea terminology, see Chapter 3. And now, let's see how green tea is made and explore some of its flavor profiles.

How green tea is made

Unlike black teas, which are mostly produced with classic air-drying methods, green teas vary in how they are made from country to country. The key is how to stop the oxidation. We address the main differences between how this is done in China versus in Japan in the section "The difference between Chinese and Japanese green teas," but all green teas are less oxidized than black teas. On our apple sequence in Figure 5-1, green teas fall more toward the left whereas black tea would be akin to the apple on the far right (most oxidized).

FIGURE 5-1:
Stages of oxidation in apples.

Photo by Lisa McDonald

Flavor profiles of green tea

A common characteristic of green teas is that they are more on the vegetal side than are black teas. But as a guide to looking for a green tea that you'll like, the question may be whether you prefer a fresh vegetal, a toasted vegetal, or something a little smoky. Although this is an extremely simplistic breakdown, it can point you to something you'll like.

TIP

One style is not better than the other when it comes to green tea production. If fresh vegetal, almost grassy, or somewhat seaweed-y is great with you, then start with green teas from Japan. If a more toasty note is what you are looking for, try a classic Chinese green tea. Both styles of tea are perfect for sipping, depending on what you are in the mood for.

INSIDER TIPS ABOUT GREEN TEA

You might hear that green tea has less caffeine than black tea, but you can't predict how much caffeine is in your teacup! See Chapter 11 for the many factors that contribute to caffeine levels. Also, you may hear that green tea is healthier than black tea, but this isn't true either. Chapter 13 explores why it doesn't matter what kind of tea you drink, and Chapter 14 considers the myriad reasons why health benefits are difficult to assess.

The difference between Chinese and Japanese green teas

REMEMBER

In China, the leaves are pan fried to stop the oxidation process. This is done in baskets, pans, or rotating drums that are positioned over a heat source. The type of heat will greatly affect the final flavor of the tea — a wood fire, electric heat, charcoal, or gas flames may be used to fire the leaves. Each year, the tea may have a different taste but will have a similar look. The individual garden's processes, whether the leaves are hand harvested or machine harvested (a more recent way), and, of course, the environment all play an important role in the final product.

REMEMBER

In Japan, the oxidation of the leaves is usually stopped with steam. The leaves retain their bright green color as well as their grassy flavor. Japanese producers take more control over consistency from batch to batch, year to year, so teas from previous years are often blended with that from the current year. Teas from various gardens can also be blended to get the right balance. Nearly all of Japan's tea is machine harvested. (Japan made the first mechanical harvester in the early 1900s.)

Looking at Chinese Green Teas

The most exquisite teas were once destined as tribute teas to the emperor. Many of these select teas are still ranked among the country's finest and consistently appear on China's "ten famous teas" list.

REMEMBER

Because China has been producing tea for thousands of years, each tea has a traditional name that has been handed down. In addition, each tea is likely to have a name that refers to where or how it was produced, and perhaps a name that describes its appearance or its quality. Individual provinces may have their own names for a particular tea. You may find variations on these names, translations, and so on, which can make things even more confusing. In this section, we go through a few representative green teas, and we've included several versions of their names, but don't get too hung up on what they're called — and don't worry about finding exactly this or that tea. Just start anywhere, and you'll surely find something that you love!

Biluochun (green snail, bi lo chun, Dongting biluochun)

Biluochun was traditionally grown only in the Dongting mountain region of Suzhou, in Jiangsu Province, although today it's grown in other areas as well. The tea's uniqueness and quality are due to the "Dongting population" of tea plants.

Dating to the Qing Dynasty, this celebrated tea is one of China's intangible cultural heritages and is usually number two on its "famous teas" list. Its name means "green snail spring," referring to the tea's spiral shape and early spring harvest (see Figure 5-2). Biluochun is hand plucked and produced in small batches (and you'll find that its price reflects this).

FIGURE 5-2:
Examples of
Chinese green
teas: biluochun,
gunpowder, lung
ching, and palace
needle.

Photos by Lisa McDonald and Jill Rheinheimer

Gunpowder

Gunpowder tea has been made for centuries in China — and was ideal for early trade. Because the tea leaves were hand-rolled into tight balls (akin to gunpowder pellets, possibly the inspiration for the name), little of the leaf was exposed to the environment, so the tea kept its flavor and quality during lengthy sea journeys.

TIP

Today, gunpowder may be hand- or machine-rolled into its signature pearls or pellets (refer to Figure 5-2). Younger leaves make smaller balls, indicating quality. These tightly rolled leaves often require several infusions to fully open. The green tea comes through with a nutty toastiness and a bit of smoke. (Read about black gunpowder tea in Chapter 4.)

Huangshan maofeng (Yellow Mountain fur peak)

Making the list of China's "famous teas," huangshan maofeng is produced in Anhui Province, near Yellow Mountain. Its name refers to its provenance; the white hairs on the buds and young leaves; and the shape of the leaves, which resemble mountain peaks. This mellow tea has a fragrant aroma.

Jasmine and other scented teas

Teas that are scented with highly aromatic flowers or fruit are considered classic teas. In these teas, the aroma and flavors of the flowers or fruit have been absorbed into the structure of the tea leaves. See Chapter 3 for more information about these traditional teas.

Lung ching (dragon well, long jing)

Once a tribute tea presented to the emperor, lung ching usually ranks number one of China's "famous teas." From Zhejiang Province, this mountain-grown tea is plucked in March to April. After withering, the leaves are pan fried, which stops the oxidation process and retains the leaves' bright green color and their flavor. The pan frying also causes the leaves to fold on themselves lengthwise (refer to Figure 5-2).

With a balance of sweet, bitter, grassy, and toasty, its unique and prized flavor owes a lot to its terroir.

Palace needle (ocean green needle)

Palace needle tea is grown in Hubei, a province in south-central China with a subtropical monsoon climate. The first leaves and buds are plucked in mid-April. The leaves are rolled into needle shape (refer to Figure 5-2), which allows the leaves to lightly oxidate, and then dried using a rather moderate temperature. The rolling process and drying temperature give this tea its unique mildly sweet flavor.

Discovering Japanese Green Teas

Around three-quarters of Japan's tea is produced from the Yabukita cultivar, which was bred in the early 1900s. This cultivar is frost resistant, high yield, and is thought to have the ideal balance of flavor (sweet, bitter, umami, and astringency).

Bancha

Originally, "bancha" referred to any tea consumed by commoners, but today it refers to tea produced from the second harvest (sencha being the first harvest). Although it's still considered lower grade than sencha because it's made with larger and more mature leaves, bancha has much to commend it. Brewed, it has a more subdued vegetal flavor than sencha, with a lighter body and a toasted note. It's refreshing iced. Bancha is often used for genmaicha and hojicha.

Genmaicha and matcha genmaicha

Roasted rice was first added to tea for economy's sake. By adding inexpensive rice to tea leaves, more cups could be brewed out of those leaves. Now, however, genmaicha (see Figure 5-3) — a blend of green tea (usually bancha) and roasted rice — is popular both within and outside Japan. Savory, starchy, and hardy, genmaicha is terrific for when you're a bit hungry and want a tea that has substance. Yet, the brininess that's characteristic of Japanese green teas is still there. Genmaicha is terrific iced. If matcha is also part of the blend, it's matcha genmaicha.

Gyokuro (jade dew)

The most labor intensive and most expensive of Japan's leaf teas, gyokuro is produced in limited quantities from a special clonal tea plant variety with small leaves. The plants are shaded for several weeks before harvest, which forces the leaves to produce more chlorophyll, resulting in a brighter green color. Shading also allows the leaves to retain more L-theanine, an amino acid that gives gyokuro its characteristic umami flavor. The bud and first leaf are plucked by hand in early spring, steamed to stop oxidation, and dried. The stems and main leaf veins are removed, and the leaves are then rolled into needle shape.

Gyokuro is brewed at a very low temperature to bring out its rich, sweet, umami flavor. Note that it can be difficult to properly brew gyokuro, which is why we often recommend kabusecha (see later in this chapter) as a less finicky and less expensive alternative.

FIGURE 5-3: Examples of Japanese green teas: genmaicha, kukicha hojicha, sencha, and matcha.

genmaicha

kukicha hojicha

sencha

matcha

Photos by Lisa McDonald and Jill Rheinheimer

Hojicha (houjicha)

"Hojicha" refers to *any* roasted Japanese green tea. A relatively new tea, hojicha was developed in Kyoto in the 1920s. Its appealing aroma and ability to convert poor teas (such as the fibrous, hard leaves of the third and fourth harvest) into an enjoyable tea probably ensured its success. Today, you can find various grades of hojicha, including premium tea. Whole leaves, pieces of leaves, stems, veins, or fannings (tiny leaf bits) can be used. (See Figure 5-3 for kukicha hojicha.)

To make hojicha, the harvested leaves and/or stems are first steamed to stop oxidation and then are put into a rotating drum, roasted at approximately 200°C (392°F), and cooled. The roasting process sets off chemical changes in the tea leaves, reducing the caffeine level. Thus, hojicha — regardless of its base tea — has little bitterness and is low in caffeine. If only stems and veins are roasted, the tea has even less caffeine because caffeine is found primarily in the leaves. Despite its toasty flavor profile, hojicha is still considered a green tea.

Kamairicha (tamaryokucha)

Rather than steamed, kamairicha leaves are pan-fried and rolled, using Chinese production methods, which gives them a slightly toastier note than that of the classically steamed teas. These leaves are often called tamaryokucha (note, however, that "tamaryokucha" can also refer to tea that is steamed rather than pan-fried).

Kukicha (twig tea, stem tea)

Composed of mostly twigs and leaf stems, kukicha is literally the undesirable stuff that's removed during gyokuro, tencha, and higher-grade sencha tea production. Although kukicha is now widely enjoyed, it had more humble beginnings. With limited land and natural resources, Japanese farmers needed to maximize what they could get out of their crops. They found that after they harvested the tea leaves, they could make tea out of the twigs that were left behind. Selling the leaf tea, they consumed the twig tea themselves.

The *kuki*, or stalks, contain little caffeine and yield a lightly creamy and nutty flavor. The stalks may be roasted to produce kuki hojicha (or kukicha hojicha) (refer to Figure 5-3).

Matcha and tencha

Tencha is the tea used to make matcha. Around four weeks before harvest, tea plants are shaded so that the leaves produce more chlorophyll and retain more L-theanine. After the leaves are plucked, the stems and all leaf veins are removed, and the remaining leaf pieces are dried. These tea leaves, or tencha, are then ground into a fine powder, or matcha (see Figures 5-3 and 5-4). Traditionally, tencha was stone-ground, and some matcha continues to be made this way. Grinding must be done slowly so that heat isn't generated; it takes around three hours to produce thirty grams of matcha. Today, this process can be mechanized, using ceramic balls, for faster grinding. Note that the time of harvest, the leaves that are harvested, and the harvesting method determine the quality of the tencha. That, in turn, dictates the quality of the matcha, and even whether it's destined for drinking or for culinary uses.

REMEMBER

There's a lot of confusion in the United States about what "matcha" means because the word is used for several very different things. Here's how to distinguish between them:

- » **Matcha:** Traditionally, matcha consists of tencha that was produced from first-harvest hand-plucked leaves and then slowly ground into a powder. It's available to buy in very small quantities, in various grades, and is very expensive.

- » **Culinary matcha:** Generally consists of tencha that was produced from second-harvest machine-harvested leaves and then slowly ground into a powder. It's available in larger quantities, is less expensive than matcha, and is best used for culinary purposes.

- » **Powdered green tea:** This is often also referred to as "matcha" outside Japan. However, it's not made from tencha. It's available to buy in larger quantities, is inexpensive, and is best used for tea lattes and whenever you want some green tea flavor.

FIGURE 5-4: Shaded tea plants; grinding matcha.

Photos by Lisa McDonald

TIP

With its vegetal and full-bodied complexity, matcha is not for everyone, although you can tweak many parameters to your personal preference. The matcha you use as well as your brewing temperature, the tea-to-water ratio, the bowl you whisk it in, and your whisking technique impact flavor. You can make thick matcha (*koicha*) or thin matcha (*usucha*). You can whisk to generate froth (which usually results in less astringency and umami flavor) or carefully whisk so that you minimize the amount of froth. Or, just put your tea and water in a bottle and shake it — done!

Sencha and Kabusecha

Invented in the early 1700s by tea manufacturer Nagatani Souen (or Soen) but popular only after World War II, first- or second-harvest sencha constitutes some two-thirds of Japan's tea and runs the gamut from very high quality to a more everyday type of tea. The finest sencha is produced from the first harvest, which takes place in May. The second harvest (June to July) is also used for sencha production, although these lower-quality leaves are often roasted to make hojicha instead.

To produce sencha, the tea leaves are steamed to stop oxidation, dried, and then machine rolled, which gives them a uniform appearance and breaks down some of the leaf cell walls, increasing flavor (refer to Figure 5-3). Sencha is brisk, full of fresh-mown grass and brine flavor, and is refreshing iced.

When the plants are shaded before harvesting, the tea is kabusecha or kabuse ("cover") sencha. With characteristics between a sencha and gyokuro, kabusecha is sweeter and less astringent than sencha, with some of the richness of gyokuro.

Finding Green Teas from Other Countries

More and more gardens are adding green tea production in countries where, previously, mainly black teas were produced. These teas often fall between Chinese and Japanese green teas in flavor and are mainly air dried.

Nepal, India, Georgia, and Rwanda are examples of countries where green tea production is slowly becoming more popular. With ever-increasing demand for green tea in the West, tea producers are trying to get into the trend and doing quite well with some amazing teas, like the green tea produced in Georgia that's depicted in Figure 5-5.

FIGURE 5-5:
Green tea from Georgia.

Photo by Lisa McDonald

Chapter **6**

Oolong (Wulong) Tea

Your journey through the world of tea isn't complete without experiencing oolong tea. Neither green nor black tea, oolongs are somewhere in-between. Some may be more vegetal and are closer to green tea in nature, whereas others lean toward black tea. Yet every oolong has undergone a complicated and lengthy production method that has generated a leaf that's complex and multilayered. These teas can — and should — be brewed multiple times, with every successive infusion bringing out new flavor nuances. Yep, you really need to try some oolong tea.

In this chapter, we look at how oolong tea is made, which takes longer and includes more steps than black, green, or white tea production. We review the various flavor profiles that oolongs may have, which reflect the manner of their processing *and* determine how you brew them. These are complex teas. Even their name, "oolong," isn't clear-cut, as we briefly consider. Lastly, we introduce a few representative oolong teas.

Taking a Closer Look at Oolong Tea

REMEMBER

Whether you choose a lighter oolong or an almost fully oxidized one, you are in for a treat. Because more steps are often involved for making these teas, there is a complexity in each cup that might be less detectable in a classic black or green tea. Also, a wide array of oolong styles is available, from almost green to almost black.

Each region, and each garden, has a style of its own, many that have been passed down over centuries, while new gardens are beginning their own traditions.

How oolong tea is made

Early in China's Qing Dynasty (1644–1911), Fujian tea producers began a new tea process, resulting in wulong — or oolong — teas. In oxidation level, oolongs fall between unoxidized green teas and fully oxidized black teas, ranging from lightly (10 percent) to more highly (80 percent) oxidized. Of all the types of teas, oolongs undergo the most complex processing, equal parts science and art.

After *C. sinensis* leaves are picked, they undergo

>> Withering on a drying rack to evaporate some of the moisture in the leaves.

>> Resting, to cool down the leaves because withering generates heat.

>> Bruising by tossing or stirring, which slightly damages the leaves and begins the oxidation process.

>> Resting, to slow oxidation.

>> Rolling, which breaks down the leaves a little more; this process is done in short spurts over a long period of time.

>> Drying, to stop oxidation.

>> Shaping, by hand or machine.

>> Final drying; some oolong teas are also roasted.

These steps can be done in various ways and for various amounts of time, and many of them are repeated — allowing the leaves to oxidize in a very slow and controlled manner. For example, the leaves may be bruised and/or rolled and dried repeatedly, which intensifies and refines the distinct characteristics of oolongs. Throughout the process, the leaves are evaluated and assessed. The producer will look at the leaf edges, for instance. Bruising causes those edges to turn red, a desired change that reflects where the leaves are in the process. (After you brew an oolong, you will often see these red edges.)

Because immature leaves are too tender to withstand this extensive processing and don't have the molecular composition best suited for oolong tea, the leaves are often harvested later in the year. Mature single leaves, or leaf sets that include three or four leaves in addition to the opened bud, are used.

Flavor profiles of oolong tea

REMEMBER

Oolongs are often described as being more earthy or woody than most black and green teas. Rarely would someone say that they had a malty oolong. The brighter or greener oolongs are more reminiscent of the more minimally oxidized green teas but with the slight heaviness of the earthy quality. On the reverse side, the darker, more oxidized oolongs tend to have a deeper, bolder flavor and a profile that's slightly more like a black tea.

TIP

Note that the oxidation level of your oolong tea determines how you want to brew it — or at least gives you a starting point. As with any tea, you can certainly tweak brewing parameters for your own preference, especially since certain oolongs will offer different nuances when brewed at various temperatures. Generally, however, you'll want to start here:

>> Less oxidized, or green, oolong teas: use a lower brewing temperature (similar to green tea)

>> More oxidized oolong teas: use a higher brewing temperature (similar to black tea)

It will probably take multiple infusions for the large, mature leaves to fully open up, with each brew giving you a slightly different experience.

Discovering the Varieties of Oolong Teas

TIP

China has been making oolong tea for nearly 300 years. This long tradition has also handed down many traditional names, along with many variations on those names. In this section, we run through some representative oolongs, but don't be intimidated by the names. Although we do want to recognize the tradition behind them, you may find these, or similar teas, by other names — plus there are new teas being produced all the time. Today, more and more gardens in various countries are trying their hand in producing this style of tea, with some stellar results. We simply want to introduce you to the world of oolongs, and we encourage you to just pick an oolong — any oolong — and try it for yourself!

Dan cong (guangdong, phoenix)

Produced in China's volcanic Fenghuang shan (Phoenix Mountain) in Guangdong Province, dan cong is produced from centuries-old tea plants that are pruned to grow as trees. The ancestors of these plants were indigenous to this area and were used to produce tea for early export to the West. There are many varieties of dan cong, or "single bush," grown at different elevations. Each will have its own flavor profile. Dan cong is one of China's "famous teas" (see Figure 6-1 for an example of this tea).

Dong ding (tung ting)

On Taiwan's "famous teas" list, the cultivar for this tea came from China's Fujian Province and was first grown on Taiwan's Dong Ding Mountain in the mid-1800s. Although Dong Ding means "frozen summit" or "icy peak," the mountain is under 2,500 feet in elevation, with a humid, cloudy, and rainy environment that's ideal for tea. Usually roasted, this premium oolong has notes of honey.

Dongfang meiren (oriental beauty)

To produce dongfang meiren, tea growers allow minute green leafhoppers to bite the tea leaves, which triggers chemical changes within each leaf as the plant fends off the pests. The leaf's response is specific to leafhopper damage — and the volatile chemicals that the leaf generates have an aroma and flavor that are pleasing to us. The leaves are harvested when they've been optimally damaged by the leafhoppers, resulting in a tea that's sweet and smooth. Note that the tea cultivar also heavily contributes to flavor, and so the quality and price of dongfang meiren reflect both the cultivar and production expertise.

FIGURE 6-1: Oolong teas: dan cong, jun chiyabari, taifu, and Tieguanyin.

Photos by Lisa McDonald and Jill Rheinheimer

High mountain

"High mountain" refers to any tea, usually oolong, that's grown at or above 3,300 feet in elevation. At higher elevations, the plants grow and mature more slowly, so these teas have limited harvests. The slow growth coupled with the unique mountainous environment also give the tea a more complex flavor. Taiwan is known for its high-mountain tea, including jin xuan (milk oolong), grown at 3,600 feet in the Alishan mountain range, and the premium oolong, li shan, grown on Lishan (Li Mountain) at elevations exceeding 8,000 feet and on Taiwan's "famous teas" list.

Jun chiyabari

Although most oolong teas are produced in China and Taiwan, the Jun Chiyabari estate in Nepal's Dhankuta district also produces oolong tea. This family-run garden works to ensure tea's future as the climate changes. They use plants from both clones and seed plants for diversity, locate their gardens higher in the mountains than is typical to offset future warming, and plant in various microclimates. As shown in Figure 6-1, jun chiyabari oolong comprises dark hand-rolled leaves sprinkled with silver tips. A more-oxidized oolong, the tea has a woody flavor, an astringent note, and an apricot finish.

Taifu

Known as "five color tea," the leaves of taifu range from beige to sienna in color (refer to Figure 6-1). This oolong is produced in northern Taiwan and is around 60 percent oxidized. This greater oxidation gives it an almost malty note, like some early picked tea from India. The earthiness gives way to an incredibly smooth cup, with every sip having a slightly different finish.

Tieguanyin (iron goddess of mercy, iron Buddha, ti kuan yin)

One of China's "famous teas," originally grown in Fujian Province, Tieguanyin is named after the deity Guanyin, the Iron Goddess of Mercy. There are *many* versions of this tea — depending on the cultivar and how the leaves are processed — although they are all under the umbrella of Tieguanyin.

If produced as a "green" oolong, the tea is buttery with a slight grassy note, although the classic earthiness of an oolong is more present than in typical green teas. Refer to Figure 6-1 for an example from Indonesia, where it was grown at high altitude.

If further oxidized and baked and/or roasted (and there are variations and degrees of this), the tea acquires greater complexity, a toasty note, and sweetness; there is little astringency. Wild-grown Tieguanyin is often called "monkey-picked tea" because it's grown at high altitude — we assure you, though, that monkeys have never been part of this tea's production. Legends, however, make great marketing tools to sell this more rare and unique tea.

Wuyi rock tea (da hong pao)

Da hong pao often refers to any number of teas produced in the eastern region of the rocky Wuyi Mountains in Fujian Province. Called rock teas, these are produced from centuries-old tea plants and from clones of ancient tea plants. There are hundreds of known cultivars in this region, some with limited numbers of plants, so leaves from different varieties may be blended to make tea. Rock teas are usually roasted, and their name describes both the plant's growing environment as well as the tea's mineral notes.

Chapter **7**

White Tea

White teas seem special, perhaps even rare. Indeed, they are delicate in leaf and flavor. These are teas that you want to carefully handle so that you don't crush the fluffy buds and fragile leaves. And if you prize subtlety and gentle flavors, these just might be the teas for you.

In this chapter, we first look at how white tea is made, and then discuss the flavor profile of this minimally processed tea. Not many white teas are produced, but we take a look at several classics.

Taking a Closer Look at White Tea

Produced for centuries in China, white tea was originally ground and then whisked into a foam. There were even competitions for the whitest and longest-lasting foam, while artists manipulated the foam into images. It wasn't until the 1700s that white tea leaves were steeped rather than being ground, and China didn't export the tea until the late 1800s.

How white tea is made

To produce white tea, buds are plucked in early spring, between late March and early April. For new-style white tea, the bud along with the first two, still immature, leaves are plucked. Harvesting is done on dry, sunny days so that the buds and leaves don't retain moisture, and care is taken to ensure that the leaves aren't damaged in any way. The tea is left to wither for up to 72 hours in the sun or in a dry room and then is quickly air dried with hot air fans to prevent oxidation. Because both buds and the undersides of immature leaves retain their minute hairs, they are silvery in color (giving the tea its moniker of "white"), while the tops of the young leaves keep their bright green color.

Flavor profiles of white tea

TIP

REMEMBER

White teas are typically more subtle in flavor and require a little more care in brewing than the tea of more oxidized leaves.

White teas are often described as being lighter in flavor, but this differs greatly depending on the type of white tea you're drinking. A larger-leaf tea like a pai mu tan or a white peony, which is a blend of buds and leaves, might allow for more flavor extraction because there is more surface area to extract from and the leaves aren't protected by the tiny hairs or fuzz like the buds alone.

Often, white teas are described as having a slight floral or even apricot finish. Much of this depends on where the tea was grown. As mentioned in Chapter 3, the terroir makes a big difference, and because white tea is minimally processed, the environment in which the tea is grown comes through in the leaf more than it does in those teas that are more processed.

INSIDER TIPS ABOUT WHITE TEA

You might hear that white tea has the least amount of caffeine — or even *no caffeine* — compared to other teas, but that just isn't true! The buds contain more caffeine than any other part of the tea plant, although the lower brewing temperature required for white tea means that less of the caffeine is extracted. You can see that this is a complicated calculation (Chapter 11 gives additional reasons for why we can't generalize about caffeine level).

Also, you may hear that white tea is the healthiest tea to drink because it's minimally processed. However, all tea contains polyphenols (antioxidants), although tangible health benefits are hard to gauge (see Chapter 14). Keep in mind that the fuzzy buds and immature leaves of white tea are the most exposed to air-borne contaminants.

Discovering the Different White Teas

White teas originated in the Fujian Province of China, but because they are becoming more popular, additional countries are beginning to produce their version of this subtle, yet delicious, type of tea.

China

Two main varieties of white tea originated in China.

Silver needle (baihao yinzhen)

Once a tribute tea presented to the emperor, silver needle remains on China's "famous teas" list. It was originally produced only in Fuding, located in the northeast part of Fujian Province. The silver needle, or baihao yinzhen, is distinct from all other teas because only one single fresh leaf shoot is picked — before it can unfurl into a full leaf. It is then withered, allowed to minimally oxidize, and then dried by baking, using a precise temperature for a controlled amount of time. Although there are very specific ways to produce this tea, there are variations from one region to the next.

Silver needle has a light aroma and liquor because the buds are coated with minute hairs, as shown in Figure 7-1. The delicacy of flavor is more pronounced with the second infusion because the buds release deeper flavors as they unfurl slightly more.

FIGURE 7-1:
Silver needle tea.

Photo by Lisa McDonald

Pai mu tan (bai mu dan, white peony)

Also produced mainly in Fujian Province, pai mu tan or white peony has a more robust flavor compared to the silver needle. Two young leaves are plucked along with the bud, as shown in Figure 7-2. After the leaf sets are picked, they are withered and lightly oxidized, with each production step ensuring minimal damage to the leaves (Figure 7-2).

Although more flavorful than silver needle, this one-bud-to-two-leaves ratio still produces a lighter cup than a black or green tea, and the tea maintains its subtle delicacy. The aroma is slightly floral; even a slight fruitiness can be detected.

FIGURE 7-2:
Leaf set and pai mu tan tea.

Photos by Lisa McDonald

Other white tea producers

With its growing popularity, tea producers from around the globe — including Nepal, India, Sri Lanka, and Taiwan, to name just a few — are trying their hand at white tea.

Figure 7-3 shows an example of a small family farm in Japan that's withering freshly picked tea leaves to produce just enough white tea for their own consumption, in the hope of perfecting the practice for larger-scale production.

FIGURE 7-3:
Drying tea leaves.

Photo by Lisa McDonald

South Indian white tea from the state of Tamil Nadu

While black teas are more commonly produced in India, smaller estates have been trying their hand at other types, like white tea. The large-leaf white tea pictured in Figure 7-4 is very minimally oxidized with very little leaf damage. The only oxidation that occurs is when the leaf is picked and transported from the garden to production; during that process, there's some breakdown of the cell walls. The flavor of this tea is subtle, with a slight dryness, yet it's bolder than a classic white peony or silver needle.

S India white tea

Malawi antlers

Photos by Lisa McDonald and Jill Rheinheimer

FIGURE 7-4:
South Indian white tea from Tamil Nadu and Malawi antlers.

Malawi antlers

Third-generation, family-owned Satemwa Tea Estate (located in southern Malawi, a small landlocked country in southeastern Africa) produces only around fifty kilograms of Malawi antlers a year. This white tea is both very rare and highly unusual. No leaves are used; instead, young shoots of the tea bush are picked and air dried. This minimal processing ensures that the shoots — which resemble antlers — retain a bit of velvety sheen (refer to Figure 7-4). Tea bushes with a longer shoot axis are selected for this unique tea.

Brewed, Malawi antlers make a wonderfully smooth tea with no bitterness and with little astringency. Fruity and a bit sweet with a slight floral note, this exquisite tea has layers of flavor.

Chapter **8**

Other Teas

T ea is nothing if not diverse — to a staggering degree. Having surveyed black, green, oolong, and white teas in earlier chapters, we still haven't covered everything. For example, did you know that tea leaves can be fermented, or that tea can be made from the trunk of the tea plant? And ice wine isn't the only beverage made from frozen plants! This catch-all chapter makes sure that you don't miss out on anything.

In these sections, we go through the various fermented teas that are produced. We then consider some specialty and unique teas.

Exploring Fermented Teas

Although you often hear that black tea is "fermented," the process is more correctly called "oxidation" (see Chapter 4). However, pu-erh and yellow teas are actually fermented — undergoing the microbially driven process that converts green tea into something special.

Pu-erh tea

Pu-erh (or pu'er) — a microbially fermented tea produced in China's Yunnan Province — is a huge category, encompassing both loose leaves and compressed cakes (see Figure 8-1 and the nearby sidebar "The pressing problem of durability"). The tea leaves are processed much like black tea but then are allowed to ferment, either naturally or with a little help, as they age.

The fermentation process differentiates the two primary types of pu-erh:

>> **Raw pu-erh.** Naturally fermented raw *(sheng)* pu-erh can be consumed after it has aged for a couple of years (young sheng pu-erh); its flavor is more like green tea.

    However, when raw pu-erh is allowed to naturally ferment and age for longer periods of time (ripened sheng pu-erh), it mellows; develops complexity; and boosts spicy, earthy, woody, and malty notes. The longer the tea ages, the more valuable it becomes, with decades-old tea commanding high prices.

>> **Ripe pu-erh.** Cooked or ripe *(shou)* pu-erh is produced from tea leaves that are subjected to microbes, heat, and moisture. This combination speeds up the "ripening" process so that within several months, the tea can either be consumed (young shou pu-erh) or can be aged. It won't, however, attain the depth of flavor of aged raw pu-erh.

FIGURE 8-1:
Assorted
pu-erh teas.

Photo by Jill Rheinheimer

THE PRESSING PROBLEM OF DURABILITY

When the Chinese first exported tea, they ensured that the product was durable because sea and land routes entailed arduous journeys that took many months. Delicate green teas could spoil or be ruined. Fully oxidized and thoroughly dried black teas such as lapsang souchong and pu-erh, however, were well suited for transport — especially if they were in the form of bricks. Tea leaves that were compressed into bricks were less exposed to the environment and thus retained more of their flavor. (Today, pu-erh is still commonly pressed into cakes, allowing the tea to maintain its quality for decades.)

Tea bricks also took up less space than loose tea, a boon for 18th-century exporters dealing with transportation costs and logistics. Lest we think this inconsequential, by the late 1700s, around **three million pounds of tea a year** were carried by camel from Fujian Province to Russia alone!

To make tea bricks, binding agents such as animal fat, flour, or even manure were combined with the tea leaves. The mixture was pressed into molds and dried, yielding a brick that weighed about 22 pounds. These bricks were cut into smaller chunks and wrapped for transport. Because tea was so valuable, tea bricks also served as currency.

TIP

Due to the fermentation process, the components of pu-erh are complex, and they interact with gut microbiomes. For this reason, pu-erh is often consumed after meals and is said to help with digestion.

Yellow tea

Made in southern China for around two thousand years, yellow tea was originally a tribute tea, enjoyed only by the emperor and other elites. Eventually the non-elite could also drink the tea, but that didn't much broaden its range. It continued to be made and consumed locally. Consequently, many regional production techniques (and secrets) have been lost over time. Today, only a few types of yellow tea are produced in small amounts by a few gardens. The process is complicated, time consuming, and costly.

Yellow tea can be produced from buds, small leaves, or large leaves, with each type having its own characteristics. Like green tea, the leaves are fried to stop oxidation, but then they're wrapped in either cloth or heavy paper to undergo a "smothering" step, or micro-fermentation. This step, often called "sealed yellowing," allows the moist, softened leaves to reabsorb their own aromatics; increases leaf oxidation; and reduces the grassiness that characterizes green teas. After smothering, the leaves are slowly roasted. These production steps may be repeated multiple times. During the process, the simple polyphenols of the tea leaf are converted into complex theaflavins, giving the tea a yellow-pigmented leaf and a golden cup.

Getting Chilly with Frost and Frozen Teas

Being frostbitten is generally a negative experience, and tea producers often go to great lengths to protect their plants from the cold. However, frozen tea leaves can result in some wonderful tea!

Nilgiri frost tea

Produced in the Nilgiri Hills (Blue Mountain) of southern India, Nilgiri frost tea capitalizes on having been touched by frost! Tea leaves are plucked during winter — either at night or very early in the morning — when frost has hit and the leaves are lightly frozen. The leaves are then allowed to thaw as part of the production process.

Leaves continually respond to their environment and to stress. When temperatures drop, temperature-sensitive plants try to prevent damage to their internal structure by making minute genetic changes and subtle shifts in proteins, amino acids, acidity, minerals, and so on. This response is specific to the threat, so frost provokes a different reaction than does cold weather. These chemical differences are reflected in the flavor of the tea.

Frozen black tea

Similar to Nilgiri frost tea production, Takatomo Katagi of Katagi Koukaen in Japan makes frozen black tea, albeit by hand. He places frozen tea leaves in a shallow bamboo basket and manually manipulates them for about half an hour so that they oxidize. Figure 8-2 shows the frozen tea leaves, the green plucked leaves, and the finished black tea. Since this is incredibly labor intensive, he produces very small quantities of this black tea and only during those years in which the leaves freeze. Due to its unique processing, which can never be precisely duplicated, the tea will have a different flavor profile from year to year, although it's often described as having a subtle sweetness.

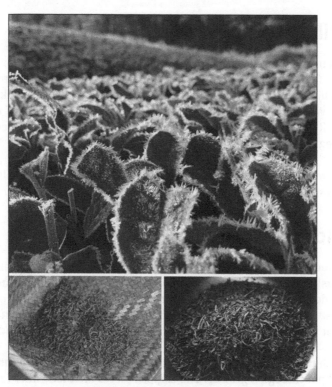

FIGURE 8-2:
Making frozen
black tea.

Published with permission from Takatomo Katagi, Katagi Koukaen

Discovering Additional Rarities

Tea leaves turn into tea depending on how they are produced, and the possibilities are truly endless. Some processing methods have been perfected over centuries, whereas others are newly developed.

GABA teas

When a tea name includes "GABA," it refers to how the tea is processed. For these teas, the leaves are often picked later in the year, and then they're cured for several days in a nitrogen chamber. This results in higher levels of antioxidants, polyphenols, and the neurotransmitter gamma-aminobutyric acid (GABA). Although GABA tea is sometimes claimed to offer greater health benefits than other tea, far more research needs to be done (see Chapter 14, which looks at why it's so hard to substantiate health claims).

Milk or milky oolong

Not to be confused with jin xuan, which is often called milk oolong for its creaminess (see Chapter 6), this Chinese specialty — a scented oolong tea — is produced in Fujian Province. Individual tea leaves are steamed over a milk and water bath, allowing the moist tea leaves to absorb the aroma and flavor of milk. Rolled into small pearls, the leaves unfurl as they are brewed, releasing a sweet, creamy flavor along with a creamy mouth feel.

TIP

Be aware, however, that inexpensive tea may be flavored with milk to mimic either this specialty tea or jin xuan oolong tea.

Old tree bancha

A unique tea, old tree bancha is produced from entire tea plants excluding only the roots! At the tea gardens of Mandokoro in Japan's Shiga Prefecture, tea plants are cut down when they are past their useful life, or at fifty years old, to allow new growth from the roots. To celebrate the plants' long lives and in appreciation for what they've provided, they aren't discarded but instead are made into tea.

As shown in Figure 8-3, the plants are first broken by hand into smaller pieces and put through a grinder. The chipped pieces are then either fed into a rotating roasting drum, heated by a wood fire, or are roasted in a small container over a wood fire and hand stirred. The finished product — comprising a few leaf pieces and chips of trunk and twigs — is boiled in water to make the aroma tea. With a caramel tobacco flavor and a soft smokiness, this tea evokes an evening spent around a campfire.

Flowering or blooming tea

TIP

Flowering teas, or blooming teas, are leaves and often flowers, bonded together in a bulb with string and left to dry. When the bulb is put into hot water, it opens. These teas are lovely and make beautiful centerpieces or decorations for tea get-togethers, so you'll want to brew them in a cup or glass teapot.

Unfortunately, flowering teas are often not made of high-quality tea leaves. Sometimes it takes several minutes for the bulb to flower or bloom, and by this time, the tea is most likely quite bitter.

FIGURE 8-3:
Making old tree
bancha tea.

Published with permission from Mandokoro Tea Garden and
Authentic Nippon LLC

Purple tea

Purple tea is produced from a genetic variant of *Camellia sinensis*; the plants are propagated by cuttings to ensure that they all produce the sought-after purple leaves. Although anthocyanin — which gives the leaves their color — is heavily studied because it's an antioxidant, it's not clear if the extra anthocyanin has any measurable health benefits for us. (See Chapter 14 to understand why antioxidant content doesn't always translate into demonstrated benefits.) However, purple strains have other advantages:

>> Because anthocyanin level and sunlight are linked, purple tea is ideal for tea gardens at high altitudes near the equator, such as in Kenya.

>> The plants seem to tolerate drought and frost.

>> The purple leaves can be made into various types of tea.

>> The full-bodied tea is delicious!

Chapter **9**

Herbal Teas

lot of herbal teas are available, and you may even have a few options in your own backyard, such as mint or lemon balm. Beyond plant leaves, herbal teas may include flowers, fruit, bark, roots, seeds, spices — anything that doesn't come from the *Camellia sinensis* tea plant. Note that many of these same ingredients may be blended into tea as well, so you may find, for instance, an orange tea that has a black tea base as opposed to an herbal orange rooibos or orange fruit tea. However, the herbal teas in this chapter don't contain a single tea leaf.

In the following sections, we look at why herbal teas are called "tea" — even though they aren't made from the tea plant. We next consider a couple of caffeine-fueled options that energize, and then we turn to those that are naturally caffeine free, discussing some of the components commonly found in herbal teas.

Why Are Herbal Teas Called "Tea" When They're Not Tea?

According to the Oxford English Dictionary, "tea" includes infusions made the same way as tea, using leaves, flowers, and/or other parts of non-tea plants. So, technically, any plant that you brew in hot water is "tea." Hmm. Does that mean that coffee is actually tea? Just wondering.

REMEMBER

In this book, we use "tea" to refer to anything made from the *Camellia sinensis* plant, and "herbal tea" for everything else. You can sound fancy and say "tisane" instead, but that's just a French word for "herbal tea."

Herbal Does Not Mean Caffeine Free

WARNING

Beware: Not all herbal teas are caffeine free! Mate, guarana, guayusa, and yaupon holly all contain caffeine. (Today, however, you're more likely to find yaupon holly grown as an ornamental shrub rather than consumed as tea.)

Guayusa

Guayusa is an evergreen tree that's native to the Amazon. Its leaves have been used ritually and medicinally for centuries — possibly even for millennia. The tea is still consumed in the region and has been woven into the food tourism industry.

Guarana

The seeds of guarana, an evergreen native to the Amazon basin, have been used medicinally for hundreds of years. The seeds are also ground and consumed as an herbal tea — but one that contains a hefty dose of caffeine! Because each seed has more caffeine than coffee beans, guarana is often used in energy drinks as well.

Mate (yerba mate, maté)

Mate contains enough caffeine to give you an energy boost comparable to coffee! Legend says that mate is a gift from the gods, and it has been enjoyed for centuries, including by larger-than-life gauchos, who became folk heroes in South American lore. Today the drink is still extremely popular in South America as well as in parts of the Middle East.

To produce mate, leaves and sometimes stems from *Ilex paraguariensis* (a holly that grows in the rainforests; also called yerba mate) are chopped and dried. Mate is traditionally brewed in a hollow gourd (*chia*) and sipped through a strainer straw (*bombilla*) (see Chapter 17). Because it's low in tannins, mate won't grow bitter, no matter how long the leaves remain in the gourd.

Herbal Teas That Won't Keep You Up at Night

Most herbal teas don't contain caffeine, so any of the naturally caffeine-free options can be enjoyed late into the evening. Although none of them have been shown to physiologically promote sleep (see Chapter 15), sipping your favorite herbal tea can certainly calm and relax.

Rooibos

Rooibos (*Aspalathus linearis*) is a legume that's native to the Western Cape of South Africa; translated from Afrikaans, *rooibos* means "red bush." Indigenous peoples were the first to turn this plant into tea, and today, rooibos remains a popular drink. It's produced only in South Africa, where the Cederberg Mountains supply the growing conditions that this bush requires.

Young branches are cut from the shrub once a year from December to April. The cuttings are finely chopped and bruised to promote oxidation, moistened and layered (a "sweating" step), and then dried. During this process, the green leaves turn red (see Figure 9-1), yielding a flavor that's somewhat woody, sweet, and creamy. When unfermented, rooibos retains its green color and has a fresh, slightly tangy flavor, somewhat akin to green tea.

Honeybush (mountain tea, cape tea)

Honeybush (*Cyclopia* sp.) is probably named for its yellow, honey-scented flowers. Native to South Africa, twenty-three species are documented, each thriving in a specific environment from coastal to mountainous. Today, 70 percent of the honeybush produced comes from these wild shrubs, according to the South African Honeybush Tea Association, although the annual harvest is small.

FIGURE 9-1: Rooibos and honeybush.

The processing stages are like those of rooibos. Twigs and leaves are chopped, moistened and layered (sweated), and sometimes heated to develop the flavor, and then dried (see Figure 9-1). Because there are so many honeybush species — each with its very own flavor — several varieties may be combined during production. Typically, honeybush has an earthy flavor, with a touch of sweetness. When unfermented, honeybush retains its green color.

Fruit teas

TIP

Fruit teas consist of fruit — whether dried, freeze-dried, dehydrated, or candied — along with spices, flowers, and/or other herbals. Unlike fruit juice, these naturally caffeine-free teas are very low in sugar. If you want a fantastic, refreshing beverage, drink them iced. If you want to amp them up a notch, make them iced and top them off with carbonated or sparkling water, as we often do with the passionfruit fruit tea shown in Figure 9-2.

Ayurvedic teas

Emerging from India's ancient Vedic period and practiced for thousands of years, the ayurvedic system of medicine focuses on balancing bodily systems through diet, herbs, breathing exercises, and lifestyle. Ayurveda, meaning the science or knowledge of life, encompasses body, mind, and spirit, and describes three energy types. These body systems or doshas are still known by their Sanskrit names: *vata, pitta,* and *kapha.*

FIGURE 9-2:
Fruit tea.

Photo by Jill Rheinheimer

Ayurvedic teas are meant to counterbalance the doshas. (Fun online tests can help you determine your dosha.) Cooling and refreshing *pitta* tea equalizes the passionate and action-oriented *pitta* dosha, whereas peppery *kapha* tea energizes the calm *kapha* dosha. Sweet and creamy *vata* tea soothes the dynamic *vata* dosha (Figure 9-3).

FIGURE 9-3:
Ayurvedic herbal teas: *pitta* (left), *vata* (center), and *kapha* (right).

Source: Photo by Jill Rheinheimer

All the rest

TIP

Although herbal teas are often consumed for presumed health benefits — and you can find a dizzying array of "wellness" teas — we suggest that you drink the ones that you love the most (and read Chapter 15 to see why you shouldn't focus overly much on what they might do for your health).

You can find practically any flavor profile: floral, tart, vegetal, lemony, minty, sweet, spicy. Some even taste somewhat like black tea (for example, blueberry leaves) or green tea (for instance, Japanese mulberry leaves).

Many herbals are beautiful, such as the Greek mountain stalks shown in Figure 9-4. While it's said that this herb is supposed to relax you, we find that just the act of brewing these pretty stalks in a favorite teacup is calming in itself. Herbal blends sometimes contain full blossoms in addition to petals, making a visually stunning tea (Figure 9-4).

FIGURE 9-4: Greek mountain and floral herbal teas.

The world of herbal tea is vast, so if you're looking for a naturally caffeine-free tea, you'll surely find something that you really enjoy. Read on to discover additional elements frequently found in herbal teas.

Flowers

REMEMBER

Flowers can serve various purposes in herbal teas. Highly aromatic lavender and rose petals and buds, for instance, may be brewed on their own or may be part of a blend to which they contribute their floral notes. Tart hibiscus can balance a sweet blend or can be brewed by itself to make a tangy tea. At other times, pretty blossoms are sprinkled into a blend for visual effect and to lend a little creaminess to the herbal tea. Bright yellow sunflower or blue cornflower petals add a pop of color and cheeriness even if they don't contribute to the tea's flavor. Sometimes that color will accentuate a tea's flavor, at least in your mind. This can work with both herbal and true teas. For example, orangey-yellow petals sprinkled into a peach fruit tea or a peach black tea will reinforce the peach flavor psychologically.

Flowers of many different plants — including what we might consider weeds — find their way into herbal teas. Dandelions and goldenrod can also be brewed (perhaps another way to rid your lawn of dandelions?). We do, however, recommend that you forage only if you know what you're collecting.

Spices

TIP

Spices are integral to many herbal blends, and although definitive health benefits remain mostly elusive, some herbal teas contain ingredients that are especially helpful when you're not feeling the best. Licorice root gives an herbal tea a viscosity that coats the throat — particularly nice when you have a cold. Blends that include peppercorns or chili pepper have a little kick that helps clear your sinuses.

Seeds

Herbal teas may consist of seeds, like fennel or caraway, or even grain. Roasted barley tea is especially popular in Korea and other Asian countries. Unhulled barley kernels were roasted at home at one time, but now they're commercially processed (Figure 9-5).

FIGURE 9-5:
Roasted
barley tea.

Photo by Jill Rheinheimer

Leaves

Leaves, of course, are often brewed to make herbal teas. Peppermint may be one of the most popular, but lemon balm, lemongrass, moringa, stinging nettle, and others may be used as tea, either freshly collected or dried.

Chapter **10**

Drinking Tea Like an Expert

When you enter the tea world, you soon discover that there are *soooo* many teas to try! You might find that you want to expand your tea cupboard as well as your tea vocabulary and tasting expertise. Teapots and other tea accoutrements may beckon. If you've read Chapter 2, you know that you can easily make a great cup of tea with just the basics. But if you're ready to enhance your tea experience, the possibilities are vast — and, far more importantly, a whole lot of fun!

We begin this chapter with a look at tea professionals and how they taste tea, and then show you how easily you can do this at home. After that, we highlight some of the inexhaustible number of tea accessories out there, focusing on those that can elevate your tea experience, while offering tips to help you decide what's best for you.

Tasting — By the Experts

Most of you have heard of a wine sommelier, an expert taster of wines. When you go to a fancy restaurant or to a fine wine shop, you may have a sommelier suggest specific wines that pair well with your meal, or one that has an interesting story, or those that go well with your dinner party menu. A sommelier is trained to identify specific flavor profiles, aromas, color, and textures. For tea, this is no different.

The term "sommelier" comes from the French and dates to the 1300s. Much like the concept of head butler in the United Kingdom, the sommelier was charged with carrying his lord's luggage as well as getting, transporting, and storing supplies — including wine. Eventually, the sommelier's role narrowed, and the title became associated only with those who chose the wine. Finally, in the mid-1900s, official training and certification courses became available, initially in Europe and then in the United States. The title "tea sommelier" wasn't used until 1998, although tea experts and shop owners have been tasting and curating tea collections for centuries.

Tea professionals

Some contention exists in the professional world about using the word "sommelier" with tea professionals because there is no one governing body when it comes to certification. With wine, longstanding recognized certification organizations certify sommeliers, whereas with tea, one can attend a weekend-long course at a convention or take a few online courses and receive a tea sommelier certificate. Many companies and organizations are popping up, ready to train you as a tea sommelier — so many that we won't list them here. A quick Google search yields more than enough options.

Is it necessary to be certified? We don't know. We do think that experience and dedication to the topic of tea is vital to running a successful business or being able to teach about tea, and it's wonderful if you want to fully understand all things tea. This training can truly be done only with time. Some European countries such as Germany have more training programs that are tea specific. I (Lisa), for example, helped design a four-year tea sommelier and tasting program. The first two years were schooling and the second two years were internships in the tea industry. But even after years of working in the industry, I haven't found a truly comprehensive program.

Often, I feel people get caught up on the term "sommelier." I prefer to use the term "tea expert." I am an official "European-trained tea sommelier," but I feel like I am learning about tea every day. Tasting new teas, visiting gardens, and interacting daily with customers eager to enter the world of tea is invaluable for a tea professional. Getting a certificate, in my opinion, doesn't necessarily make you an expert. In many countries, the term "tea master" is used. This title can be earned only with years of dedication and knowledge, far surpassing what can be learned in a weeklong seminar or online course.

Words the experts use

There are so many fancy words and so many teas to describe! I am torn here because my training taught me to describe tea in such depth, using very specific words.

I was once at a wine tasting; the gentleman hosting knew my credentials as a tea sommelier, so I think he was aiming to impress. He described a wine as such: "A deep red but with a slight aubergine hue. Flavors of currants, black, not red; peach pit; nectarine skin; and subtle blackberry notes give way to a tobacco-scented, earthy, and mineral-filled spiciness. Though medium-bodied, the mouth feel is heavy, and, in the end, the dark cherry, red currant, and hazelnut shells with an herbaceous bite finish each sip with a robust woodiness." He looked at me and asked what my thoughts were. I politely said, "Yeah, it's good."

We experts can get a bit carried away with over-the-top descriptions of our favorite beverages. It's fun, don't get me wrong. I love having tea tastings at my store with excited people ready to experience something new. Some words do help describe what we are experiencing when tasting. Just remember, we all may experience flavor differently, and you should never feel as though you don't have a good-enough palate to taste what someone else is tasting.

I often use words that can help people relate to something more common. For example, I like to compare first- and second-flush Darjeelings with bananas. Trust me, you'll see where I am going with this. You know when you take a bite of a greener, slightly harder banana and it has a slight bite to it and leaves your mouth a little dry? But when you eat a riper, slightly browner banana, the flavor is sweeter and the mouth feel is more coating than drying. This is exactly the same way that a first-flush Darjeeling "feels" versus a second flush.

How experts taste tea

When doing my tea training, we would sometimes taste more than 20 teas at once — often even 50 or more — following this procedure:

Examine the leaf

The first step is to examine the leaf. This differs from wine tasting. Unless I am at the vineyard where the wine is produced, I cannot experience the grape from which the wine was made. But with tea, I can see the leaf from which the tea is made and can examine it for color, cut, level of oxidation, size, and so on. It is also important to smell the leaves. I bring them as close to my nose as possible, often rubbing some between my fingers to break them up a little. This can help release a bit more aroma.

Brew the tea

Next is to simply brew the tea. Well, this isn't always so simple. There are different water temperatures, amounts of leaf, time of brewing, and so on (we talk about this more in Chapter 2). However, when a tea sommelier or tea master is doing a tasting to find a new tea or to compare teas, we often brew them stronger than we would for serving. This allows us to really get a sense of all the elements of flavor.

We brew the leaves in tasting sets. The brewing cup has ridges to hold back the leaves as the tea is poured into the tasting cup. The wet leaves are then placed on the inverted lid so they can be examined. Figure 10-1 shows an individual tasting set, and Figure 10-2 shows how professionals might taste multiple teas during a tasting.

FIGURE 10-1:
Tea tasting set.

Photos by Jill Rheinheimer

Photos by Lisa McDonald

FIGURE 10-2:
Tea professionals
taste multiple
teas at a time.

Smell the tea and leaves

After the tea is brewed, it is time to smell again. I smell both the wet leaves and the tea itself. You can almost taste the tea through the aroma.

Taste the tea

Time to taste the tea. I sip the tea as quickly as I can. It almost sounds like I am inhaling it. This allows for the tea to cool but also hits all areas of my palate. I usually take a second normal sip to experience the tea as I would normally drink it. Our tongues taste different things in different regions, so it is important to give your entire mouth a taste. We go into more detail about this in Chapter 20, but Figure 10-3 is a good diagram to see where flavors fall with sipping.

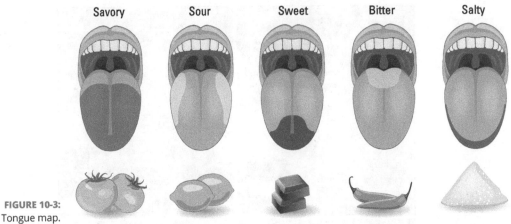

FIGURE 10-3:
Tongue map.

Source: John Wiley & Sons, Inc.

Describe the tea

Finally, I put words to my experience. After tasting tea after tea, it can be hard to keep them straight. I often keep a checklist next to each tea. The list might include a scale of dark to light or bitter to smooth; I might also rate color hues. My notes vary, depending on the teas being tasted and the purpose of the tasting.

For example, when I was on a tasting and buying trip in Japan, I was looking for a new sencha for my store. For each tasting round, tea farmers would set out a row of 12 to 20 samples of tea leaves and a cup of each one brewed. I looked at the leaves, smelled them, and rated them based on my criteria. My note scale includes criteria like "color: dark green to light green 1–5" and "leaf size: long to short 1–5," and so on.

After rating the leaves, I sipped each tea quickly. I often had only a few minutes before the next round so I would have to quickly narrow my selection to two or three. A quick "look, sip, and push away" method is what I used. After I had my choices narrowed down to two or three cups, I went back and spent a little more time with the smaller selection.

In some tastings, I had to choose 1 tea out of 20 in fewer than 5 minutes. I have seen tea buyers do this over and over, sometimes tasting up to 100 teas a day. Because we don't have the time for fancy tasting notes and flowery language, we often use rating scales. It's only when we have more time that we can use better words to describe our tasting experience.

When I hold tastings at the store for customers, industry trainings, or private groups, I like to use tasting note cards with more descriptive terms (see Figure 10-4 for an example). We can talk about our experiences and, through discussion, have a better sense of what we are tasting.

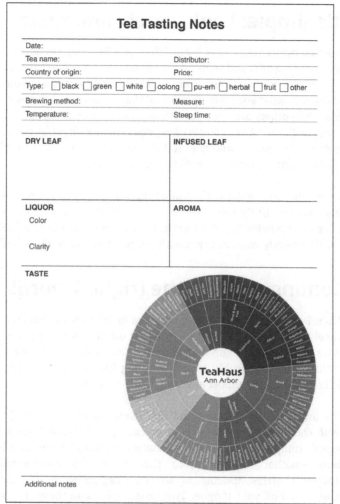

Tea Tasting Notes

Date:

Tea name: Distributor:

Country of origin: Price:

Type: ☐ black ☐ green ☐ white ☐ oolong ☐ pu-erh ☐ herbal ☐ fruit ☐ other

Brewing method: Measure:

Temperature: Steep time:

DRY LEAF   **INFUSED LEAF**

LIQUOR   **AROMA**

Color

Clarity

TASTE

Additional notes

FIGURE 10-4:
An example of a tea tasting note card.

Source: Illustration by Jill Rheinheimer

Tasting — And Figuring Out How to Describe What You Taste

There's no reason to leave the tasting to the experts. You are the best judge of what you like, and when tasting, everyone is right.

It's simple: Look, smell, and taste

REMEMBER

The title pretty much says it all! When you first open your package of tea leaves, take a deep whiff, and then take a close look. After you brew your tea, notice the color of the brew and its aroma. Taste it, while thinking about what you feel in addition to what you taste. You'll find that some teas give you a pucker-up sensation while others are silky smooth or even coat your mouth. Do there seem to be layers of flavor? After you swallow, does the tea linger at the roof of your mouth or down your throat, and does it differ in flavor from what first hits your tongue? Finally, examine (and admire!) the brewed leaves.

TIP

Essentially, you're doing the same things as a tea professional, and the more teas that you mindfully taste, the more you'll discover and learn. You don't need fancy or expensive tea. Start with the ones you already have! (Keep in mind that you'll generally want to begin with lighter teas and work toward stronger ones.)

Coming up with the (right?) words

When I do a tea tasting with customers or friends, I often give them our tasting wheel (Figure 10-5) to help them figure out words to best describe their experiences. It is a bit more fun than using a rating scale. If you have ever been to a wine tasting, you've probably seen something like this before. The same words can describe flavor for almost anything you are tasting.

REMEMBER

It is important to keep in mind that many flavors are actually composed of the same chemical compounds. A great example is isoamyl acetate. For some, this organic compound can taste like bananas, whereas for others, it has a distinct pear flavor. Another is benzaldehyde. This organic compound smells and tastes like peaches, cherries, apricots, or almonds, depending on the chemical compound experienced on your tongue. Two tasters can taste these compounds differently. My friend Phil, who wrote Chapter 21 on tea cocktails, is a chemist who works as a distiller. He explained this to me one day at a whiskey tasting when I could swear that I tasted pears when my colleague said he tasted bananas. Though I, to this day, say that I was right, we both tasted what we tasted, and neither of us were wrong.

TIP

Again, it is helpful to learn words that best describe your tasting experience — but it's important to remember to enjoy the experience and worry less about sounding like an expert.

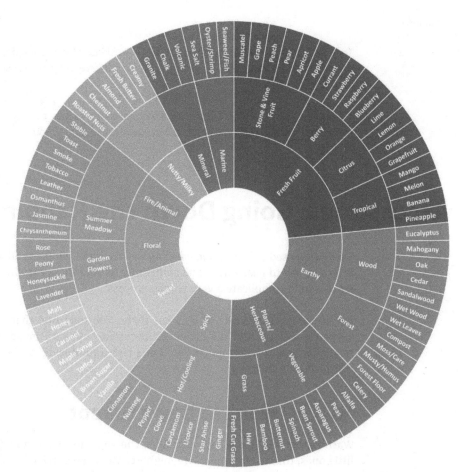

FIGURE 10-5.
TeaHaus tasting
wheel.

**TECHNICAL
STUFF**

YOUR GENES PLAY A ROLE

Although you can train your palate and become more aware of flavors, don't worry if what you taste seems to be at odds with what other people are describing. You may even be able to blame it on genetics! Many people, for instance, don't like cilantro because to them it tastes soapy — they can perceive unappealing aldehydes that others can't. In a study of more than 400,000 people, researchers compared beverage consumption to the participants' genetic markers for three bitter compounds:

- Propylthiouracil (PROP), found in tea

- Quinine, found in tea and coffee

- Caffeine, found in tea and coffee

(continued)

(continued)

They found that people who perceive higher intensities of PROP and quinine tend to drink tea (but not bitter tea), whereas those who perceive a higher intensity of caffeine tend to drink coffee.

Therefore, keep in mind that when you taste and compare teas, the flavors that you pick up are partially due to your genetic makeup, are unique to you, and are always correct.

Accessories: Going Down the Rabbit Hole

Tea is supposed to be fun and easy! As we stress in Chapter 2, all you need are tea leaves, a way to heat water, and something to hold those brewing leaves. There's no reason to complicate a very simple process.

Yet, there are thousands of teas out there. You may find that your tea cabinet keeps expanding. And the danger of becoming a tea aficionado? So many tea-related accessories can tempt you! Let's risk a tumble down the rabbit hole and consider your choices.

So, you want to buy a teapot

Warning: Buying one teapot may open the gates for a veritable flood! Big ones, little ones, thrift store finds, late-night-can't-sleep purchases.

Remember, however, that you don't *need* a teapot. They simply are fun accessories that sometimes can really expand your tea experience. So, if you're ready to venture into the warren, here are some of your options. And don't worry. We'll give you tips along the way to help you decide what's best for you.

Teapot material

All teapots are designed to hold hot water, but the material used to make the pot impacts heat retention and how your leaves brew. It may even change how your tea tastes!

POTTERY

We classify pottery teapots into three categories that cover most of what you'll come across: traditional Japanese, Chinese Yixing, and everything else. The "everything else" section launches our discussion, because if you're going to buy just one teapot, we suggest these all-purpose pots:

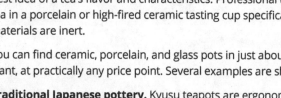

>> **High-fired ceramics, porcelain, and glass.** Ranging from utilitarian to exquisite works of art, these versatile teapots are the ones that we highly recommend for your first teapot. Yes, they are breakable, but that's pretty much their only downside. These are what we reach for nearly anytime we need a teapot.

They are inert, meaning that they don't impact the flavor of your tea. Easily cleaned, they don't retain any flavor or aroma. Therefore, they can be used to brew any kind of tea. Delicate teas, such as green and white teas, work particularly well in these pots (especially in porcelain and glass pots, whose walls are very thin and consequently don't retain enough heat to damage delicate tea leaves).

These pots are also ideal for comparing teas to each other or simply to get the best idea of a tea's flavor and characteristics. Professional tasters brew each tea in a porcelain or high-fired ceramic tasting cup specifically because these materials are inert.

You can find ceramic, porcelain, and glass pots in just about any size you want, at practically any price point. Several examples are shown in Figure 10-6.

>> **Traditional Japanese pottery.** Kyusu teapots are ergonomically designed, with a hollow handle at a 90-degree angle to the spout (see Figure 10-6). Usually made of clay, they can also be found in porcelain or glass. These teapots, generally on the small side, are ideal for green tea.

For very small, or individual, servings, a houhin (hohin) or shiboridashi can be a lot of fun, especially if you want to experiment with brewing styles. These handleless pots can be made of unglazed or glazed clay or of porcelain; they are meant to hold a lot of leaves and just a little water. You brew the leaves very briefly and then rebrew them repeatedly. Since neither type of pot has a handle, you'll want to use them for teas that require lower brewing temperatures so that you don't burn your fingers!

The shiboridashi, as seen in Figure 10-6, has more of a lip than a spout; a very small gap between lid and pot body allows the liquid to pour out (the functionality directly reflects the potter's skill). A shiboridashi works best with large leaves, whereas the houhin, which has a filter in its spout, can take smaller leaves.

>> **Chinese Yixing earthenware.** Some consider the Yixing teapot the best of the teapots (see Figure 10-6 for an example). Although handmade pots (entirely shaped by hand; wheels aren't commonly used) are the most valuable, Yixing pots are also mass produced. The high-quality clay from China's Yixing area is found in multiple colors, including purple, red, and yellow. Beware, though: Many fakes are on the market.

ceramic

porcelain

china

glass

cast iron

kyusu

Yixing

shiboridashi

FIGURE 10-6: Examples of teapots.

Photos by Jill Rheinheimer.

A porous, unglazed clay pot has several advantages:

- It holds the heat well.

- The clay interacts with the tea, bringing out flavor nuances and impacting mouth feel, particularly for black tea, roasted green and oolong teas, and pu-erh; every type of clay interacts uniquely.

These same qualities, however, can be problematic:

- Because a clay pot retains the heat so well, it stays too hot for delicate teas.

- Because the clay interacts with the tea, it can dampen bright notes.

- Flavors remain in the pot, which is why it's recommended that you use only one tea, or very similar teas, in your pot.

- The pot must never be washed (just rinsed with hot water and allowed to air dry).

TIP

We don't suggest that you buy an unglazed clay pot until you've experienced a lot of different teas and know that your favorites will benefit. These pots are not very versatile, must be handled with care, and are expensive. However, for the right tea, they can definitely enhance what you taste in the cup.

METAL

Metal teapots are often associated with a culture or country. Sterling silver may evoke American silversmiths, for example. See Chapter 17 for a further discussion of teapots within cultures. Here are some various metals to consider:

>> **Cast iron.** Although these heavy teapots may seem extremely durable, it's important to know that most of them are *not* designed to be used on a stove burner. The direct heat may warp the metal and/or damage the enamel interior, allowing iron to leach into your tea. Either way, the pot will rust. To use your teapot safely, first pour warm water into it; dump that out and then add your tea leaves and brewing water — which you've heated in a water kettle. (Note that a Japanese *tetsubin,* which does not have an enamel interior, *can* be used on a stovetop.)

TIP

Cast iron teapots are often beautiful works of art (refer to Figure 10-6). They retain the heat well, keeping your tea warm for longer periods of time, but for this same reason, we don't recommend them for brewing delicate white tea.

>> **Stainless steel, bronze, brass, and other alloys.** Metal teapots are traditionally used in North Africa and India (see Figure 10-7). Moroccan mint tea is boiled right in the pot, which is set on a gas burner. The pot's graceful spout facilitates a "high pour," which cools and slightly froths the tea.

WARNING

Metal from a pot's body and from the soldering can leach into hot tea, giving it a metallic taste (and possibly a few toxins). Stainless steel pots are thought to be the safest.

A samovar, commonly used in Turkey and Russia, can be made of various metals, including copper, iron, brass, nickel — or even silver or gold! The teapot itself sits atop the samovar, which heats the water (see Figure 10-7).

For a closer look at tea traditions, see Chapter 17.

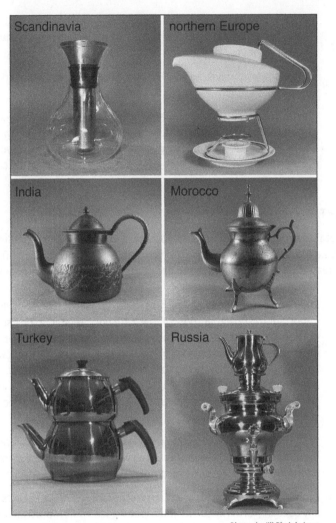

FIGURE 10-7:
Examples of
teapots from
various regions of
the world.

Photos by Jill Rheinheimer

>> **Silver.** Whether sterling silver or silver plate, these teapots add an air of
elegance to your table. Although sterling silver is inert, some people notice
a metallic taste in their tea. However, the metal retains heat well, and tea
brewed in sterling can be brighter, which may improve or diminish the tea,
depending on the tea and on personal preference. Silver-plated pots are far
less expensive and are often made in similar styles or as reproductions of
their pricy cousins. A word of caution: It's possible for heavy metals to leach
out of the solder used to attach the spout.

Teapot size

Before buying a teapot, seriously consider how you want to use it. Are you brewing a pot just for yourself, or are you entertaining? How many servings do you need that pot to hold? Teapots are readily found in a range of sizes.

Keep in mind that you want your tea leaves to brew only for the recommended time. After that, you want to remove the leaves from the pot (for instance, by removing the brewing basket) — or you need to pour out all the tea to prevent over-brewing, in which case you may not want a huge pot unless it has a brewing basket.

Also, if you plan on brewing tea that can be resteeped multiple times, such as oolong, you'll probably want a small pot. Trust us — some tea leaves can be steeped so many times that even a diminutive teapot may sometimes seem too large!

Teapot shape

The shape of your teapot affects how the leaves are exposed to the water, but whether that changes the flavor of your tea is a matter of debate. The primary issue is whether the leaves have enough room to unfurl and maintain sufficient contact with the water.

Other considerations

Teapots may come with removable brewing baskets, or a mesh filter may be built into the pot. Alternately, there may be an integrated strainer at the base of the spout to prevent leaves from escaping the pot. These latter ones work well with intact leaves or large leaf pieces, whereas removable basket filters can also be used for teas composed of smaller pieces, such as CTC (cut-tear-curl) teas. Brewing baskets also allow you to easily remove the leaves from the pot. If your leaves remain in the pot, you'll want to pour out all the liquid so that your tea doesn't over-brew and become bitter.

Ergonomics matter. Because you're pouring hot tea, you want to get a pot that you feel comfortable using. A large pot may be quite heavy when it's full, so make sure that you like the handle and the pot's balance. If you must hold the lid as you pour, you'll need to use two hands.

And maybe some teacups

You need to drink your tea from something — and anything will work. Still, drinking tea is multisensory. You hear the tea being poured; you see the color of both tea and teacup; you smell the aroma; you feel the teacup in your hands and on your lips, and you feel the liquid in your mouth; and, finally, you taste the tea.

Because most sensory information comes from what you see, the appearance of your tea and teacup influence what you taste. Also, because most of your tactile receptors are on your fingertips, lips, and tongue, the cup's shape, size, and material impact how you perceive your tea — including its bitterness, astringency, overall taste, and aftertaste. Tea in one cup may seem weak and lackluster, but that exact same tea in a different style of cup may be amazing.

The teacup, then, is a vital part of having tea, and the right cup can heighten your experience. But with thousands of cup choices, how do you even begin?

First and foremost, if you have a favorite cup, then your tea will taste perfect in that cup. You do not *need* anything special to enjoy tea! But if you're intrigued or you want different cups for different types of tea, well, then you're sliding deeper into that rabbit hole!

A note regarding aroma

A good teacup should maximize how you experience tea's aroma, which is part of how you taste. The width, depth, and material of the cup all impact aroma because they either direct the aroma to your nose or they do not. A narrow cup directs aroma more precisely than a shallow cup. Just something to keep in mind as you experiment with cups.

Size

If you're pouring from a teapot, ideally your cup size should match your desired number of servings. For instance, when you and a friend share tea, two 16-oz cups won't work well if you're using one 12-oz teapot.

Remember that you'll want small cups if you're having very expensive tea (you really want to savor the good stuff!), are sampling or comparing teas, or if you're going to be rebrewing your leaves multiple times.

Material and porosity

Just as for teapots, material matters. Inert high-fired ceramics, porcelain, and glass won't interact with the tea, but they still can influence how you experience it. Thin-walled cups, such as porcelain and some glass cups, allow the tea to glide over your tongue differently, and more fully, than when you drink from a thicker-walled cup. Also, a thicker cup allows faster and larger intake.

Perception also plays a large role (remember, most of your sensory information comes from what you see). Tea presented in a delicate or an elegant cup may seem vastly different from that very same tea served in an everyday mug. When you factor in social setting as well, it's easy to see how your perceptions are fluid. Kitchen table versus fancy soiree, workout clothes versus evening dress?

Unlike inert and nonporous cups, some glazed pottery cups may interact with your tea. For example, a Jian ware cup (or Japanese tenmoku or temmoku), which has a high iron content, can sometimes change the tea in subtle ways — but for the right tea, flavor improves. These cups might absorb certain elements, bring out desired notes, or soften a tea.

Porous unglazed clay cups will very likely impact your tea. Flavor and aroma may sink into the cup itself so that both are diminished. Or, the clay may interact favorably with the tea, enhancing it. Each type of clay will interact differently with any given tea.

Stoneware falls somewhere between nonporous porcelain and highly porous unglazed clay. These cups often have thicker walls and lips, and unless designed for tea, they're better suited for coffee. That being said, the heft of stoneware can feel really nice in your hands, especially on a chilly day! Your perception impacts what you taste.

Handle

TIP

If you're drinking tea that was brewed at a high temperature (such as black tea), you'll probably want a handle on your cup. Handleless cups can get too hot to comfortably hold. Also, if you want a big cup of tea, it's easier to use one that has a sturdy handle.

Heat retention

Cups that have thin walls, are wide, are shallow, or are made of glass all allow heat to be lost more quickly.

Color

The depth, width, and interior color of your cup will change the color of your tea. Eighth-century Chinese scholar and tea connoisseur Lu Yü preferred drinking green tea from a celadon or greenware tea bowl because the color enhances the color of the tea. In a white vessel, some green teas take on a reddish hue. The color doesn't change how your tea tastes, but it can alter how you perceive your tea.

Convenience

Travel mugs and disposables always have their place! Many are available on the market, and most are designed to fit into car cupholders.

GAIWAN: TEAPOT OR TEACUP?

First used during China's Ming dynasty, the *gaiwan,* or "lidded bowl," remains popular. It's essentially both a teapot and a teacup! You brew your leaves in the cup and then use the cover to hold the leaves back as you drink. Alternately, in gongfu style, you pour the liquor into a small pitcher from which you fill tasting cups. (See Chapter 17 for a closer look at the *gaiwan* and the gongfu tea ceremony.) The following photo shows a *gaiwan* and a gongfu set.

gaiwan

gongfu set

Photo by Jill Rheinheimer

Other convenient accessories

There seems to be no end of various tea accouterments that you can pick up. Truthfully, you don't need any of them (see Chapter 2 for the basics), but they *can* make things convenient.

Tea tins

REMEMBER

You really want to protect your tea from moisture, strong aromas, air, and light. For this reason, avoid plastic containers and glass jars, and store your tea away from the stove and from foods and spices with strong aromas. We suggest using tins that have tight lids (many even have double lids) and are dedicated to tea. Tins range in size, price, and style; you don't need anything fancy.

TIP

Note that tins will absorb the aroma of whatever's stored in them. It's very difficult to remove lingering odors, so we recommend that you store the same type of tea, or a similar tea, in each tin. For example, if you store a high aroma tea in your tin, you won't be able to later use that same tin for a delicate classic white tea.

Tea-measuring spoons and scales

TIP

Although you can be super fancy and get a scale to weigh your tea, Jill prefers a tea-measuring spoon, whereas Lisa just eyeballs it. If you're starting out in tea, though, a measuring spoon is a good way to help you figure out how many leaves you want to use. Because tea leaves can often be large, wiry, or fluffy, spoons designed for measuring tea have a deeper bowl and are easier to use than the teaspoons in flatware sets (which are usually shallow and vary wildly in size).

Timers

It's best to begin with the given recommendations for brewing your tea, including brew time. There's no need for anything elaborate. A cheap kitchen timer is fine, although you can always use the timer on your phone or watch.

Water kettles

From simple stovetop kettles to smart electric kettles, you have many options. Some electric kettles may adjust by 5-degree increments, but this is close enough. Temperature-controlled kettles are handy if you brew a lot of green and white teas, which require lower temperatures. These kettles turn off automatically when they reach your desired temperature, so you don't have to pay attention as the water is heating.

Infuser mugs

TIP

A very quick and easy way to brew loose tea leaves is with an infuser mug, which includes a compatible brew basket. Simply measure your leaves into the basket, fill the mug with water, and use the lid to retain heat and aroma during brewing. When you remove the brew basket, set it on the flipped lid (most of them are designed to be coasters). Infuser mugs work well with most teas (just remember that large, intact leaves brew better in a roomier brew basket rather than a small one).

Strainers and brewing baskets

REMEMBER

Although many different types of strainers are available, the best ones allow the tea leaves to fully unfurl and the water to freely circulate around them. You never want to overcrowd your tea leaves.

If your teapot doesn't have an integrated web in its spout or its own brewing basket (built in or removable), you can usually find a removeable brewing basket that will fit. Alternately, you can brew your leaves loose in the pot and then either use a spout filter or just pour the tea through a brewing basket or kitchen strainer as you fill your teacups. Remember, however, that when you can't remove the leaves from the pot, you'll want to pour out all the tea to prevent over-brewing. (Note that this doesn't apply to herbal teas; they can safely brew for hours.)

TIP

Our favorite brewing basket is made by Finum. Its cylindrical shape and super-fine stainless-steel mesh allow good water flow while preventing even the tiniest bits of leaf from escaping; therefore, it's well suited for any type of tea. It's also very easy to use and clean, is available in cup and pot sizes, and lasts for years.

REMEMBER

Tea balls and eggs are also popular, but we don't recommend them for teas that consist of large pieces of leaf or intact leaves, or for high-quality leaves. They simply don't allow enough room for the leaves to fully open and to interact with the water properly. Figure 10-8 demonstrates how some teas comprise large, intact leaves that have been rolled into small balls. When exposed to hot water, the leaves unfurl, and you can see why they need a lot of room to properly brew. Save your tea balls for CTC teas or similar teas; just be careful that you don't overfill them.

FIGURE 10-8:
Some tea leaves, like the oolong here, have been rolled into small balls that open up during brewing.

Photo by Lisa McDonald

Novelty filters (think unicorns, sloths, flamingos) are fun but often aren't ideal. They can be fussier to use and harder to clean than a brewing basket, plus many of them don't allow your leaves to yield their optimal flavor; use them as you would tea balls.

TIP

You can also make your own teabags, which is convenient for traveling or for those days when you just aren't up to brewing tea (we all have them!). Simply measure your favorite tea into paper filters (available in several sizes) and store them in an airtight container.

Coasters and tea trays

TIP

If you have stone countertops, we advise setting glass, porcelain, and unglazed clay teapots and cups on something to cushion them, such as a cork coaster, before filling them with boiling water. This helps prevent breakage. A tea tray — which consists of a grate that sits atop a tray that collects liquid — also works well for this purpose, plus it protects your table or counter from drips and stains. Tea trays are customarily used for gongfu brewing and although not essential, they are practical when brewing with a Yixing pot.

Cozies and warmers

Although you may think "grandma," a tea cozy truly does keep the tea in your teapot warm (and cozy). You can find a variety of cozies — from traditional to quirky to stylish. Alternately, tea-candle-lit warmers fit nicely under many teapots.

Tea pets

We mustn't forget these most whimsical and useless of tea accessories: the tea pet! Usually made of unglazed clay, tea pets generally sit on the tea tray with your tea set. When you prewarm your teapot or cup, pour the discard water over your tea pet, and then let it keep you company while you enjoy your tea (see Figure 10-9). Or, you can share your tea by pouring a little over your pet. Over time, the unglazed clay will take on the color of tea.

FIGURE 10-9:
Tea pet.

Photo by Jill Rheinheimer

3
Getting Curious about Caffeine

Deconstruct caffeine. Learn what it is, how it operates in your body, and how it works synergistically with the amino acid L-theanine that's found in tea leaves. Unravel why you can't predict how much caffeine is in your cup of tea, and probe common misconceptions about caffeine in tea leaves.

Compare decaffeination methods and see why it's hard to find quality decaf tea.

Chapter **11**

Caffeine: Tempest in a Teacup?

Yes, caffeine is a psychoactive stimulant, and most Americans use it. Daily.

Admittedly, "psychoactive stimulant" may sound a bit alarming, but it simply means that caffeine affects your mind (psychoactive) and increases your level of physiological activity (stimulant). Many of us practically depend on these benefits to get us started in the morning or to counteract a midafternoon slump.

But drink one too many cups? Use coffee or an energy drink too late in the day? Jitters, anxiety, or exasperating insomnia may be the unwelcome consequence. Caffeine can be the proverbial double-edged sword.

So, how do we make caffeine work better for us? And what is the story between caffeine in coffee and caffeine in tea? Isn't it all the same thing?

In this chapter, we read the tea leaves to explain what caffeine is, how it works, and why you experience caffeine differently when drinking tea (relaxed alertness) versus drinking coffee (wham!). We also discuss the numerous factors that impact how much caffeine is in your teacup and look at some of the misconceptions surrounding our favorite stimulant.

The Ins and Outs (or Ups and Downs) of Caffeine

Caffeine. Almost everyone has an opinion about it. Some find it necessary, whereas others avoid it at all costs or even outright malign it. We, however, embrace caffeine completely, trusting that its stimulatory effects will help us power through our day.

Yet, there *is* that tipping point when "just enough" turns into "oops, too much." Let's take apart this psychoactive stimulant to see how it operates — and to figure out how to stay in the safe zone.

Caffeine, a Stone Age drug?

Although caffeine was formally identified in the early 1800s by German chemist Friedlieb (or Friedrich) Ferdinand Runge, who called it *kaffein* for the compound found in *Kaffee* (coffee), it was discovered eons earlier by Stone Age night owls who needed to wake up early for the morning mammoth hunt. Well, maybe not.

However, it is believed that our prehistoric ancestors did intentionally chew plants containing caffeine. After all, if you were going to grab a plant to-go, wouldn't you pick the one with that little something extra?

Eventually, humans figured out that you can extract more caffeine by brewing those special plants in hot water. That is, make tea. Stories ascribe the first cup of tea to around 3000 BCE, when tea leaves allegedly blew into Chinese emperor Shen Nong's cup of hot water.

However, tea plants seem to have been cultivated thousands of years earlier, during the late Stone Age. In 2004, archaeologists working in China's Tianluo Mountains unearthed pottery shards and rows of what looked like tea plant roots. Archaeobotanists and other scientists confirmed the identification of *C. sinensis* (tea plant) and dated the roots to the Hemudu culture (5500–3300 BCE).

So, yes, caffeine was a Stone Age drug.

What caffeine is

TECHNICAL STUFF

Caffeine is the common name for the chemical trimethylxanthine, a xanthine alkaloid. Alkaloids contain nitrogen (N), are found mostly in plants, and affect us physiologically. Although caffeine is a benign alkaloid, other examples include stronger drugs (such as morphine) and poisons.

Trimethyl refers to caffeine's three methyl groups, each of which consists of one carbon (C) and three hydrogen (H) atoms. The chemical also contains oxygen (O); its complete molecular structure is $C_8H_{10}N_4O_2$.

Because caffeine is a chemical that's made by plants, it's also called a phytochemical (*phyto* meaning "plants"). Phytochemicals may give plants certain advantages, but they aren't necessary for their development.

At room temperature, caffeine is a white crystalline powder with a bitter taste. The bonds between its atoms are very strong, so caffeine won't melt until it gets extremely hot (460°F). It does, however, dissolve in water, especially in boiling water, a factor that comes into play whenever you brew tea.

Caffeine naturally occurs in the leaves, nuts, fruit, or seeds of some sixty plants, including coffee beans, tea leaves, kola nuts, guarana berries, mate, yaupon holly, and cacao. Its presence in unrelated plants resulted in various names for the chemical — theine (tea), mateine (mate), and guaranine (guarana) — but they all mean caffeine.

The caffeine-producing plants also derive several benefits from the stimulant. When the plant is very young and vulnerable to pests, caffeine acts as a natural pesticide, paralyzing and killing insects that try dining on it. As the plant matures, caffeine concentrates in the tender new leaves, which are the most susceptible to pests.

Caffeine can also leach into the soil from leaves that have fallen to the ground, thereby discouraging rival seedlings from surviving. And, happily for both parties involved, the caffeine found in a plant's nectar gives a pollinator enough reward to prompt a return visit. The caffeine buzz that bees receive even boosts their memory of the flower's scent.

How caffeine works

We know that caffeine can really give us a shot of energy, but how does it do it?

When you ingest caffeine, it quickly gets absorbed into your gastrointestinal tract. And unlike a lot of other things that you consume, 100 percent of the caffeine can be absorbed, and 100 percent is available for your body to use!

Your liver processes most of the caffeine and sends it throughout your body via your blood. Caffeine reaches all tissues and affects your central nervous, cardiovascular, respiratory, and renal systems as well as metabolism. It readily crosses from your blood into your brain, where it both shuts down the signal that would normally tell you that you're sleepy and stimulates the central nervous system.

The caffeine molecule is very similar to a neuromodulator, adenosine, that helps induce sleep, particularly deep sleep. During the hours that you're awake, adenosine accumulates. It binds to and activates adenosine receptors, thereby reducing neural activity. When enough receptors are activated, your brain tells you it's time for bed. As you sleep, your body metabolizes the adenosine, and the cycle begins anew in the morning.

When you ingest caffeine, however, the caffeine molecules bind to the adenosine receptors, shutting out the adenosine. Because caffeine only blocks but doesn't activate the receptors, neural activity never declines. This allows dopamine and serotonin levels to increase, improving memory, mood, motivation, and feelings of pleasure. At the same time, caffeine stimulates noradrenaline neurons, giving you a burst of adrenaline. (More on the benefits of caffeine coming up in the next section.)

REMEMBER

Because caffeine stays in your body for hours, you can see why having a highly caffeinated drink too close to bedtime may be ill-advised. For the average adult, it takes 4 to 6 hours for *half* the caffeine to clear from the body. Smoking shortens the half-life, whereas other factors (some diseases, pregnancy, certain medications for example) increase it.

The benefits of caffeine

Whether hunting mammoth or parking spots, we've been taking advantage of caffeine's stimulatory effects for millennia. With the right dose and timing, we can exploit it for our benefit. Just look at all the great things that caffeine does:

>> Works within minutes

>> Keeps you awake

This does *not* mean that you should rely on caffeine during a potentially dangerous situation.

>> Increases alertness

>> Improves cognition; may help short-term memory

>> Stimulates metabolic rate

>> Can improve the performance of endurance sports athletes

>> Sharpens focus and concentration

>> Improves reaction time

>> Improves coordination and motor skills

>> Boosts mood

>> Helps us carry out mundane tasks

>> Reduces inflammation in some people

>> May protect against dementia and Parkinson's disease

>> May treat diseases that damage the blood-brain barrier (Alzheimer's and Parkinson's disease, for example)

>> May improve lung function

>> Treats apnea and other conditions in preterm babies

>> Enhances the efficacy of pain relievers by improving the absorption of analgesics, making them act more quickly

>> Counteracts sleepiness caused by medicines (e.g., antihistamines, for example)

>> Possibly has anticarcinogen properties, particularly in tea

Finally, caffeine is built into our lives. That morning cup of tea or coffee kickstarts our day, brightening our mood while waking us up. The benefits encompass the physiological and psychological, yes, but just as importantly, they also include the merits of ritual.

The drawbacks of caffeine

Caffeine usually isn't classified as an addictive substance because it doesn't affect the brain in the same way that other addictive drugs do. Still, you can build up tolerance to it and become dependent on it. If you then abstain from caffeine, your body may let you know, responding to the sudden caffeine deficit with unpleasant symptoms such as

>> Headache

>> Fatigue

>> Anxiety

>> Depression

>> A change in alertness

>> Irritability

>> Brain fog

WARNING

On the other hand, *too much* caffeine can precipitate the same problems, plus a few more:

>> Counteraction with sedatives

>> Interaction with certain medicines

>> Insomnia

>> Jitters

>> Heartburn or indigestion

>> Vomiting

>> Trouble focusing

>> Temporarily increased blood pressure and/or heart rate

>> Headache (yes, caffeine can prevent, cause, *and* treat headaches)

It's possible to overdose on caffeine, but it's rare (and usually associated with high-energy drinks or caffeine in tablet form, or in combination with other agents).

REMEMBER

Your response to, and tolerance for, caffeine is unique to you.

TECHNICAL STUFF

L-THEANINE, TEA'S SECRET INGREDIENT

Amino acids, which are found in plant and animal tissues, are the building blocks of proteins and are, thus, critical to life. Your body makes 13 (nonessential) amino acids; the food you eat provides an additional 9 (essential) amino acids. More than 200 amino acids have been identified so far, including an amino acid that is currently known to be present only in the *Imleria badia* (also called *Boletus badius* or *Xerocomus badius*) mushroom, in guayusa (a plant native to the Amazon rainforest), and in tea leaves. This unique and rare amino acid is L-theanine, or theanine — and most of the amino acids in tea are theanine.

Theanine chemically resembles the amino acid glutamate, the most prevalent neurotransmitter in the brain. Essential for brain function, glutamate assists with learning and memory formation and is required to produce gamma-aminobutyric acid, which helps regulate and calm the nervous system. Similarly, theanine appears to improve cognition and help calm the nervous system; it also seems to increase feelings of well-being.

The Magic of Caffeine plus L-theanine, the Calming Factor

The caffeine molecule is the same no matter what plant it's in. However, you may have noticed that tea doesn't give you the same jolt that coffee does. In tea, a couple of things mitigate caffeine's stimulatory effects.

First, polyphenols in tea bind with caffeine (especially in black tea) and control its absorption by your body.

Second, tea has the amino acid L-theanine, or theanine (see the nearby sidebar, "L-theanine, tea's secret ingredient").

Amino acids are integral to tea. They're responsible for umami, that savory, brothlike character that's so prized. But the amino acid theanine has another trick up its sleeve.

Like caffeine, theanine affects your central nervous system. It's absorbed by your body, enters your blood, and crosses the blood-brain barrier. When in the brain, theanine is thought to

>> Increase serotonin levels (modulate mood, anxiety, happiness, and so on)

>> Raise dopamine levels (provide feelings of pleasure)

>> Increase gamma-aminobutyric acid levels (regulate and help calm the nervous system)

>> Possibly lower cortisol and stress levels (cortisol is the stress hormone that's released by your body, including in response to fight, flight, freeze, and fawn hormones)

>> Improve cognitive function, including learning and memory

>> Protect neurons (such as viability and function)

>> Serve as an antioxidant (acts against oxidative stress)

>> Boost immune function (bolster the body's defenses)

>> Reduce inflammation, often triggered by oxidative stress

>> Increase alpha wave activity (alpha waves help you relax and focus; they are the goal of biofeedback, meditation, and mindfulness)

Theanine helps reduce stress and anxiety, improves mood, and promotes calmness, all things that can blunt caffeine's negative effects.

However, theanine also seems to work synergistically with caffeine to improve brain function and attention. Although scientists don't yet fully understand the process, theanine appears to give us the best of caffeine's stimulatory effects — but wrapped in calmness.

REMEMBER

So, even though tea contains the stimulant caffeine, polyphenols help ensure that it's released more slowly while theanine boosts alpha-wave activity; and caffeine and theanine work together to give you a "calm alertness" that's unique to tea.

Determining How Much Caffeine Is in Your Cup (Hint: It's Complicated)

You may want to know how much caffeine you're getting, especially if you want to make sure that you're not going to be wide awake when you're supposed to be fast asleep. Overall, a cup of tea generally contains less caffeine than a cup of coffee (see Chapter 23), but how do you calculate how much caffeine is in any given tea?

Unfortunately, there's no easy answer for this. There are thousands of different teas you can drink, and a plethora of factors impacts the caffeine level in every one of those teas. Without testing each specific tea in a laboratory, it's nearly impossible to project its caffeine level.

REMEMBER

Experiments have shown that tea type (black, green, oolong, white, pu-erh, yellow) *does not* predict caffeine level either. The following sections explain why.

First, the tea plant itself

For any agricultural crop, including tea, both environment and growing conditions affect each individual plant. However, the plant's genetic makeup also partially determines its response. For example, a cold-tolerant tea cultivar will react to chilly weather differently than a cold-sensitive cultivar. These changes occur at a molecular level and will govern to some extent what we taste in our teacup.

Caffeine is part of this equation, and, therefore, the levels of this molecule can be modified by many factors including

>> Tea plant variety (*Camellia sinensis* var. *assamica* has more caffeine than *Camellia sinensis* var. *sinensis*) and cultivar

>> Origin of plant (a clone has more caffeine than a seedling)

- » Age of plant (older plants contain less caffeine)

- » Stress on the plant (for example caused by pests, wind, pruning)

- » Soil conditions (for example a higher nitrogen level means a higher caffeine level)

- » Climate (plants in warmer climates may have more caffeine)

- » Rainfall (the plants are very sensitive to rainfall — too much rain and intense rainfalls damage the plants; too little rain stresses them)

- » Altitude (plants grow more slowly at higher altitudes)

- » Growing season (the faster the plant grows, the more caffeine it contains)

- » Shading versus full sun (shading increases the caffeine level)

- » Leaves plucked (buds and young leaves contain more caffeine than older and more mature leaves; stems contain less caffeine than leaves)

Second, how the tea is processed

After the tea leaves are plucked, the processing steps induce changes in the leaves' molecular composition. However, withering and oxidation do not impact caffeine levels. In other words, regardless of how long the leaves are withered or oxidized to produce the desired tea type (black, green, oolong, or white), caffeine content remains the same. On the other hand, post-production roasting may alter caffeine levels to some extent. Thus, roasted green tea, roasted tea stems, and more heavily roasted oolong teas may contain somewhat less caffeine than other teas.

Tea leaves may be left intact or they may be cut, depending on the type of tea being produced. Cut-tear-curl teas and fannings (leaf dust and tiny leaf bits often used in teabags) have particularly small pieces of leaf. Although cutting the leaves doesn't change their caffeine level, the increased surface area of these small bits allows more caffeine to be extracted when they're exposed to hot water.

Pu-erh is a fermented tea; as the leaves ferment and age, caffeine starts breaking down over the years. A well-aged pu-erh, then, may contain less caffeine than other teas. (Find out more about this type of tea in Chapter 8.)

If tea leaves are blended with caffeine-free herbals, there will be less caffeine simply because there are fewer tea leaves.

Third, the caffeine-to-theanine ratio

In addition to caffeine, the amount of theanine also comes into play because it impacts how you experience caffeine. (For details about theanine, see the "The

Magic of Caffeine plus L-theanine, the Calming Factor" section earlier in this chapter.) A greater caffeine-to-theanine ratio means you'll get more of caffeine's effects. Conversely, if there's more theanine than caffeine, the stimulant is blunted to a greater extent. Theanine levels, however, can widely vary, making it challenging to predict the caffeine-to-theanine ratio of any given type of tea.

All tea leaves contain theanine, but sunlight converts some of the theanine to polyphenols (remember, polyphenols bind with caffeine, which helps control the rate at which caffeine is absorbed by your body). Conversely, when tea plants are shaded before harvest, the leaves retain more theanine. Therefore, both polyphenol and theanine levels impact how you experience caffeine:

>> Tea grown in sunlight: less theanine but more polyphenols

>> Tea grown in shade: more theanine but also more caffeine

Processing may also change theanine levels, with more oxidized teas (black, some oolongs) sometimes having lower levels of theanine than less oxidized teas (green, white, some oolongs). Generalizations are mostly unreliable, although studies do indicate that pu-erh seems to have very little theanine.

REMEMBER

The upshot? The caffeine-to-theanine ratio helps determine to what extent you experience the stimulatory effects of caffeine, but it's difficult to predict that ratio. Any individual tea may fall widely outside caffeine and theanine averages.

Still, we can say that when you drink pu-erh, little or no theanine is available to offset the caffeine, so you will likely get caffeine's full stimulatory effects.

Fourth, how you brew and drink your tea

Finally, we come to the one thing that you can control: how you make and take your tea:

>> **Amount of tea.** Since tea leaves contain caffeine, the more leaves you brew, the more caffeine in your cup.

>> **Type of tea leaf.** When you brew intact tea leaves, caffeine will be extracted more slowly than with cut leaves, although that also means that every time you rebrew intact leaves, you'll continue to extract caffeine. Intact leaves that have been rolled into curls or tight balls may require several brewing sessions to open completely; they'll release caffeine throughout the process.

WARNING

Note, however, that if you cram large, intact leaves into a vessel or brewing device that doesn't provide enough room for the leaves to unfurl, less caffeine (and flavor) will be extracted. You'll also have a very suboptimal cup of tea.

Small pieces of leaves, especially the fannings used in tea bags, will release caffeine very quickly. Such teas can be brewed only one time because the caffeine and flavor go hand in hand; there's little or nothing worth drinking after the first brew. Yet, even after several minutes of brew time, the leaves still contain and will continue to release caffeine.

>> **Water temperature.** The hotter the water, the more caffeine extracted. If your green or white tea tastes bitter, you may have brewed the delicate leaves in water that was too hot and, therefore, pulled out too much bitter caffeine. More oxidized oolong teas and fully oxidized black teas tolerate — and may require — higher brewing temperatures.

>> **Brewing time.** The longer you brew your leaves, the more caffeine you get in your cup. Black teas often require longer brewing times than green and white teas. Note that if your tea is overly bitter, you may have brewed your leaves for too long and have too much caffeine in your cup. (If you let your tea leaves or teabag remain in your cup while you're drinking, well, you'll keep getting caffeine.)

>> **Which steep it is.** You may want to rebrew your tea leaves, especially if you have intact leaves, which will continue to release flavor over several steepings. However, no matter which steep of the same leaves you're on, you will get caffeine. This is true for intact leaves, cut leaves, and fannings in teabags. See the following section for more about this often-misunderstood point.

>> **Adding milk.** Although milk doesn't change caffeine levels or their effects, if you add a lot of milk to your tea, you are drinking less tea and, therefore, are getting less caffeine.

>> **Amount consumed.** The more tea you drink, the more caffeine you will consume.

REMEMBER

So how much caffeine *is* in your cup? Unfortunately, it's so complicated that it's anyone's guess. However, because caffeine works synergistically with theanine, which calms, and because the polyphenols in tea help control caffeine's release, you're likely to experience the caffeine in tea more gently than that same caffeine in coffee.

TIP

It's also helpful to brew your leaves correctly and monitor how much you drink. If you're drinking multiple cups of tea, you'll generally get somewhat less caffeine by steeping the same loose tea leaves several times rather than by using a new teabag each time. If you're having tea with a friend, consider making a pot of tea and then enjoying it in small teacups, which allows you to have multiple cups while consuming a lower quantity overall.

Paying attention to your tea is also helpful. You may love the calm alertness you experience with your favorite tea, but you may also find that you do better drinking it in the morning. For evening sipping, you may want to turn to a naturally caffeine-free herbal tea (see Chapter 9). Fortunately, there are thousands of teas and herbal teas so there truly is something for everyone, day or night!

Misconceptions and Myths about Caffeine in Tea

Misleading stories about caffeine in tea are everywhere! We think this is very unfortunate because you may have limited yourself to certain types of tea, believing that you were reducing your caffeine consumption. Or you may have incorrectly brewed your tea, thinking that you could reduce the caffeine level.

But we're here to clarify some of this confusion so that you have a better understanding of why some of these myths are truly fallacies.

Caffeine is bad for you

Far too often, caffeine seems to get a bad rap. It's blamed for headaches or a quickened heartbeat or sleepless nights. Caffeine tolerance may even be confused with addiction. However, in moderation, caffeine can be beneficial. Why, then, is our understanding of caffeine often muddy?

For starters, the way that caffeine operates in the human body is complex, and you may react to caffeine very differently than another person does. I (Jill) can even provide a real-life example! My husband had argued for years that caffeine helps him both focus and *sleep*. Okay, that made no sense to me. Then our daughter mentioned to her doctor that she, like my husband, finds that caffeine helps her sleep — and was told that this is true for some people who have attention deficit/hyperactivity disorder (ADHD).

What are we to make of this? A stimulant as a sleeping aid? Intrigued by the anecdotal accounts, researchers have begun to parse this out. Although the science isn't there yet, perhaps one day caffeine will join the arsenal of ADHD strategies.

And there's the whole question of caffeine and headaches. Earlier in this chapter we point out that caffeine causes, treats, *and* prevents headaches. At first look this may seem contradictory, but knowing how you personally react to caffeine will help you use it to your advantage.

For example, many chronic migraineurs who drink caffeinated beverages acknowledge that it's important to have about the same amount of caffeine every day, at roughly the same time of day. By standardizing caffeine intake to some extent, it's less likely that caffeine will trigger or worsen a migraine. Caffeine doesn't necessarily need to be avoided; rather, it may simply need to be managed.

For non-migraineurs who don't drink caffeine regularly, a cup of coffee or tea may alleviate a mild headache. On the other hand, too much caffeine or a sudden withdrawal from caffeine can cause a headache. Perhaps ironically, you can treat that headache with a pain killer that includes caffeine as an active ingredient.

REMEMBER

Caffeine isn't bad. You just need to be aware of how it operates, how you experience it, and the optimal times to have it.

Caffeine is not classified as an addictive substance, yet you can grow tolerant to it. If you find yourself depending on caffeine to help wake up or to provide a boost of energy, is that a problem? You need to decide what's best for you, but it's helpful to know that caffeine tolerance is not the same as drug addiction. Caffeine does not affect the brain in the same manner as addictive drugs, nor does its use impinge on society. Withdrawal symptoms, if any, may be mildly unpleasant but are short-lived.

Although caffeine is a mild diuretic, research suggests that it doesn't cause dehydration. If you want to drink more fluid in a day, tea counts! In fact, many researchers unequivocally state that drinking tea is healthier than drinking water. And it's decidedly better than sugar-filled beverages.

Despite warnings of old, caffeine won't stunt the growth of children or teenagers. Caffeine remains in the body of a child much longer than in the average adult, though. If you let your children have a bit of tea, mornings are the best time. (Note, however, that if young people ingest excessive levels of either caffeine or caffeinated sugar-filled drinks, or if they mix caffeine with drugs and/or alcohol, other problems may ensue.) If you aren't used to caffeine or if you have too much of it, you may notice your heart beating a little faster. However, recent research suggests that caffeine does not increase your risk of cardiovascular disease. (We actually embrace that revved up feeling when launching into spring cleaning, for example!)

WARNING

Do note that your body's response to caffeine is unique to you. You should always check with your doctor if you are concerned or if you wonder whether you should eschew caffeine.

REMEMBER

Taking advantage of caffeine's boost of focus and alertness seems to offer more benefits than problems. While scientists continue to probe this age-old stimulant to maximize its potential, sit back and enjoy your cup of tea.

You can avoid the caffeine by throwing out the first steep or "washing out" the caffeine

The story goes that you can give your tea — and this usually refers to teabags — a quick rinse or wash (30 to 45 seconds) in hot water. Throw that brewed tea out, and then rebrew your largely decaffeinated tea leaves. But this myth does not hold water, hot or otherwise!

Studies have shown that brewing tea leaves for 30 seconds removes less than 10 percent of the caffeine; brewing them for a minute removes less than 20 percent. It would take around 10 minutes to remove some 90 percent.

Therefore, you would need to brew your tea for 5 to 10 minutes to remove half-to-most of the caffeine. Imagine that you do indeed brew a teabag for this amount of time, throw that tea out, and then rebrew that same teabag. Trust us, you do not want to drink that tea. It will have *no* flavor.

But what about loose tea leaves, especially if they are intact? Although intact and larger pieces of leaf release caffeine more slowly than finely cut leaves, caffeine extraction still requires around 5 to 10 minutes. However, optimal brewing times for most teas are *under three minutes*. If you over-brew your leaves so that you remove enough caffeine to make a difference, your tea leaves will have little flavor left to give. That second brew will taste bad or even be unpalatable depending on the type of tea. For instance, if you brew a delicate green tea for 10 minutes rather than for its recommended 1 minute, the leaves will be ruined and they cannot be brewed again. Certain oolong and pu-erh teas may still release some flavor after prolonged brewing, but you're really missing out on the best flavors and qualities of the tea — not to mention that most of the polyphenols and other compounds that make tea a healthy beverage have also been largely depleted by that time.

And keep this in mind: If you give your tea leaves a quick rinse or wash — *and this is especially true for rolled or curled leaves* — you've given the leaves just enough time for them to start unfurling. Some studies have shown that the next time those leaves are exposed to hot water, they'll be at the stage where they'll release the *most* amount of caffeine.

TIP

Trying to rinse or wash out caffeine simply cannot be done at home. If you don't want much caffeine, buy decaffeinated tea; if you don't want any caffeine, drink a naturally caffeine-free herbal tea instead. Many terrific options are available!

Caffeine is separate from flavor

This perpetuated myth is just that: a myth. When hot water hits tea leaves, all the elements that give the tea its flavor are extracted along with the caffeine. In fact, flavor and caffeine are so intertwined that if you try to brew your tea leaves long enough to remove the caffeine, you've also removed the flavor and all the beneficial micronutrients.

Multiple components are responsible for tea's aroma, flavor, astringency, and micronutrients:

» Alkaloids (caffeine, theobromine, and theophylline; caffeine is the primary alkaloid in tea, contributing bitterness)

» Amino acids, including theanine (depending on the amino acid, contributes umami, sweetness, or bitterness)

» Polyphenols (depending on the polyphenol, directly impacts flavor in many possible ways, including astringency, briskness, bitterness, smoothness, grassiness, mouthfeel, or depth; also responsible for the color of the brew)

» Volatiles (combine to contribute flavor, aroma, and complexity)

Thousands of polyphenols and hundreds of volatiles exist. Change some and you change the tea. The balance of these components is fluid; everything that changes the caffeine level in the tea plant (see preceding sections) also impacts these elements.

Consider a plant beset by pests. The stress of being bit causes the leaf to protect itself, which it can do at a molecular genetic level by changing the levels and balance of caffeine, amino acids, polyphenols, and volatiles. A plant is so adept that it can identify its foe, whether caterpillar or type of bug, and counter with tactics specific to the attack. If you make tea from a plant that's actively defending itself from pests, the chemical composition of those leaves will be different from that of a plant that wasn't under stress. That tea will taste differently.

Even if the caffeine level doesn't change, the other components do, so you will have different ratios. There will be a new flavor profile. Depending on the dominance of the other flavors and characteristics, caffeine may be more pronounced or less noticeable.

Intriguing studies suggest that besides contributing its own characteristic bitterness, caffeine may also play a role in how we taste or perceive flavors, including that of caffeine itself. Many as-yet unanswered questions remain:

>> Do we learn to enjoy caffeine's bitterness over time?

>> Does caffeine work with taste receptors in the brain, changing how we perceive it?

>> Does the composition of our saliva play a role?

>> Is it simply a matter of our age, since we often become less sensitive to flavors as we grow older?

>> And, a hotly contested topic, does caffeine *enhance* other flavors?

Right now, science remains on the fence, but regardless of exactly how caffeine operates, it is integral to the flavor of tea. When you remove it, you have changed the tea for the worse (see Chapter 12).

Certain teas have less caffeine than other teas

All tea has caffeine. We're going to repeat this: All tea has caffeine, including decaffeinated tea (see Chapter 12). This also includes white tea, which is frequently purported as having little or no caffeine. Of all the types of tea, white tea is the least processed and, therefore, is considered a "delicate" tea. This may make you think it's also low in caffeine, but that's not necessarily true. Several things are at play here.

All tea types (black, green, oolong, white, pu-erh, yellow) can be made from the exact same leaves plucked from the exact same plant on the exact same day. That means that theoretically they would all have the same level of caffeine. Although some studies suggest that the withering and oxidation processing steps might change caffeine levels, other research indicates that this change is minimal.

However, if the tea has a lot of buds and/or immature leaves, it will have more caffeine because those buds and young leaves have the highest levels found in the plant. This reflects caffeine's role in protecting the most vulnerable leaves.

White tea, which is often comprised of delicate buds and immature leaves and is the least processed tea, must be brewed at low temperatures so that you don't ruin the delicate leaves. Lower brewing temperatures extract less caffeine. But, on the other hand, the tea leaves themselves contain more caffeine to begin with. You see the difficulty.

You may also hear that green tea has less caffeine than black tea. Again, this may or may not be true. It depends on the exact green tea that you're drinking and on the specific black tea that you're comparing it to. However, you may extract less caffeine from green tea because these less-oxidized, delicate leaves are brewed at lower temperatures, often for less time, than black tea.

The stems of tea plants contain less caffeine than the leaves, so teas made of stems or shoots — such as Japanese kukicha and Malawi antlers — theoretically would have less caffeine than tea made from leaves. We'd also expect roasted teas to have less caffeine than their nonroasted counterparts. However, because so many factors are involved in caffeine content, we can't predict caffeine levels with much accuracy.

So, although we may be tempted to say that generally x tea has less caffeine than y tea, we don't really know unless we've tested the teas in a laboratory.

That leaves us with only two generalizations:

>> Matcha is made from tencha, which is produced from tea leaves that have been shaded and, therefore, contain more caffeine. After the stems and veins of the leaves are removed, the leaves are ground into a powder. Because you ingest entire leaves, you get 100 percent of the caffeine contained in them.

>> Pu-erh has little theanine to offset its caffeine.

TIP

In the end, we recommend that you simply drink teas that you enjoy. If a particular one seems to have too much caffeine for you, we suggest drinking less of it, maybe using a fancy but small teacup to make it special. Have a scone or cookie with your tea because food can help cushion the impact of caffeine. Drink the tea slowly, savoring its aroma, mouthfeel, and flavor.

Alternately, you can try using fewer leaves or brewing them at a slightly lower temperature or for less time. Depending on the tea, you might blend the leaves with a caffeine-free herbal so that you use fewer tea leaves. You can always dilute the tea with milk, although some teas aren't as amenable to this as others.

REMEMBER

Remember, many, many teas are available. Don't get bogged down by worrying that some have more caffeine than others. Just enjoy sampling different teas and find the ones that you love!

Chapter **12**

Less Is Not Always More — Decaffeinated Tea

or many of us, caffeine in tea provides an amazing "calm alertness." But what if you aren't one of these people? What if caffeine sends your body into overdrive, or your doctor has recommended that you avoid caffeine? When you brew tea, you can't predict how much caffeine is in your teacup (really, it's impossible; see Chapter 11 for the reasons why this is so), so let's consider your options when you simply can't take a chance on how much caffeine you're getting.

If your goal is zero caffeine, go directly to Chapter 9 because herbal teas are your friend. (Most of them, anyway.) But if you're fine with a touch of caffeine, then this chapter's for you.

Here we explore the different methods used to decaffeinate tea. We also explain the problems inherent in that process, which is why finding high-quality decaf teas can be a real challenge.

Removing Caffeine from Tea Leaves

If you drink coffee (it's okay; some dedicated tea drinkers also enjoy that *other* beverage!), you know that you can easily get decaffeinated coffee and that some of the options are very good, even indistinguishable from the real deal. That's because decaffeination occurs early in the process while the coffee beans are still green. Then, after the caffeine's been removed from the beans, they are roasted, which alters their chemical structure and heavily contributes to flavor. Thus, decaf beans offer much of the complexity and many of the characteristics that you find in regular coffee.

In tea, however, decaffeinating is nearly always done *after* the tea leaves have been processed, *after* they have been made into black, green, oolong, or white tea. This makes it rather tricky. How do you get rid of the caffeine yet keep all the good stuff?

Decaffeinating methods

Caffeine can be removed from tea, although none of the methods are ideal. Here are the ones you may come across as you consider your decaf tea options.

Organic solvents

Although it doesn't sound like a good idea to expose tea leaves to organic solvents (chemicals), it's a relatively inexpensive method that works. Methylene chloride and ethyl acetate, for instance, readily extract caffeine from tea leaves with either of these methods:

>> Tea leaves are put into water or are steamed so that they soften; the water is then replaced with the chemical solvent. At room temperature, caffeine molecules move from the leaves into the solvent, and the solvent is then removed.

>> Tea leaves are blanched, which extracts the caffeine into the water. The chemical solvent is added, attracting the caffeine molecules, and then the solvent is removed. The tea leaves reabsorb at least some of the caffeine-free liquid.

Methylene chloride was widely used into the 1970s, when it was largely discontinued over concerns of ozone depletion and residual chemical in the tea leaves. Some countries have now banned it as a decaffeinating solvent.

Ethyl acetate is sometimes promoted as a "natural" decaffeinating method because some fruits naturally contain the compound. This is a bit disingenuous because the decaf process usually uses synthetically produced ethyl acetate. Same chemical but not totally natural in the way the word might imply. Anyway, the FDA approved this solvent in the early 1980s, and it continues to be used. However, drawbacks exist. Ethyl acetate is difficult to remove, so the leaves may have a chemical taste to them. Plus, most polyphenols are lost in the process.

Water

Another comparatively inexpensive decaffeinating method uses water as the solvent, simply subjecting freshly harvested tea leaves to boiling water (basically "making tea"). Most caffeine molecules will transfer from the leaves into the water within a few minutes if the leaves are immature or buds; mature leaves require more time. The caffeine is then removed with a carbon filter.

Although this process works well with coffee beans, it's hard on tea leaves, which are easily damaged. Teas that have been decaffeinated by this method often taste watered down, with a substantial loss of flavor and theanine (see Chapter 11 for more on theanine).

When this method (often called the "Swiss water method") is used to decaffeinate tea leaves that have already been processed, far too many polyphenols are lost, particularly in black tea (which is why you can't decaffeinate your own tea leaves; see Chapter 11 for more information).

Carbon dioxide

Using naturally occurring carbon dioxide (CO_2) as a decaffeinating solvent is expensive, but this method has several advantages:

>> Doesn't use organic solvents

>> Is nontoxic

>> Is quick

>> Retains more flavor and polyphenols compared to other decaffeinating methods

TECHNICAL STUFF

First identified in the mid-1700s, CO_2 in gaseous form is an essential part of the earth's atmosphere. Under high pressure and temperature, CO_2 enters a supercritical state, having both gas- and liquid-like properties. The decaffeination process takes advantage of this state.

Like a gas, CO_2 enters wet tea leaves, and, like a liquid, its small molecules attract and bind to the small caffeine molecules found within the leaves. The resulting linked CO_2–caffeine is then filtered out. Because CO_2 doesn't bind to larger molecules, the leaves' flavor and polyphenols remain mostly intact.

REMEMBER

Still, some volatile components and other flavor compounds are lost. Although more can be retained by tweaking pressure and temperature, it's a balance. How much caffeine needs to be removed? How much of everything else can be retained? You can't remove all the caffeine *and* keep all the flavor and polyphenols. However, this method is currently the best option out there.

Putting the caffeine to other uses

Where does that extracted caffeine go? Although a tea drinker may not want the caffeine, plenty of other people really *do* want that caffeine!

After caffeine has been separated from the tea leaves, it's purified and then dried. Nearly all the caffeine extracted by supercritical CO_2 is saved and reused, primarily by beverage companies that add caffeine to water, alcoholic beverages, and soft drinks. Energy drinks? Fueled by caffeine.

The pharmaceutical industry is the second-largest buyer of caffeine, incorporating it in pain relievers, antihistamines, flu and cold medicines, and dietary supplements. In neonatal intensive care units, caffeine both prevents and treats apnea in preterm infants.

Caffeine tablets and gum provide a shot of energy, but if such products seem too pedestrian, the food industry is happy to oblige. Caffeinated potato chips, anyone?

The Problems with Decaffeinating Tea

Because demand is high for caffeine itself, and because more people are turning to decaffeinated tea, you'd think there'd be plenty of decaf tea options. But if you've spent any time trying to find a really fantastic decaf tea — or a top-shelf decaf classic tea — you're probably more than a bit frustrated.

So why *are* decaf teas generally inferior to their non-decaf counterparts? Why are there so few classic teas? Why hasn't anyone come up with a better process? Let's look at some of the issues involved.

Degradation of tea leaves

The decaffeination goal is clear: remove caffeine while retaining everything else, including polyphenols, theanine, flavor, and quality. Unfortunately, caffeine contributes to flavor, so when it's gone, the tea has been changed (see Chapter 11).

Still, if you need your tea to be decaf, you can probably live with that. The problem, though, is that during the decaffeinating process, the tea leaves are subjected to exactly those variables that compromise them: liquid and heat.

Currently, no way exists around this. Leaves that have already been made into black or green or whatever tea — with an already completed flavor profile — must be moistened in some way and then the caffeine removed. Things aren't going to improve; the tea leaves will degrade.

The tea industry's response to this problem?

>> Only lower-quality tea leaves are decaffeinated.

>> Cut-tear-curl tea, fannings, or tea leaves that have been cut into small pieces are chosen over whole-leaf tea for decaffeination because

- Caffeine extracts more quickly out of smaller leaf pieces and ground leaves.

- They're less expensive than whole-leaf teas.

>> Fully oxidized black teas are often chosen over more delicate white and green teas.

>> Labor-intensive oolong teas are rarely decaffeinated.

>> Decaf teas are often blended to boost flavor.

>> Herbals, fruit, spices, and so on are often added to the decaf tea leaves to compensate for the lower-quality leaves or to mitigate their loss of flavor.

In other words, you won't be seeing decaf versions of rare, premium, or expensive teas anywhere.

(And we truly aren't judging anyone here — this is the current reality of the situation; we would be the last ones to advise a company to try decaffeinating high-end tea leaves.)

Cost

Decaffeinating tea leaves adds both time and cost to the product, even if the cheapest possible method is used. And that CO_2 process, which best retains the flavor along with many of the health benefits of tea? You're talking high cost, specialized equipment, and considerable energy requirements.

When you also consider that only lower-quality and cheaper leaves are used to produce decaf tea, the problem compounds. How much money should a company sink into tea leaves that are on the lower end of the spectrum to begin with? Can they recover their investment?

As one way to minimize risk, companies decaffeinate only large runs of popular teas that they know will sell.

Demand

If you're a decaf-tea drinker, we're sorry but you are in the minority, at least right now. This may change as more people, particularly in North America, move to what they perceive as a healthier lifestyle and eschew caffeine. Demand overall, however, isn't high enough for companies to offer much more than a handful of decaf teas. Stuck in a cycle of low demand and few options, there's little to inspire companies to invest in costly decaffeination plants or to research and develop alternate decaffeination methods.

Exacerbating the issue is the very real fact that tea drinkers have plenty of exceptional no-caffeine options to turn to. The herbal tea industry is robust, offering seemingly unlimited choices. You can even find herbals that are strikingly similar to tea, such as blueberry leaves (which taste much like black tea) and Japanese mulberry leaves (like green tea). And for the health conscious, particularly if you view herbal tea as a panacea? Many companies are happy to market products geared specifically toward you.

With abundant and excellent herbal teas readily available, tea companies have less incentive to bother with the expense and time needed to produce decaf teas that simply don't measure up to their caffeinated counterparts.

Decaffeinated does not mean caffeine free

REMEMBER

Caffeine free is not the same as decaffeinated, so all *Camellia sinensis* teas have at least some caffeine. If you want a caffeine-free beverage, you must choose one that never had any caffeine to begin with (see Chapter 9 for your many options).

TIP

Still, decaf teas are very low in caffeine. They are required to have less than 2.5 percent of their original caffeine level, and they generally contain 1–2 percent. Labels on each tea merely say that they're decaffeinated, so if you're somewhat sensitive to caffeine, you may want to enjoy decaf tea earlier in your day. If, however, you need to avoid all caffeine, you'll want to stick to the herbal teas that are naturally caffeine free.

4
Spilling the Tea about Health Benefits

Learn about polyphenols: what they are, how they change during tea production, and why we care. Find out why it doesn't matter whether you drink green or black tea.

Distinguish between health claims and health benefits, and between real-world applications versus observational and lab studies. Survey some of the numerous studies into the potential health benefits of tea — for your body, mind, and spirit — and understand what we know so far.

Evaluate research reliability and bioavailability issues that complicate herbal tea studies. Review some of the research on herbal tea and identify which herbs show promise.

Chapter **13**

Tea and Its Powerful Antioxidants

You've read it over and over: "*Drink this type of tea and fix/prevent/reduce [ailment du jour].*" Unfortunately, many people make their tea decisions accordingly, even drinking teas that they don't enjoy. We're here to tell you that if tea truly fulfilled all those promises, we'd be the healthiest (and thinnest) people around, because we drink a *lot* of tea!

So what accounts for all the hype? Well, there *is* a reason why people have for millennia turned to tea as beverage and medicine. Tea leaves are filled with polyphenols, which are potent antioxidants. These compounds help protect the plant, and they potentially offer significant health benefits to us (see Chapter 14 for a deeper probe into this topic). But, just as importantly, polyphenols are largely responsible for the huge choice of teas that we enjoy!

In the following sections, we explain what polyphenols are and why they are critical to tea production. We also compare the polyphenols found in green versus black tea. Because the polyphenols aren't the same, there's often confusion over which tea is "better" to drink. We then address that very question and consider whether one tea is healthier than another.

Polyphenols and Why They Matter

Although the word "polyphenols" is tossed around all the time, what exactly does it mean? The dictionary definition — a compound with at least one phenolic hydroxyl group — is not particularly helpful to those of us who aren't chemists. But think of polyphenols as micronutrients that are found naturally in plants and that potentially function as antioxidants and anti-inflammatories in your body. With that, it's clear why you want them in your diet!

TECHNICAL STUFF

In the tea plant, polyphenols are phytochemicals (chemicals made by the plants), but are also secondary metabolites, which means that the plant produces them from other compounds. Sunlight is a driving factor to convert the plant's amino acids, including theanine, into polyphenols; tea plants that bask in sunshine have more polyphenols than those that are in the shade. As you'd expect, the level increases as the growing season progresses, with summertime leaves possessing more polyphenols than springtime leaves.

Taking advantage of the relationship between sunlight and polyphenol content, some tea growers in Japan intentionally cover their plants for a few weeks. The lack of sunlight forces the leaves to retain more theanine and produce fewer polyphenols, changing the flavor characteristics of the tea (see Chapter 5).

Polyphenols concentrate in the buds and emerging leaves of tea plants, although they are present in all leaves. At the microscopic level, each leaf is made up of thousands of plant cells, each one protected by cell walls. Within each cell, soluble polyphenols are confined to sacs called vacuoles. If the leaves are damaged — whether by pesky insects or enterprising tea producers — the cell walls break and vacuoles rupture. Oxygen enters and, at the same time, polyphenols are exposed to cell enzymes. With the trifecta of polyphenols, enzymes, and oxygen, oxidation and polyphenol conversion begin.

We can embrace this cascade of events for at least two reasons:

>> When the leaf is still attached to the plant, oxidation helps protect the plant from pests by making the damaged leaf less palatable.

>> When the leaf is in a tea producer's factory, oxidation gives us black tea, which differs strikingly from unoxidized, or green, tea.

No matter whether black or green, however, processed tea contains thousands of polyphenol compounds, which heavily contribute to the flavor and character of the brew. Yet, those polyphenols do more than simply ensure that our tea options are plentiful.

Researchers believe that the polyphenols and alkaloids (primarily caffeine) found in tea are responsible for the beverage's many presumed health benefits. Consequently, polyphenols are heavily studied. We know that they do act as antioxidants (and thus as anti-inflammatories), possibly protecting us from a slew of diseases, aging, and more — although tea in a laboratory setting and tea in our teacups are not always comparable (see Chapter 14 for specifics). Still, the staggering potential of tea's plentiful polyphenols continues to spur scientists to substantiate current evidence and optimize real-life applications.

TIP

Yep, as the common saying goes, "Tea is always a good idea." So, when you next enjoy a cup of your favorite, take a second to drink it in. That aroma? That flavor? It directly reflects the specific combination of polyphenols contained within the leaves (plus, we're pretty sure it's good for you!).

So, now, let's home in on the specifics that differentiate green from black tea, because it's all about the polyphenols.

Green Tea and Its Polyphenols

TECHNICAL STUFF

In green tea production the leaves wither after they're harvested, but there's minimal cell wall disruption (unlike black tea production, which capitalizes on cell damage). The goal for green tea is to retain the existing polyphenols and prevent oxidation. Therefore, the carefully handled leaves are heated to deactivate the enzymes found within the cells, rendering them unable to interact with polyphenols. The polyphenols, then, don't change; they stay as simple polyphenols, or monomers.

The simple polyphenols in green tea include phenolic acids and flavonoids. Flavanols (or tannins) are the most prominent flavonoid, and catechins are the most common flavanol. The primary catechins are

>> Epicatechin (EC)

>> Epicatechin-3-gallate (ECG)

>> Epigallocatechin (EGC)

>> Epigallocatechin-3-gallate (EGCG)

Catechins dissolve in water and give brewed tea its color (green, yellow, or very light brown), flavor (for example, vegetal, grassy, earthy), bitterness, and astringency. In fact, catechins comprise one-third to nearly one-half of green tea's water-soluble solids.

Remember that tea is an agricultural product, so catechins change according to the plant's growth cycle. Although EGCG is, overall, the most abundant catechin, the leaves contain more EGCG during spring (in the beginning of their growing season) than during other seasons of the year. In the teacup, higher levels of EGCG yield a smoother liquor, which is why spring teas are so prized.

Later in the growing season, EGCG levels are lower, and the flavor characteristics of EC dominate. The tea is less smooth and has a grassier taste.

Of the catechins, EGCG seems to be the most promising for potential health benefits and continues to be extensively studied (see "The benefits of green tea" section later in this chapter).

Black Tea, with Polyphenol Conversion

TECHNICAL STUFF

To produce black tea, leaf cell walls are intentionally broken, allowing cell contents to mix and oxygen to enter. Enzymes interact with the oxygen and polyphenols, and oxidation is underway, chemically converting the simple polyphenols or catechins into complex polyphenols. Tea producers manipulate this process to get exactly the tea that they want. For example, they tightly manage leaf damage — a wide spectrum that runs from simply bruising the leaves to grinding them up.

During oxidation, most of the catechins (monomers) convert into complex polyphenols or derived tannins:

>> Theaflavins (dimers)

>> Thearubigins (polymers)

These complex forms give oxidized teas their robust character. Theaflavins, which develop first, account for black tea's orange and red pigments, bright taste, and briskness. As oxidation continues, however, theoflavins degrade and thearubigins develop, contributing brown pigments, mellowness, and depth of flavor to the tea. Thearubigins comprise around one-third to more than half of black tea's water-soluble solids.

The ratio of theaflavin to thearubigin is one aspect of tea quality, and some sources recommend a one-to-ten ratio. Tea producers, then, may slow the oxidation process to allow more thearubigins to develop, resulting in a more complex (and darker-colored) cup of tea.

BREWING OVER TEA SEDIMENT?

You may sometimes find a little sediment in your tea (here, we're talking about classic teas, which don't contain spices or other ingredients that often cause turbidity and heavy sediment). Sure, tiny bits of leaf may have escaped your filter, but we're referring to small, dark particles that settle to the bottom of your cup. Not to worry! These specks are simply the result of polyphenols binding to proteins.

Many types of polyphenols are in tea, including tannins; the largest group of tannins are ellagitannins. When you brew your tea, the ellagitannin strictinin reacts with the hot water and breaks down into ellagic acid, which then combines with proteins in the tea, creating the sediment you see in your cup. Because there's not much strictinin in most types of tea, sediment is generally minimal.

Still, manufacturers of ready-to-drink tea prefer not to have any sediment, so, as you'd expect, research abounds. Sugar, especially fructosyl, reduces sediment in green tea — but then you have fewer polyphenols, less caffeine, and, well, added sugar. Calcium has also been studied. It binds with organic acids, so the more calcium in the brewing water, the cloudier the tea.

This brings us to water. The dissolved solids that are in your water — minerals, metals, salts, and so on — affect both sediment levels and the taste of your tea. You don't want to use distilled water because there aren't enough minerals for optimal flavor, yet hard water contains too much calcium and magnesium. Most tap water works well for brewing tea, although you may find that filtering the water yields better flavor. Bottled spring water is another option.

On the other hand, if oxidation occurs very quickly, thearubigins don't have the opportunity to develop, and the tea remains brisk and astringent. This is why cut-tear-curl (CTC) teas — heavily damaged leaves that rapidly oxidize — are in-your-face bold (and often drunk with milk).

Unlike green tea leaves, which retain much, or even most, of their original color, oxidized tea leaves generally range from coppery-brown to black in color due to chemical changes in the chlorophyll. Buds, however, turn golden. This is because they contain little chlorophyll; during oxidation, the honey tones of degraded polyphenols come out.

The Best Tea to Drink

Although you may hear that green tea is better for you because the catechins haven't been converted into more complex forms, don't immediately throw out the black tea that you love and switch to green tea! Both green *and* black tea have antioxidant properties. Let's take a look.

The benefits of green tea

The catechin EGCG that's found in green tea is often called a "natural drug" and is the golden child of current research. Laboratory studies suggest that this strong antioxidant may indeed be helpful to treat or prevent many chronic diseases, including those that damage the brain.

Intriguingly, EGCG also may have some of the same advantages that theanine offers (see Chapter 11 for details about theanine in tea). Preliminary research suggests that EGCG may promote alpha, theta, and beta wave activity in the brain, helping us calm down and focus.

However, even though it's delicious, and even if you drink copious amounts of it, green tea is not guaranteed to give you *all* the benefits of EGCG that have been demonstrated in the lab. The tea may be loaded with polyphenols, but there may not be enough to have a measurable effect, or your body may be unable to access them. Assessing definitive health benefits is very complicated (see more about this important point in Chapter 14).

REMEMBER

The upshot? If you like green tea, drink it. Green tea has lots of polyphenols.

The benefits of black tea

Like catechins, theaflavins and thearubigins are antioxidants. The conversion from simple to complex polyphenols does not appear to change their antioxidant properties in any substantial way. Although numerous studies focus on the catechin EGCG found in green tea, plenty of work also supports the similar antioxidant capacity of theaflavins and thearubigins.

Moreover, many of the health benefits suggested by studies of green tea are also supported by research on black tea, including possible protection against dementia, cancer, viruses, and bacteria. Note, however, that whole leaf teas appear to contain more robust antioxidants than CTC teas.

But, as mentioned in the previous section, consuming polyphenols isn't a promise that health effects are tangible.

REMEMBER

In a nutshell? If you like black tea, drink it. Black tea has lots of polyphenols.

Does it matter which tea you drink?

So many teas! And so many voices out there telling you to drink this or that tea.

REMEMBER

But tea shouldn't be this difficult. Instead, you should drink tea only because you like it, and you should drink only those teas that you like. Because it really doesn't matter which tea you drink.

All tea contains polyphenols, and all tea polyphenols are antioxidants. It doesn't matter whether you're drinking tea that contains mostly catechins (green tea) or mostly theaflavins (black tea). This is a win-win situation for tea drinkers!

Note also that if you want to drink the tea that contains the *most* polyphenols, just drink the tea that you love. (Bonus: You'll end up drinking more of it because you enjoy it.) Calculating the number of polyphenols in any given tea is futile, just like figuring out caffeine levels (see Chapter 11). Every individual tea must be tested in a lab, and generalizations are challenging. For example, some studies have demonstrated that white tea contains more polyphenols than green, whereas other studies have shown the opposite. Levels vary widely even within a type of tea. As with caffeine, polyphenol quantity depends on a plethora of factors including

» Type of tea plant

» Geographic location

» Growing conditions and stress on the plant

» Time of harvest

» Which leaves are harvested

» How the tea is produced

» How you brew your leaves

TIP

Now if you still think that you "have" to drink green tea because it's "healthier" — *even though you don't like it* — put that thought away, right now, please. Just drink the tea you most enjoy!

Green tea was originally thought to be healthier than black tea for numerous reasons:

>> Early studies came out of primarily green tea-drinking countries such as China and Japan.

>> Green tea-drinking countries were ideal for studies involving large groups of people. Researchers could find communities in which most people were drinking the same tea — grown and produced from the same tea garden and brewed and consumed in a similar manner.

>> EGCG is undeniably a potent antioxidant, and, to our knowledge, green tea contains more EGCG than anything else we ingest (remember, though, that polyphenol quantity doesn't always translate into concrete health benefits; see Chapter 14).

>> Extensive studies of black tea began relatively recently; therefore, a larger body of work exists for green tea.

However, as research continues, we're learning how much more we need to learn. Although thearubigins aren't well understood and EGCG continues to reveal surprises, results for *all* types of tea continue to be promising.

REMEMBER

In the end, *all* tea contains polyphenols, and *all* polyphenols contribute to your health. Drink the tea that makes you happy!

Chapter **14**

Investigating the Health Benefits of Tea

Back in the Stone Age, our ancestors discovered tea. However, they weren't content with getting their caffeine fix by foraging in the wild. No, these ambitious mid-3000s-BCE farmers planted tea rhizomes near their homes — and precipitated a burgeoning industry. Early influencers, they knew that tea has it all: terrific flavor, a caffeine boost, and a promise to heal body and soul.

So, now, grab your favorite tea and consider whether it truly is a magic elixir. *Will your cup of tea provide tangible health benefits?* Although the question is straightforward, the answer is complicated and often unclear. There's plenty of hype and many sweeping claims, but what's the truth behind it all?

In this chapter, we analyze why health claims don't always translate into actual health benefits. We examine the research — how it's done, why laboratory results don't always apply to real-world situations, and why assessing tea is so complex. Finally, we see how tea potentially plays a role in preventing, mitigating, or treating illness, disease, stress, and aging.

Seeking the Truth behind Health Claims

Enjoyed for its flavor and for providing calm alertness, tea has been used medicinally for centuries. Sore throat? Add a bit of lemon and honey to hot tea. Headache? Have a cup of tea.

We know that tea hydrates, which improves cognition, cardiovascular health, digestion, and so on. But, more exciting, tea leaves are brimming with polyphenols (see Chapter 13 for an introduction to polyphenols). These potent antioxidants have inspired decades of research and prompted many a health claim.

Health benefits versus health claims

Tea is a treasure trove, but how do we unlock its potential and access its benefits? There are many tantalizing health claims, but do any of them hold water?

Calculating the specific benefits of any plant-based food or beverage is extremely complicated. First, you must determine what polyphenols are present. Well, that part's been done! We know a lot about what's in a tea leaf.

But then you must figure out whether any of those polyphenols are available in a useful form to your body after you've consumed the food or drink. Bioavailability — or how much of a specific polyphenol is absorbed and has an active effect — is often the sticking point because

TECHNICAL STUFF

>> No correlation exists between how many polyphenols are in each food item and how many of them are biologically available in your body.

>> Every polyphenol has a different bioavailability in your body.

>> Generally, your body can't absorb polyphenols as they are; rather, the polyphenols must undergo a chemical reaction that enables them to be absorbed.

>> The polyphenols must be metabolized and absorbed rather than simply eliminated from your body.

>> The metabolites may not have the same bioactivity as the original polyphenols.

>> A polyphenol that isn't well absorbed may still be highly effective because it isn't readily eliminated.

Further, even if you know that certain polyphenols are theoretically available for your body's use

>> The exact number of polyphenols in any specific food or tea can't be predicted (see Chapter 13).

>> Compounds within a food can enhance or diminish antioxidant effects (for example, the polyphenols and caffeine in tea work synergistically).

>> The bioactive compounds derived from a food may interact — synergistically, anti-synergistically, or in an additive manner — with compounds from other foods, or even metals.

We don't really understand a lot of this yet despite a huge amount of research. The polyphenols in tea have been identified, we know that they have great potential, and it appears that green and black tea have similar antioxidant capacities. However, we have a long way to go.

Many studies focus on optimizing bioavailability. For example, it's been shown that when you drink tea, antioxidant activity in plasma increases. However, studies of green tea extract indicate that not many of tea's catechins, such as EGC and EGCG (catechins are a type of polyphenol; see Chapter 13), are absorbed. Alternately, the catechins may not be broken down, absorbed, or metabolized efficiently.

Ascorbic acid (vitamin C) and citric acid contain flavanones that are more available and better absorbed than tea catechins. When either of these acids are added to tea extract, substantially more of tea's polyphenols are absorbed. In fact, adding citrus to any type of tea seems to increase antioxidant properties. Therefore, will adding a squirt of lemon to your tea give you more polyphenols? It's hard to know. Many of the studies done so far have been in the laboratory, using animal models and/or tea extracts. (Unlike a brewed cup of tea, an extract is a concentrate, so it contains far more bioactive compounds than you get in a cup of tea.)

REMEMBER

Thus, even though tea has plenty of polyphenols, and even though these polyphenols potentially offer many health benefits, we can't necessarily say that drinking tea provides polyphenols that are bioavailable and effective.

This is where health claims often diverge from demonstrated health benefits. Say you hear that drinking tea can prevent you from falling ill from a virus. Laboratory studies may suggest such a benefit, and theoretically it may be true. However, those studies might have evaluated an isolated and concentrated catechin in cell cultures. It's unlikely that drinking tea will be enough to safeguard you — it's impossible to know how many polyphenols are in your specific cup of tea, whether there are enough polyphenols to have an effect, or whether the polyphenols are even available for your body to use in fending off that virus.

BEWARE THE SNAKE OIL!

We are bombarded by irresistible come-ons all the time. Drink *this* to cure *that*. Articles push the tea du jour while ads and slick packaging peddle "wellness" herbal teas. In fact, some wellness-type teas profess to boost your health in so many ways that you might think that you've discovered a veritable fountain of youth! In all this noise, how do you navigate? Is it possible to evaluate the tempting claims that clamor for your attention (and dollars)? Are any of them grounded in truth?

Well, sensationalism sells, and wellness-type teas are becoming big business. Unfortunately, there's little scientific proof for herbal tea efficacy. Although there's considerably more research on tea itself, it's difficult to calculate and measure tangible health benefits. Keep in mind, too, that all tea types (black, green, and so on) come from the exact same plant. We suggest that you ignore anything that overpromises or pushes a specific tea, herbal or not. Rather, drink the tea that you most enjoy. And, while you wait for the kettle to heat, read both this chapter and Chapter 15 to better understand why claims are no guarantee of benefits.

REMEMBER

Health claims are usually based on science, but a positive result from a lab experiment doesn't mean that you'll reap the same benefits when you drink a cup of tea. Too many claims overreach, promising effects that are feasible theoretically — but not realistically. The science behind polyphenols and how they work in the human body is complex with a lot of moving parts!

TIP

We suggest that if you like tea, drink it! Don't worry about which tea will supposedly alleviate this or that health problem — just drink whatever tea you love. Overall, any tea is a healthy option, even if specific health benefits remain elusive.

The reliability of the research

Thousands of studies have been done on tea and its components. Conducted worldwide by individuals and by large corporations, studies run the gamut from theoretical to on-the-ground analyses of what people drink daily. Experiments are sophisticated, well designed, and far-reaching. After all, tea — second only to water as the most-consumed beverage worldwide — is big business.

Yet, tea also intrigues those seeking new avenues for medicine, hoping to build a novel and potentially powerful complement to current drugs and treatments. There are many excellent ways to isolate, analyze, and compare the components of tea, allowing targeted experiments and applications. The research to date is solid, but it's only a beginning.

Beyond the laboratory, there are observational, self-reported studies, which probe the link between drinking tea and people's health (and sometimes involve thousands of people). However, we need more double-blind clinical studies to pinpoint measurable effects — but this is difficult. A nearly unlimited number of teas are available, with differing and even fluctuating polyphenol and caffeine levels. Much work remains to be done.

Real-world applications versus observational and laboratory studies

Delving into tea research takes you in various directions; in the end, it's likely that laboratory-based experiments, theoretical analyses, and probing the links between people, tea, and disease will eventually converge to yield therapies for treating illness and disease. Meantime, research continues — on all these fronts.

Analysis on the ground

Researchers may analyze large groups of people: how much tea they drink, what they eat, how active are they, how many of them have cardiovascular disease, and so on. Although these epidemiological, observational, and/or self-reported studies can generate useful information and identify trends, there is an element of subjectivity.

For example, if asked how much tea per day you drank over the past ten years, how accurate would your answer be? If asked how many portions of vegetables you ate daily, would you tend to estimate upward? We may think we walk a lot — until we get a pedometer.

If you're the researcher, you must figure out cause and effect. Does drinking tea lead to greater mobility in the elderly, or do more-mobile people happen to drink tea? Or do tea drinkers tend to have healthier diets overall, resulting in better health and, hence, greater mobility?

And there's always the question of what constitutes a "cup" of tea? Two ounces, twenty ounces? How strongly was the tea brewed? And what type of tea are we talking here?

Studies undertaken in Asian countries usually focus on green and oolong tea, whereas those conducted in Western countries often focus on black tea or a combination of tea types — because that's what people in those areas generally drink. It's not really a matter of selecting which tea type to examine. Rather, the study evaluates whatever tea the subjects are already drinking.

Designing measured, cause-and-effect clinical trials is vital, but the many variables must be minimized. For instance, different tea cultivars have different antioxidant capacities. If the study subjects drink different teas, then cause and effect can be muddy. To circumvent this, tea supplements or extracts may be used instead.

When observational surveys and clinical trials produce promising results, they spur further study — and, often, a lot of media attention. Keep in mind that

REMEMBER

>> Promising and preliminary results are just that: promising and preliminary, not definitive.

>> Observational studies encompass many variables.

>> What you're able to extract when you brew a cup of tea is not the same as what's in a supplement.

>> Supplements, such as green tea dietary supplements, don't necessarily provide more health benefits than drinking green tea.

WARNING

>> You shouldn't try to self-medicate by drinking tea *and* taking tea supplements because excess amounts can cause liver damage. Even the supplements alone can pose problems, especially if you have a medical condition (or take certain medicines) that might put you at risk. It's always a good idea to check with your doctor before taking tea supplements.

Analysis in the lab

In a lab, you can isolate specific components from tea and then tightly control the testing conditions. It's not the same as studying what happens in a person's body, but it'll provide information about how a component might work.

The catechin EGCG is one of the most promising compounds in tea; it's frequently called a "natural drug" for its efficacy against viruses, among other benefits. However, EGCG isn't stable and doesn't easily penetrate membranes. Therefore, to make it available within the human body at a dose high enough to have an effect, it might be isolated and then chemically altered. Or it might be encapsulated, which gets the phenol to where it needs to be, in an effective concentration. Likewise for other polyphenols. They can be extracted, perhaps concentrated, or possibly encased in something else.

By isolating specific phenols, scientists can determine what they do, but these studies are often carried out in cell cultures or animal models. When a phenol is found to have a specific effect, that result does not necessarily have real-world applications. Exposing a group of cells to a polyphenol is vastly different from you obtaining that same polyphenol from food you eat, for all the reasons given in preceding sections!

Rather, these experiments contribute to our knowledge of what polyphenols do and how they do it. Because tea polyphenols are natural and nontoxic, scientists hope to use them in their isolated form to build novel drugs and create new therapies that will augment our current options.

Something to note about tea — it's difficult to separate the caffeine from the polyphenols (which is why decaf tea isn't very good; see Chapter 12). Polyphenols and caffeine can interact, creating unique complexes, particularly in black tea, and they appear to work synergistically. Clearly this complicates research. What's responsible for an outcome: caffeine, a particular polyphenol, or both? Isolating specific compounds helps clarify what each one does.

Theoretical experiments, done virtually by software (see the nearby sidebar, "Check out these libraries"), may sometimes precede laboratory work. Databases help scientists refine experiment design, saving time and resources.

What these studies mean to you

REMEMBER

Researchers *do* know a lot about tea, and we can be encouraged by that — so long as we're careful that we don't read too much into scientific studies because

>> Laboratory results don't guarantee similar results in humans.

>> Many experiments involve small sample sizes.

>> Much of the work is preliminary, so results need to be verified, replicated, and honed.

REMEMBER

Tea has tremendous potential, but we're only at the cusp of unlocking its secrets. Tea-derived therapies may eventually complement current medical treatment, but meanwhile, as scientists continue to plug along, we recommend that you simply enjoy your tea. We can't say it will prevent this or cure that—but we do know that simply having tea can be an overall healthy choice for body, mind, and soul.

TECHNICAL
STUFF

CHECK OUT THESE LIBRARIES

There are libraries — or databases — of compounds that scientists can access, which enable them to screen hundreds of compounds. For example, they can design a computer program that runs through the library and flags any compound that can bind with a compound of interest. Endless experiments can be conducted virtually, ruling out dead ends and allowing scientists to design targeted research experiments, using only those compounds that show promise.

(continued)

(continued)

Both natural product libraries and synthetic compound libraries have been developed. Natural products encompass plant and animal sources (including bacteria and fungi), extracts from natural products, and synthetic compounds extracted from natural sources.

With the demand for new drugs to address current needs, some scientists are shifting back to natural products, which fell out of favor with the advent of the pharmaceutical industry. Natural compounds offer several advantages:

- They've resulted when a species has developed protection against infections and infestations — and against being eaten out of existence; this defense system includes polyphenols and their antioxidant properties.

- These phytochemicals (biologically active compounds found in plants) are more structurally complex than synthetic compounds.

Compared to a synthetic product library, a natural product library contains fewer compounds. This facilitates efficacy by smaller and/or less well-funded research groups.

Looking at the Potential Role of Tea in Illness and Disease

The polyphenols in tea generate laundry lists of possible benefits:

>> Some are "anti-" ones, meaning that the compounds in tea may work against or counteract the disease or illness. These include antiaging, antiallergic, antiangiogenic, antiarthritic, antibacterial, anticarcinogenic, anticataract, anticavity, antidiabetic, antifungal, anti-inflammatory, antimicrobial, antimutagenic, antineoplastic, antinociceptive (pain), antiobesity, antioxidant, antiseptic, and antiviral.

>> And some are protective: cardioprotective, chemoprevention, neuroprotective, and probiotic.

No wonder tea is so heavily researched — what doesn't it potentially do?!

But how can tea do all this? How can its polyphenols be implicated in so many disparate health conditions?

OXIDANTS AND ANTIOXIDANTS

TECHNICAL STUFF

In our bodies, cellular mitochondria use oxygen to produce energy, which results in some byproducts, usually reactive oxygen species and reactive nitrogen species. Also called free radicals, these reactive species are unstable molecules. Although they are essential for bodily functions, sometimes there are just too many of them. This harmful imbalance is called *oxidative stress* — and stressful it is. Cells and DNA are damaged, we age, and various chronic and degenerative diseases may be triggered or exacerbated.

Unfortunately, mitochondria aren't the only source of free radicals. Inflammation, bacteria, stress, or even too much exercise can also generate these harmful oxidants. We can blame external factors as well, including exposure to smoke, toxins, certain solvents, radiation, and some foods.

Luckily for us, our bodies don't passively tolerate all this instability without fighting back. We're programmed to combat oxidative stress by sending out *anti*-oxidants that either have been made by our bodies or have been obtained from the food, beverages, and supplements that we've ingested. These antioxidants react with and remove the oxidants, thereby mitigating or even helping to prevent cell and tissue damage and the onset or progression of chronic diseases. Some studies suggest that antioxidant polyphenols may also trap reactive carbonyl species, an alternate method for disabling these unstable molecules.

REMEMBER

In whatever manner they work, we do know that antioxidants are critical for our health. By including plentiful amounts of polyphenols in our diet, we help our bodies do their job even more efficiently and effectively. Note, however, that we must consume polyphenols daily because our body doesn't store them for future use.

Well, within your body, cells communicate with each other continually; any incoming message or signal triggers a series of reactions. Called cellular signaling pathways, they cause something to happen, whether bad (progression of a disease) or good (interrupting that progression, for instance). Although we don't completely understand how the polyphenols of tea function, they offer vast possibilities because they work at the cellular level, and they appear to operate on these cellular communication pathways.

For these reasons, tea's potential has been investigated in preventing, alleviating, or even curing myriad health problems. Let's take a look.

Disease

Oxidative stress (see the nearby sidebar, "Oxidants and antioxidants") is probably a major cause of cancer, cardiovascular disease, diabetes, kidney disease, liver disease, and osteoporosis and is involved in some neurological diseases (see the section, "Neurological") such as depression, multiple sclerosis, and Parkinson's disease. Oxidative stress can also trigger inflammation, potentially leading to inflammatory diseases such as asthma or rheumatoid arthritis.

Because tea works against inflammation and oxidative stress, researchers strive to tap into that potential. The following sections offer some examples.

Cancer

Many studies have focused on how polyphenols may help fight cancer, but there are few definitive conclusions. In some studies, tea seems to protect against various cancers, whereas in other studies, tea apparently has no effect against those same cancers. Although that seems disappointing, every study contributes to our body of knowledge.

So far, lab studies have demonstrated that both black and green tea have anticancer properties, perhaps with several underlying mechanisms. The polyphenols may interfere with cancer cell signals and/or disrupt the cell cycle. This might then prevent cancer cell growth.

Therefore, researchers are testing to see whether tea can discourage cancer from returning or prevent it altogether (chemoprevention). For instance, oxidative stress can damage cellular DNA, causing cancer. The catechin EGCG, found primarily in green tea, appears to curb damage to the DNA, which, in turn, lessens the damage to cells. Before you jump on the green tea wagon, however, note that black tea has also been shown to protect DNA.

Studies also probe tea's ability to control cancer cell progression. If the natural compounds found in tea could be used to slow or block cancer cell growth, we may eventually have an additional tool for managing incurable metastatic cancer. Lab-generated EGCG analogs — which increase EGCG's stability within the body environment — may even induce cancer cells to die.

Intriguing skin cancer studies have been conducted. Whether applied topically or consumed, it appears that caffeine works with the polyphenols in tea to inhibit cancer cells. Several mechanisms of action, including tea's antioxidant properties, may be at play.

REMEMBER

Despite the many studies on tea, no decisive proof confirms that it prevents or cures cancer. Results are inconclusive, sometimes contradictory, usually preliminary — yet frequently promising.

Cardiovascular disease

High blood pressure often leads to cardiovascular disease, and although some studies indicate that black tea lowers blood pressure, others have shown there's no effect.

Tea may help lower low-density lipoprotein (LDL cholesterol, the "bad" cholesterol), which, in turn, might decrease the risk for cardiovascular disease and stroke. The catechin EGCG may work with the anticoagulant heparin to protect blood vessels against plaque; EGCG binds to a protein that forms amyloid deposits and, thus, changes them into less-damaging molecules.

Both black and green tea have been linked to a lower risk of dying from a stroke and other cardiovascular issues, and it's possible that tea may protect neurons during a stroke. However, there's little evidence that drinking tea, green or otherwise, prevents stroke or heart attacks. A 2021 study again verified those conclusions — but did find that tea seem to improve the prognosis and functional recovery of stroke and heart attack *survivors*.

REMEMBER

Future research must also tease out other factors — such as a person's diet, lifestyle, and overall health before suffering a stroke or heart attack — to figure out how large a role the tea itself plays in these results.

Diabetes

The polyphenols in tea appear to slow the rate at which the body absorbs glucose, which could help prevent diabetes from developing. The polyphenols do this by inhibiting a type of enzyme (carbohydrate hydrolyzing enzymes). Incidentally, many such inhibitors are derived from plants.

REMEMBER

However, diabetes is a complicated disease, making research difficult. Even if tea has an impact, it may not overcome a person's genetic tendency to develop the disease.

Osteoporosis

Tea is linked to a lower risk of osteoporosis, although many studies are inconclusive or contradict other studies. It seems that long-term tea drinking may preserve bone mineral density, thereby protecting against fractures.

Several theories seek to explain how tea might affect bones. For instance, is it tea's fluoride and/or flavonoid content, or does tea decrease bone resorption or promote new cell growth? Hopefully, future studies will shed light on this.

Immune system and infection

In general, drinking hot liquids, including tea, helps relieve some cold symptoms.

Tea is linked to a lower risk of dying from pneumonia, and its polyphenols show promise for preventing and treating flu. If extracted and used to design a new drug, a tea-derived treatment may one day complement current drugs. Meanwhile, some observational studies have noted fewer cases of flu in populations that drink tea or were given capsules of catechins and theanine.

Specific polyphenols found in black, green, oolong, and pu-erh tea have been identified as virus inhibitors. They appear to dampen virus replication. (Theaflavins in black tea and polyphenols in green tea can affect *proteases*, enzymes that are critical to some viruses.) In addition, they can affect how viruses enter host cells and have been shown to partly prevent them from entering at all. At the same time, the polyphenols don't hurt the host cells. However, scientists stress that this work is preliminary and often theoretical; medicinal application remains distant.

TIP

Besides tea, many plant extracts are under study as potential antiviral treatments. A polyphenol-rich diet may help you fight secondary infections — reason enough to eat a lot of plants and drink tea!

Polyphenols are also antibacterial. EGCG may work synergistically with antibiotics to combat antibiotic-resistant bacteria — but, so far, only in a lab setting. There's some indication that green and black tea may help prevent tooth decay and periodontal disease, although other studies suggest drinking tea can cause cavities.

Neurological

Polyphenols from tea even reach your brain — an important point because other antioxidants tend to work elsewhere in your body, leaving the neurons in your brain vulnerable to free radicals such as reactive oxygen species (see the sidebar, "Oxidants and antioxidants"). Because your brain demands a lot of oxygen (about 20 percent of what you breathe in), there's plenty of opportunity for oxidative stress. High levels of free radicals in the brain may pose a greater risk of neurodegenerative disease.

REMEMBER

Because the antioxidants in tea reach the brain, the possibilities are exciting — what if drinking tea combats neurological damage? The research is encouraging! Still, we don't totally understand how the whole thing works. Currently, it's thought that both black and green tea polyphenols (and maybe the amino acid theanine as well) may protect your brain by

>> Getting rid of reactive oxygen species and reactive nitrogen species (free radicals)

>> Helping your body make antioxidant enzymes

>> Protecting existing neurons from damage and maintaining their viability (neuroprotective)

>> Boosting new neuron production

>> Binding with transition metals

>> Increasing the number of enzymes that work against toxins such as lead

This neuroprotection, in turn, may cushion you from Alzheimer's disease (see the section "Aging Well, with a Nod to Tea" later in this chapter), stroke (see "Cardiovascular disease" earlier in this chapter), cognitive impairment and decline, depression, and Parkinson's disease, for instance.

In fact, tea — any tea — is linked with a lower risk of cognitive impairment, cognitive decline, depression, and developing Parkinson's disease. Ongoing studies probe how the catechins might work. Is it their neuroprotective role and/or their antioxidant capacity, for instance? Multiple signaling pathways within the brain are implicated in Parkinson's disease, so tea is intriguing because it seems to act on those same pathways in a neuroprotective manner.

Pain

Tea can potentially mitigate pain because it's an anti-inflammatory and an antioxidant, damping down inflammation and oxidative stress. Observational studies indicate that tea drinkers report less body pain. Research continues, with the goal of boosting (or replacing) traditional drugs.

Note, however, that tea can irritate the bladder, especially for those with bladder pain syndrome. Also, the caffeine in tea can prevent, treat, and cause headaches (see Chapter 11).

Topical treatment

TIP

Spent tea leaves have been used as a home remedy for ages. Try applying a poultice of brewed leaves to itchy bug bites. A used teabag, chilled, can reduce swelling (like under your eyes). Wet tea leaves can stem bleeding, reduce inflammation, and, due to its antibacterial properties, perhaps help to prevent infection.

Weight control

Will tea help you lose weight? If only it were that easy. Because it contains no calories, having tea in place of caloric drinks will lower your overall calorie consumption. Some studies suggest that caffeine works synergistically with the polyphenols in tea to play a role in weight control, whereas others indicate little correlation between caffeine and polyphenols. Experiments have shown that tea may increase energy expenditure; promote lipid metabolism, breaking down fat; discourage precursor fat cells from turning into fat cells; and suppress appetite.

TIP

Although there's little hard evidence to date that you'll lose weight by drinking tea, the groundwork has been laid for future studies. Meantime, tea makes a great substitute for high-calorie snacks and sugary sodas!

Aging Well, with a Nod to Tea

We all want to know how we can stay healthy as we grow older — but many of us seek an easy way to do that. Strength training? Ugh. Drink more tea? Sure thing!

Surveys of large populations of elderly people can help to identify what protects us as well as help define the lifestyle that best promotes continuing health. Of course, a person's genetic makeup partly reflects their health and affects their functional level (including both physical and mental activity). Still, tea often seems to be part of the equation.

Cognition and dementia

Oxidative stress damages neurons in your brain, which can lead to cognitive decline and dementia. Because tea polyphenols are neuroprotective (see the section "Neurological," earlier in this chapter), their potential is heavily investigated.

As you get older, your neurons begin to show damage and you lose neural plasticity, making it harder for you to learn and to form new memories. However, tea polyphenols may help neurons recover. It appears that the brain structure of long-time tea drinkers doesn't experience the same decline but instead continues to exchange information more efficiently — in terms of global brain organization, how the two hemispheres interact, and the nodes or synapses (the juncture across which the neurons send information on to other neurons) within the frontal cortex.

Some studies suggest that caffeine also guards against dementia and cognitive decline, and green tea extract and L-theanine supplements may sharpen memory and alertness.

Eating a diet rich in flavonols (a type of flavonoid, under the polyphenol umbrella) may help prevent or delay Alzheimer's disease. The flavonol kaempferol, which is found in tea, among other foods, is especially promising. It's been shown to alleviate oxidative stress, for example. Tea may protect by binding hydrogen peroxide and beta-amyloid (a protein; the plaques of Alzheimer's disease) and by hindering tau proteins (the tangles associated with Alzheimer's disease).

Besides kaempferol, tea contains the flavonols quercetin and myricetin. An observational study showed that elderly people who drank tea and ate various foods that contained these flavonols were more physically and mentally active than those who didn't.

Will tea stave off dementia? It looks promising, especially when tea is coupled with a healthy diet. While we wait for more definitive answers, we're going to grab another cup of tea, just in case (and maybe have a bit of broccoli or kale)!

Motor function and muscle strength

Tea drinkers sometimes seem be more physically active in their day-to-day activities than non–tea drinkers, possibly due to fewer broken bones (tea may help preserve bone density); better leg muscle strength, which helps prevent falls and frailty (tea polyphenols may help preserve strength); and better motor function.

Functional leg strength and power are critical for the elderly to remain independent. When leg muscles weaken, people begin to have trouble dressing themselves, or they may struggle to get in and out of chairs. They are prone to falls, and they may lose both mobility and functionality.

Life span

Multiple factors contribute to life span. For instance, as we note earlier, having good muscle strength, especially in the legs, helps guard against falls and broken bones. This, in turn, allows greater mobility, which facilitates physical activity and protects independent living. And *that* enables fuller participation in the community, improves mental outlook, and on and on.

Keeping disease at bay is also crucial. As seen in this chapter, tea may help protect against illnesses that damage our bodies and those that ravage our minds.

Further, tea polyphenols may delay aging itself. One of the markers of aging is telomere length. These bits of DNA, found on the ends of chromosomes in your cells, help stabilize the chromosomes. They also seem to reflect how much oxidative stress and inflammation you've experienced — the greater the damage, the shorter the telomeres. Thus, they are associated with a range of health problems. It appears that drinking tea may help preserve telomere length, although preliminary research suggests this applies to men more than to women, who tend to have longer telomeres even without tea.

Although it's impossible to say that drinking tea will lengthen your life, a growing body of work suggests that it contributes to your overall health, which certainly impacts life span in some measure.

Stay Calm and Drink Tea: Relieving Stress

As the saying goes, "Sometimes all you need is a good cup of tea."

It's long been known — scientifically and anecdotally — that we seem more prone to illness when we're psychologically stressed. Perhaps stress suppresses our overall resistance or impacts our body's immune processes. Whatever the reason, reducing stress is a worthy goal! Fortunately for tea drinkers, tea is linked with a lower risk of anxiety and psychological distress.

Granted, simply holding any hot beverage has benefits. You project the warmth of what you are holding to other people and situations, transferring physical sensations to the psychological. You might view strangers in a more positive light, for instance.

Drinking hot liquids impacts you on multiple levels. For one, it can make you happier. If that hot drink has caffeine (even a little bit), your anxiety decreases, which improves your mood and gives you more energy.

Tea specifically may decrease your cortisol level (cortisol is the "stress hormone," released whenever you experience stress or fear) and help you recover from stressful events. Note that tea doesn't reduce stress. Rather, it helps you recuperate from stress.

This recovery may be due to several things. Tea contains the amino acid theanine and many polyphenols, including the catechin EGCG. Theanine promotes calming alpha waves in your brain (see Chapter 11) and appears to lower cortisol levels. EGCG seems to increase alpha, theta, and beta brain wave activity, helping you relax and focus. Fewer platelets activate, which is good for cardiac health. Anxiety decreases; you relax.

Even when incorporated into confectionaries, matcha is calming because it contains a lot of theanine as well as arginine, an amino acid that enhances theanine's calming effects. (Note, however, that "matcha" refers to finely ground, shade-grown, high-quality tencha. Powdered green tea, in contrast, contains little theanine; see Chapter 5.)

The ritual of making tea — the meaning that "having tea" holds for you — may also contribute to tea's calming influence.

Thus

>> Ingesting tea (physiological) helps mitigate stress (psychological).

>> "Having" tea (psychological) helps change compounds in our body (physiological).

Whatever way it works, sipping a cup of hot tea after experiencing stress may be just what you need.

Tea for Two: Enhancing Your Social Life

As this chapter demonstrates, tea research is in its infancy. Studies are frequently ambiguous or even contradictory. Yet, the preponderance of evidence suggests that tea contributes to your health, protects cognition, and improves mood — all conducive to an active lifestyle. When you feel good, you're likelier to engage socially.

Elderly people who drink tea seem to be more socially active. They're more apt to join community events and activities; they socialize, volunteer, and exercise. They also report having more social support systems than non–tea drinkers.

REMEMBER

We also know that tea promotes calmness, both through its theanine and through the ritual of making and having tea. When you make tea, you might pause and pay attention to what you're doing, which relaxes you. When you make tea for others, you demonstrate your care for them, and you foster community. "Having tea," then, involves meaning and intention. You actively connect with others and form bonds, thereby creating and strengthening a social support system.

Chapter **15**

Investigating the Health Benefits of Herbal Tea

When you survey your herbal tea options, you quickly discover that there are a *lot!* Fruity, floral, earthy, sweet, tangy — you're sure to find flavors that you absolutely love. And there's something so accessible about herbal teas. You can walk out to your garden or neighborhood park and harvest your own leaves or berries. Did you know that sunny dandelion petals, especially those shade-grown flowers, can be brewed into tea? Fresh mint and lemon balm leaves are delightful together.

Tea made from herbaceous plants — herbal teas — have been used medicinally for, well, probably forever. Over the years, specific plants became associated with certain health conditions, as people thoughtfully applied their botanical expertise. Therefore, how valid are the many health claims that swirl around herbal teas today?

Here, we assess the evidence behind the claims and consider the reliability of the research and whether it has real-world applications. We look at why it's difficult to determine tangible health benefits, and then we take a closer look at some specific herbal tea ingredients to see where the science is today.

Seeking the Truth behind Health Claims

You generally can't go wrong with drinking herbal teas. They hydrate; most of them are naturally caffeine free; and they contain polyphenols, or antioxidants, which are good for you. But, best of all, many herbal teas are tremendously flavorful, making terrific alternates to tea *(Camellia sinensis)*. However, herbal teas are sometimes pushed for their presumed health benefits more than celebrated for their flavor, which can be misleading.

Health benefits versus health claims

With their deep history of use — as tea, food, and medicine — we assume that herbs are healthy for us. And they are! Personally, we love to end our day with a naturally caffeine-free herbal tea, whether steaming hot on a chilly winter evening or refreshingly iced on a sultry summer night. Essentially calorie free and filled with natural ingredients including herbs, spices, and fruit, we can feel good about what we're drinking.

REMEMBER

However, enjoying herbal teas as part of a healthy diet differs from using them as medicine. Of course, if ginger seems to quiet your nausea or chamomile helps you sleep, there's no harm there. Drink whatever you enjoy, and if it seems to make you feel better, then that's great. Just recognize that most health claims about herbal tea are simply that: claims, not demonstrated benefits.

You see, there's been research, some of it very encouraging, but few health claims have been clinically proven at this point. We simply don't have enough information. As with tea, the potential is there, but we don't fully understand how to access those benefits (see Chapter 14).

Using herbal tea as medicine is appealing because people have been doing just that for thousands of years. It's a natural remedy, and herbs are readily available. In fact, a lot of current research focuses on tea and herbal teas precisely *because* they've long been used medicinally. If we can substantiate the anecdotal benefits, then we may have new treatments to supplement our current options.

The problem? We just don't know how effective these herbs are, especially when ingested as tea. There are far too many variables to demonstrate their efficacy, and not enough testing has been done. Note, too, that they aren't necessarily benign. (They may interact with other medicines, for instance.)

Many research studies use concentrated extracts, rather than cups of tea, because it's far easier to prove cause and effect with an isolated compound that can be tested in a controlled laboratory setting. But lab results don't guarantee that you'll get the same result when you drink an herbal tea. Further, even though a plant contains compounds that theoretically benefit you, those compounds aren't necessarily available for your body's use (see the upcoming section, "Bioavailability complicates things").

TIP

Most health claims are tenuous, so until we have hard evidence, ignore the hype about herbal teas and focus instead on their flavor. Explore the many options out there and find the ones that you really love to drink!

The reliability of the research

You might think that we'd know a lot about the health benefits of herbal tea. After all,

>> The herbal tea market continues to grow.

>> Herbal teas have been used medicinally — globally — for millennia.

>> At one time, physicians were well versed in botany because most medicines were, well, plants. It wasn't until scientists were able to extract the active ingredients from plants, ushering in the age of the pharmaceutical industry, that drugs — rather than plants in the form of herbal medicines — were more widely used. Today, according to the University of Maryland Medical Center, nearly a quarter of pharmaceutical drugs still come from botanicals.

>> There's currently great interest in developing nutraceuticals. A pharmaceutical alternate, nutraceuticals are foods or supplements that usually contain a lot of polyphenols and may have medicinal benefits. (Note that in the United States, nutraceuticals are in the same FDA category as food additives and dietary supplements, and mostly aren't regulated.)

Unfortunately, research on herbal teas has lagged behind that on tea (*C. sinensis*), which means that the overall body of work is less robust. Too few analyses and tests on herbals have been done — and many of those have been small, were poorly designed, included too many variables, or were inconclusive. We simply don't have enough to go on.

This can be frustrating. These herbs have been used for generations, and there are countless anecdotal accounts of their efficacy, so why isn't the existing body of research more robust?

For one, there are lots of herbs to look at! In addition, there can be tremendous variability within a species. For example, if people study the same herb — but that herb was grown in different environments — the herbs (and, therefore, the studies) may not be comparable. This makes it even harder to determine specific health benefits.

Also, with resources and funding often limited, investigators will pursue the most promising leads first — and that's been tea, which is loaded with potent polyphenols and is the second-most consumed beverage worldwide.

REMEMBER

Therefore, because we don't fully understand how the active components of herbs work in the human body, we must be careful what we claim. Yes, most plants are good and part of a healthy diet, but, to date, research doesn't support more specificity than that. Drink herbal tea because you like it!

Real-world applications versus observational and laboratory studies

Compared to research on tea (see Chapter 14), relatively few observational and lab studies focus on herbal tea — which makes real-world applications a stretch. There are herbs such as rose hips and blackberry leaves with demonstrated antioxidant capacity. The polyphenols in tea, however, have garnered far more attention for their potentially extensive medical applications.

Many observational studies using herbal teas or supplements have involved small numbers of subjects (often under 100 people), unlike those of tea, which might include tens of thousands of people. This does make some sense. An entire village in China may drink *C. sinensis* var. *sinensis* green tea that's been produced from one tea garden, for example. But to find lots of people who all drink the same variety of Greek mountain herbal tea? That's much harder.

As with tea research, it's easier to ascertain cause and effect when an active ingredient can be isolated and evaluated in the lab. But so many herbs abound, sometimes with multiple varieties, that the workload is staggering. If preliminary work on one herb doesn't seem fruitful, researchers may simply move on to other herbs. And, as we discuss more comprehensively in Chapter 14, lab results don't guarantee the same results in the human body.

Sometimes, herbs are studied more for their potential as food additives than as tea:

» An herb's antioxidants might help stabilize a food item, perhaps preserving nutrients or preventing lipids from oxidizing.

» Herbs add nutrients, enriching foods such as bread or pasta, which are routinely eaten. These tactics can improve people's overall health. However, even adding an herb to bread, for instance, demands research. How much can be added before it compromises the bread? Does the bread still rise, and does it taste good and look appetizing? Is there enough of the herb to be beneficial?

TIP

When you read an online article that makes health claims, first consider whether it seems reliable and well researched. If the authors link to their sources (ideally, primary research articles), try checking them out to see how the studies were done. Were only a handful of people observed or tested? Was the study lab-based, using an isolated compound on a cell line or an animal model? How applicable are these results to you when drinking a cup of tea? Remember, the devil is in the details.

Bioavailability complicates things

Plants contain polyphenols, which are antioxidants (see Chapters 13 and 14); these can be identified, isolated, and studied. However, polyphenols vary from species to species and even from plant to plant, so it's impossible to predict how many polyphenols are in your cup. Further, you don't know how many of these polyphenols are available — or if they're available — for your body to use (see Chapter 14 for a fuller understanding of this problem).

REMEMBER

Whenever you eat or drink something, the polyphenols usually must undergo a chemical reaction so that your body is able to absorb them. "Bioavailability" refers to how much of a polyphenol is absorbed and has an active effect. Whatever a food or beverage contains *before you consume it* has little correlation to how much your body gets *after digestion*. For example, mangiferin is honeybush's most powerful antioxidant — in the lab. When you drink honeybush tea, mangiferin has a low bioavailability. In other words, honeybush contains this potent antioxidant, but your body can't use it.

In addition, whenever food is processed and/or cooked, its antioxidant properties and bioavailability change. Fermented ("red") honeybush and rooibos have substantially lower polyphenol levels than their unfermented counterparts ("green"). Fruit must be processed to make it shelf stable. For example, fruit may be dried, dehydrated, or crystallized. Solidifying or acidifying agents, oil, or rice flour may be added. Such processes impact polyphenol levels and bioactivity.

Many illnesses and diseases are caused by oxidative stress and inflammation (see Chapter 14), which is why it's critical to eat lots of polyphenols every day. Because we know that polyphenols *can* counteract oxidative stress and inflammation, researchers hope to harness that potential to build novel therapies to complement current medicine. A cup of herbal tea may not be effective. However, what if we could isolate an active component contained in that tea and put that isolate into a form that your body could absorb and use?

REMEMBER

Currently, there's little definitive evidence to back the many health claims about herbal teas — yet research continues, especially for those herbs that have shown the most promise so far. Meanwhile, we suggest that you drink the herbal teas that you love, making them part of a healthy lifestyle.

Evaluating Common Herbal Teas

In this section we look at many common herbs — by no means an exhaustive list — along with some that may be in wellness-type teas, to see where the science falls. What are some possible health benefits, and how supported are the claims?

Some herbal teas are thought to offer greater health benefits than others, but sometimes that's just because more research has been done on them or because they've been better publicized. Although we separate herbal teas into two categories — those that seem more promising versus those that remain in limbo — don't take this dichotomy as concrete. Our listings are loosely based on how much scientific scrutiny there's been and on whether that inquiry has been promising so far. As we mention earlier in this chapter, scientists have only begun to explore the staggering possibilities of herbal tea.

Some that show promise

These herbal teas have demonstrated some encouraging study results, and they can certainly be part of a healthy diet. However, it's not clear that they provide any definitive health benefits, particularly when consumed as tea.

So, if you like them, drink them for your enjoyment! Most are naturally caffeine free, ideal for evening sipping or for those sensitive to caffeine. And if you think that they seem to help your overall health, consider that a bonus!

Ashwagandha (winter cherry)

Long used in India in the ayurvedic system of medicine, ashwagandha is said to confer vitality. Although it's not clear how the herb works, it does appear to enhance stamina and energy as well as alleviate stress, at least for some people. Additional, and larger, studies need to be done. Because preliminary studies have been encouraging, researchers continue to probe the herb on many fronts, including its possible role in cognition and neuroprotection, cancer, and inflammation, among others.

Blackberry leaves

Curious scientists tested blackberry leaves — a byproduct when wild blackberries are mechanically harvested — to determine whether they could provide natural antioxidants. It turns out that the leaves seem to have more antioxidants than their berries! With these promising results, various cultivars have been screened to find those that have the highest antioxidant activity, with the hopes of eventually using them for tea and as a food additive.

Cinnamon

This aromatic spice — often part of herbal tea blends — has been used medicinally for millennia. Cinnamon, the inner bark of the *Cinnamomum* spp. tree, is harvested during the rainy season when the bark is more pliable. Cassia cinnamon, native to southern China, is the variety more likely to be found in your kitchen because it's cheaper and has a stronger flavor, but the higher-quality Ceylon variety, native to Sri Lanka and parts of India, appears to offer more health benefits.

In laboratory studies, cinnamon has been shown to aid insulin function and protect cognition. It has measurable antioxidant, anti-inflammatory, antiviral, and antibacterial properties. However, much more research needs to be done. As with tea (*C. sinensis*), the properties of cinnamon depend on many factors besides its variety. Where and how it's grown, as well as the concentration used in the study, impact its effects.

Cornflowers

Frequently sprinkled into both tea and herbal tea blends, cornflowers owe their blue color to the plant pigment and flavonoid anthocyanin. The pH condition determines the color of anthocyanin: alkaline, blue (for example, cornflowers, chicory, blueberries); neutral, purple (for example, violet, lavender); and acidic, red (for example, hibiscus, red roses, red raspberries). Anthocyanin is heavily studied because it's an antioxidant, but since cornflowers are usually added to tea and herbal blends for visual appeal, it's highly unlikely there are enough petals to have an impact.

Fireweed

Native to much of North America (with related plants indigenous to Europe), fireweed is well adapted for survival, repopulating areas following fires and volcanic eruptions. A flowering perennial, it belongs to the evening primrose family.

Traditionally, fireweed was used medicinally in North America, Europe, Scandinavia, Russia, and China. Applied topically, it served anti-inflammatory and antiseptic purposes. Ingested, it was used to treat a wide range of ailments, from the minor complaint to serious illnesses. With its many polyphenols, current research suggests that fireweed indeed has anti-inflammatory, antioxidant, and antibacterial properties, among others. The main polyphenol, oenothein B, has potential in cancer research as well. Comprehensive studies are needed.

Fruit

Fruit teas are in the herbal tea category because they don't contain tea leaves. Although you can find nearly any fruit incorporated into a fruit tea, you may notice that apple is a common ingredient. You may not even notice an apple flavor — like when apple juice is used as the base for other juices. Apple adds sweetness while allowing other flavors to shine.

Although all fruit is healthy, remember that processing changes polyphenol levels, and bioavailability is complicated. Anthocyanin-filled acai berries are considered a superfood, but that doesn't mean that the berries in your tea have a meaningful bioavailability. Calculating the specific health benefits of a fruit tea blend is challenging.

Greek mountain (shepherd's tea, ironwort)

A perennial in the mint family, Greek mountain, or ironwort (*Sideritis* spp.) thrives in a high-altitude environment. There are around 150 species of ironwort, located mostly in the Mediterranean area.

Ironwort appears to reduce anxiety. Some species and the tea made from them have been shown to have higher antioxidant and anti-inflammatory activity than other species. The plant's flavonoids, diterpenes, and volatile components seem to be responsible for these potential benefits, although the body of research remains small at this point. Still, preliminary research supports ironwort's traditional application as an antioxidant, anti-inflammatory, and antimicrobial, as well as its anecdotal effectiveness for calming stress.

Guarana

With its caffeine kick, guarana has been long enjoyed in the Amazon basin — and just might lead to a longer life! Studies are beginning to tease apart how guarana seeds might extend life and help protect cognition. As with tea (*C. sinensis*), its polyphenols may work with caffeine. Despite its many health claims, not enough research has been done to demonstrate how guarana operates in the human body.

Hibiscus

A member of the mallow family, hibiscus ranks as one of the top traded herbal products (by volume), both locally and internationally; more than 200 varieties are grown.

Hibiscus has been used medicinally through the ages, and, even when dried, the calyx has antioxidant properties. Although said to lower blood pressure, its effects are modest, and the studies are small. Similarly, it doesn't seem to have much impact on cholesterol levels. However, a lot of the preliminary research is promising, and studies continue.

Honeybush (mountain tea, cape tea)

Native to South Africa, honeybush probably takes its name from its yellow, honey-scented flowers. Left unfermented, it's known as green honeybush; when fermented, it's called red honeybush. Although it's high in antioxidants, fermenting substantially changes polyphenol levels. Additionally, even within the species, different types of plants vary in antioxidant level.

Honeybush is said to have many health benefits, but there's been almost no research to substantiate its anecdotal benefits. It has a complicated composition, although studies are starting to identify its components. Honeybush appears to act on cellular signaling pathways, and so may work to protect against cardiovascular disease, gene mutations, and other health issues.

Although encouraging, the lab-based results remain preliminary. Its low bioavailability complicates matters. When you drink honeybush, its most powerful antioxidant, mangiferin, is poorly absorbed and degrades into less usable metabolites.

Japanese mulberry leaves

Growing as a small tree or shrub, the Japanese mulberry (Moraceae family) is native to Japan's mountainous areas. For centuries it has been cultivated for its leaves, which are fed to silkworms — and consumed as tea. Mulberries have traditionally been used to treat diabetes; however, lab studies are now beginning to confirm it can lower blood glucose, even when consumed as tea made from mulberry extract (tablets of mulberry twig alkaloids also appear effective). Additional work investigates mulberry leaf extract's ability to combat diseases caused by oxidative stress and inflammation. Current studies are promising.

Licorice

This sweet root shows some promise against bacteria, viruses, inflammation, and fever, apparently due to its chemical component glycyrrhizin. Ongoing studies target its potential antioxidant properties and potential against cancer as well. Although evidence is building for the root's effectiveness, researchers caution that we still need more data.

WARNING

Licorice tea can sooth a sore throat. Just be aware that too much licorice can be toxic, potentially causing dangerously high blood pressure, potassium loss, and muscle weakness. Some products now contain licorice that's had the glycyrrhizin removed, making it safer for consumption.

Mate (yerba mate, maté)

Produced from a holly found in South American rainforests, mate may be natural, toasted, or roasted. Mate's trifecta of caffeine, theobromine, and theophylline crosses the blood-brain barrier to give an energy boost that's comparable to coffee. The herb also contains many vitamins and minerals.

Although mate contains antioxidants, and lab studies suggest it's an antimutagen, other studies have linked it to various cancers. The cancer risk, however, is contested because some study subjects also used tobacco and alcohol, compromising the results. In addition, animal research hasn't shown that mate is associated with cancer.

Most of the preliminary work on mate's antioxidant activity has been encouraging, although the studies are largely lab based; much more research must be done.

Moringa

Native to Africa and Asia, the versatile moringa plant has been used medicinally; for food and spice; to treat malnutrition; in the cosmetics, biodiesel, and oil industries; as forage; for water treatment; and as fertilizer. Its leaves, pods, and seeds are nutritionally dense, containing large amounts of vitamins C and A, calcium, protein, potassium, and iron — qualities that researchers hope to eventually exploit as a food additive. Dried leaves contain plenty of polyphenols, and numerous animal studies suggest that they have great potential. However, few studies have been done in humans.

Nettle (stinging nettle)

This widespread plant has long been used for both food and medicine. With its antioxidant, anti-inflammatory, and antimicrobial potential (among others), it merits further research, although its bioavailability appears to be low. There's some suggestion that nettle tea may ease pain caused by inflammation such as from arthritis; preliminary studies on its effects on cancer cell lines are encouraging. Overall, however, studies are limited at this time.

Rooibos

A legume native to the Western Cape of South Africa, "rooibos" means "red bush." Although it's called the "Long Life Tea" in Japan, it's not been well studied, and researchers are only beginning to tease out possible health benefits. When fermented, rooibos is called "red"; unfermented, it's "green." Fermenting affects the polyphenol levels, and within the species, different types have different levels.

Rooibos's composition is complicated. As with tea *(C. sinensis)*, the active components appear to work on cellular signaling pathways, possibly protecting against damage to DNA. Due to rooibos's antioxidant and anti-inflammatory capacity, it may potentially treat cardiovascular disease and related issues. However, results are preliminary and currently not medically applicable.

Rose hips

Found just below the petals of the rose, the rose hip is a pseudo-fruit that contains the plant's seeds. Rose hips have long been used medicinally. Although scientists are still parsing out potential benefits, it seems that rose hips have a lot to offer. They contain vitamin C, along with flavonoids and organic acids that hinder the vitamin C from oxidizing, which keeps more of it available for your body's use. Vitamin C is essential; it may also help protect cognitive ability.

Rose hips are anti-inflammatory and antioxidant; plus, they contain additional compounds that have been shown to work against disease. Therefore, rose hip extracts are heavily studied for their potential to prevent or treat diseases and illnesses caused by oxidative stress and inflammation. Studies on their neuroprotective properties are particularly exciting, with the hopes that treatments for illness such as Alzheimer's disease may be possible. Note, however, that much of this research has tested extracts in cell cultures in a lab.

The jury is still out

REMEMBER

Unfortunately, the jury remains out for many herbal teas. For some, the evidence for demonstrated health benefits remains unconvincing. For the most part, however, we simply don't know enough about these plants.

TIP

Still, these *are* plants, which contain polyphenols and are good for us. Therefore, you can't go wrong with these herbal teas. They are unlikely to have specific health benefits to any measurable effect, but they can be part of a healthy diet — plus, many of them make lovely tea! Enjoy them for their flavor, and let's just leave it at that while we await additional research.

Astragalus

Although long used in traditional Chinese medicine to help prevent disease, astragalus has been little studied in the Western world. Many of the existing studies on this herb are poorly designed or are inconclusive.

Barley

One of the world's oldest cultivated grains, barley has been documented archaeologically as early as 8000 BCE; it continues to be among the top five crops grown worldwide. Although many purported health benefits are touted, there don't seem to be any compelling health benefits specific to barley tea.

Cistus incanus

A member of the rockrose family, *Cistus incanus* has been investigated for its antioxidant, anti-inflammatory, and antibacterial capacity, for example. As with most plants, its environment affects its polyphenol levels. Several small studies suggest that drinking this herbal tea may help prevent cardiovascular disease, but much more work needs to be done. It's also been studied for use as a food additive.

Chamomile

Although this delicate flower is said to induce sleep, there's little evidence to that effect, especially when ingested as a cup of tea. Studies have evaluated various parameters of sleep (time, onset, quality, and so forth) and found that chamomile has little effect. As a dietary supplement, chamomile may help reduce anxiety; its anti-inflammatory capacity is also being studied. Note that if you're allergic to ragweed, you may also be allergic to chamomile.

Dandelion

Although native to Europe, the dandelion has a firm foothold in North America. All parts of the plant have been used medicinally, but there's no scientific support for this.

Echinacea

Native to North America, echinacea has been used medicinally for centuries. Although some research suggests that it may help prevent a cold, it may not have a significant effect. Currently, no other health claims are supported by science. The extracts used in research aren't standardized, precluding comparison, and many studies are poorly designed and inconclusive.

Elderberries

From European or black elder trees, these berries have traditionally been used to treat flu and upper respiratory infections. A few studies using supplements seem to agree, but there's currently not enough evidence.

Ginger

This hot spice, like peppermint, is commonly said to help settle the stomach and relieve nausea. The plant is native to Asia where it's been used medicinally in China for thousands of years. Studies have been done — but with supplements, not ginger tea. It appears that supplements may help with mild pregnancy-induced nausea.

Ginkgo

The *Ginkgo biloba* tree can live more than 4,000 years; its leaves and seeds have been used medicinally for millennia. Ginkgo has been studied for its possible use to treat various conditions, including cognition and dementia, anxiety, diabetes, cardiovascular disease, and more, but results are inconclusive or contradictory.

Ginseng (Asian ginseng)

Native to the Far East, ginseng has been taken as a tonic for thousands of years. Studied for its possible neuroprotective capacity, there's currently little scientific evidence for its efficacy; higher-quality studies are needed.

Goldenrod

Goldenrod, a perennial in the sunflower family, is native to North America. Its genus name, *Solidago* spp. refers to its use in traditional medicine, "to make whole." Native Americans used its leaves and flowers to treat various illnesses and wounds. Although there've been some studies on its pharmacological activity, results are inconclusive.

Lavender

Although this fragrant flower, a member of the mint family, is said to help with anxiety, and lavender oil has some similarity to benzodiazepines (such as valium), science currently doesn't support this claim. Studies have been done, but they're insufficient.

Lemon balm

There have been few studies. Although some preliminary work suggests that lemon balm, part of the mint family, may have multiple benefits and appears to be loaded with antioxidants, there's just not enough information.

Lemongrass (lemon grass)

Native to tropical and semitropical regions of Asia and India, lemongrass has been consumed for centuries. Preliminary studies indicate that lemongrass has antioxidant, anti-inflammatory, antibacterial, and other potential benefits, although it appears that when the grass is dried, many of these properties are lost. In addition, it's unclear how the components of this grass work molecularly; more research is needed.

Milk thistle (silymarin)

Native to Europe, milk thistle has been little studied. Although the herb was traditionally used to treat liver ailments, preliminary experimental results have been inconclusive or statistically insignificant.

Mint

The Lamiaceae (formerly Labiatae) or mint family includes 236 genera and more than 7,000 species. Spearmint, peppermint, and nana mint are among the mint varieties used for refreshing teas. The leaves contain the essential oil menthol, which binds to a specific receptor on sensory neurons, sending a message to the brain: "cool."

Although there's some indication that mint may aid digestion, very little research has been done on the leaves. Most studies have focused on extracted peppermint oil for its potential to ease nausea caused by surgery, chemotherapy, and pregnancy. Unfortunately, the results are not conclusive.

Valerian

Promoted for sleep, most studies haven't shown that valerian has any effect on people. Some animal studies have been more promising, but it's still unclear what components of valerian might be responsible or how they work. Further, harvest date impacts the levels of valerian's active compounds, adding another variable.

The many misconceptions around turmeric

With its saturated yellow color and unique flavor, turmeric elevates many a meal! The spice is produced from the rhizome of the *Curcuma longa* L. plant, which is in the ginger family and is native to Southeast Asia. Turmeric has been used in Chinese traditional medicine and Indian ayurvedic medicine for generations, and it remains popular today for presumed health benefits.

Turmeric contains polyphenols (antioxidants) called curcuminoids. Curcumin, which gives the spice its color, has been studied for its potential against oxidative stress, inflammation (including cognitive decline), viruses, and more. In breast cancer research, there's some indication that curcumin may work with the tea catechin EGCG. Like the polyphenols in tea, it may operate in cellular signaling pathways.

There are several sticking points of curcumin, however. It's not stable and is easily degraded. Even as a supplement, it's not well absorbed and is quickly metabolized and eliminated in the human body, so its bioavailability is extremely low. Scientists have tried encapsulating it and have combined it with other compounds such as piperine (found in black pepper) to improve its bioavailability.

Despite the compound's promise, we still don't know much about it. Curcumin formulations vary widely, so experimental results often can't be directly compared. Many studies have been poorly designed, with too many variables. Others are simply too small in scale or have yielded contradictory or inconclusive results. We need larger, well-designed studies that probe curcumin's bioavailability, including how that changes when curcumin interacts with other foods that are ingested at the same time. Importantly, we need to know whether, and how, curcumin impacts health in a significant, replicable way.

REMEMBER

As part of your tea, this insoluble spice is unlikely to improve your health because it simply isn't available for your body's use. However, research continues as we seek to tap its potential.

The problem with claims about herbal blends

Many wonderful herbal blends are available, including so-called wellness teas, which often claim copious health benefits. If you enjoy drinking these teas, that's terrific. Besides simple hydration, they contain plants and spices, which are good for you and may help maintain your overall health.

The caveat? Herbal tea blends are unlikely to give you specific health benefits.

For example, if you want to know exactly what a particular tea blend will do for you, you must calculate

>> How much of each ingredient is extracted during the brewing process

>> Which polyphenols are present in every ingredient extracted

>> The level of each polyphenol present (This varies by plant variety, growing conditions, time of harvest, processing, storage, and more.)

>> The bioavailability of each polyphenol

>> How that bioavailability changes in the presence of the other ingredients in the tea blend. For instance, do the ingredients work synergistically? Might they work against each other?

>> What the polyphenol does in your body

>> Whether the polyphenol has a measurable impact on your body

Thus, for any herbal tea blend that promises health benefits, who has evaluated its efficacy? How have those studies been done? This is staggeringly complicated. (See Chapter 14 for more about bioavailability.)

REMEMBER

Wellness-type teas can certainly be part of a healthy lifestyle; if you like them, great! Beware, however, of overreaching health claims. Some benefits may be theoretically, but not realistically, true. Other claims aren't supported by science at all. Also, remember that a cup of any other herbal tea — or tea (*C. sinensis*) — may be just as healthy as a "wellness" tea. Drink whatever you most enjoy!

But if It Works for You, Then It Works

We can't stress this enough: If you love herbal tea, and if you believe that it helps you focus or quiets your stomach, then it works for you (although, as with anything, it's best to consult a doctor if you have any health concerns). We ourselves find that ayurvedic vata tea excels at coating and soothing a sore throat.

Herbal teas have a long tradition of use — as medicines, home remedies, tonics, replacements for tea, or flavorful drinks on their own. Many of them haven't been scrutinized until fairly recently, when researchers began to wonder how we might better harness their potential or even develop new therapies to augment current medical treatment. Although we still don't fully understand how they work in the human body, the very fact that these herbal teas have long been used and enjoyed speaks to their value. Further, never discount the impact of the psychological on the physiological.

REMEMBER

Finishing your day with a soothing cup of chamomile tea may be wonderfully relaxing, enough to promote a peaceful night's sleep. Regardless of what science does or doesn't say, if an herbal tea works for you, then it works.

5

My Cup of Tea — Around the World

Travel the world and visit major tea-producing regions.

Appreciate tea's deep history, steeped in culture, ceremony, tradition, and regional customs.

Better understand the tea industry, including the lives of tea workers, tea certifications, tea purity and quality, the balance between tea and the environment, and the future of tea.

Chapter **16**

Exploring Tea-Producing Regions of the World

M any times, people talk about how the English love their tea, but how often do we step back and consider just where, exactly, this beverage comes from? Well, it definitely doesn't come from England! But did you know that 30 percent of tea comes from Kenya? Or that tea is produced in the Black Sea region and even in New Zealand?

In this chapter, we explore the world's major tea-growing and tea-producing areas, plus we take a look at several minor players. We aim to give you a good idea of where your tea comes from and perhaps a new appreciation for its incredible diversity.

Looking at Where Tea Is Grown

Tea-producing regions are expanding. Where tea was once grown only in China and India, you can now find tea gardens in all parts of the world. Geographically, tea is still best suited to areas around the equator (between latitudes 43° north and

30° south), within its natural limits, as shown in Figure 16-1. However, cultivars have been developed that enlarge the growing area, allowing the plants to do well in other climates. For example, drought-resistant cultivars can better tolerate less rainfall, whereas cold- or frost-resistant cultivars may flourish at higher elevations or in colder climates that original tea plants couldn't tolerate.

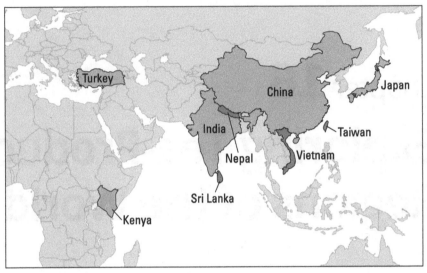

Source: John Wiley & Sons, Inc.

FIGURE 16-1:
World map showing major tea-producing countries.

Besides the suitability of the climate, other factors limit tea production. For example, although certain regions within the United States may be amenable to tea plants, commercial ventures just haven't lasted or have only niche markets, partly because profit margins are low and the quality of the tea isn't as high as that of other countries.

Where topography allows, producers plant and prune plants specifically for mechanical harvesting. In more mountainous areas, plants grow in clumps and must be hand harvested. Wild-grown plants must always be hand harvested. In Figure 16-2, you can see how the homogenous rows of plants (top photo) are well suited for mechanical harvesting, unlike the clumps of plants growing on a hillside (middle photo). Although they are well tended, the topography of the environment and the nature of these plants mean they must be harvested by hand. The wild-grown plant (bottom photo) also clearly requires hand plucking.

Note that any tea can be produced from any tea plant variety. This includes black, green, oolong, white, pu-erh, and yellow tea!

REMEMBER

FIGURE 16-2:
Types of tea gardens.

Photos by Lisa McDonald

Asia

Although many countries in Asia, such as Bangladesh, Thailand, and Malaysia, produce some quantity of tea, here we consider select countries.

China

China is the birthplace of tea. It's believed that the plant has been cultivated and consumed in the country for well over 5,000 years. And with the discovery of tea leaves in Jing Emperor Liu Qi's tomb in north central China, we have physical evidence that it was taken to non-tea-growing regions at least 2,100 years ago. The famed Silk Routes were established in 130 BCE and conveyed tea, along with other luxury goods, to the rest of Asia, the Middle East, the Mediterranean, and Russia.

Camellia sinensis var. *sinensis* is native to China; there are endless regional culti-vars, allowing individual regions to produce teas specific to them. Today, China produces 40 percent of the world's tea, exports the most tea of any country, and continues to supply the world with the entire spectrum of tea — black, green, oolong, white, pu-erh, yellow, and scented — all of which were originally developed within the country. The Chinese continue to be the only producer of yellow tea.

The country's major tea-growing regions include Jiangbei, the northernmost area, which produces primarily green tea; Jiangnan, which produces the most tea in the country; southern China, known for producing mainly black, oolong, and white tea; and the southwest area of the country, considered the birthplace of tea. The tea is largely mechanically harvested although a lot of tea is hand plucked as well.

The Chinese drink primarily green tea, and much of their black tea is exported, although younger people are beginning to drink more black tea.

India

Tea has a long history in India, with historical accounts indicating that it was consumed by 750 BCE. The British government established the tea industry in India in 1824, and today, India is second only to China in tea production. India produces mostly CTC (cut-tear-curl) black tea that's largely consumed domestically. The better-quality, orthodox tea (less than 10 percent of the tea produced) is typically exported and is not readily available within the country. India is now trying to rectify this by improved marketing, branding, and education. In addition, efforts are being made to produce greater amounts of orthodox and organic tea using sustainable methods, and to increase exports. Although tea in Darjeeling and Assam require hand plucking, other areas are exploring the use of mechanical harvesting to reduce production costs, especially in light of current labor shortages.

Assam

Assam, a state in northeastern India, is one of the world's largest tea-producing regions. *Camellia sinensis* var. *assamica* — a robust variety that's typically used to produce strong, black tea (see Chapter 4) — is native to this region. The first tea company was established in Assam in 1839, and today, lowland-grown tea plants thrive in the floodplain of the Brahmaputra River, which bisects the region. The majority of Assam's 800 registered tea gardens are located in this river valley. Fast-growing sal trees also like Assam's rainy, hot, humid environment, and forests of these trees have a greenhouse effect that helps protect the tea plants from the sun. The first harvest, or first flush, begins in February. The May–June second flush, however, yields the highest-grade Assam teas, characterized by a full-bodied, spicy, and malty flavor. Assam tea constitutes over half of India's total tea production.

Darjeeling

Also in northeastern India, but situated on the southern slopes of the Himalaya Mountains, is Darjeeling, which produces the Champagne of black teas (see Chapter 4). The tea gardens in this area consist of the *sinensis* variety, which was smuggled in from China in the 1800s and which thrived in the mountainous environment. At altitudes of 2,600 to greater than 6,500 feet, these gardens produce high-quality tea processed in the orthodox method. Five harvest seasons are possible: first flush, an "in-between" harvest (that is, between the first and second flushes), second flush, monsoon, and autumnal. However, the first- and second-flush teas underwrite the rest of the year. Darjeeling tea was accorded the first geographical indication of India, meaning that its quality is attributable to its geographic origin. Many of the plants are more than 100 years old. Currently, fewer than 100 gardens remain in operation, and Darjeeling tea accounts for approximately 1 percent of India's total production.

South India

Tea gardens located in the mountains of Southern India produce around 18 percent of the country's tea. In Nilgiri, tea is picked year-round. In some areas, cycles of drought and sporadic but intense rainfall have prompted farmers to replace tea with other, more resilient, crops.

Indonesia

The Southeast Asia nation of Indonesia includes thousands of islands with rich, volcanic soil. In the 1600s, the Dutch East India Company used the country as a trade hub and eventually tried growing their own tea with plants from China. When the plants didn't take, the *assamica* variety from India was brought in, thereby beginning the country's tea industry. Today, in gardens on Java and Sumatra, tea is harvested year-round; most is processed with conventional methods for black and green tea and is used in blends for bulk markets. Some oolong tea is also produced.

Japan

Brought from China in the 700s, tea was originally reserved for monasteries and royalty. Finally, in the 1300s, tea became available to all social classes and now is embedded in Japanese culture. The first tea garden in the country was on Japan's largest lake, Biwa-ko. Today, the Shizuoka District produces nearly half of the country's tea.

Tea gardens are located primarily in south and central Japan and on the island of Kyushu. Three-quarters of the tea produced comes from the Yabukita cultivar, which was developed in the early 1900s from the *sinensis* variety of tea plant. This cultivar was selected for its balance of flavor, yield, and ability to withstand frost.

The machine harvester was invented in the early 1900s in Japan, and today, most tea in the country is mechanically harvested. Machine harvesting helps ensure uniformity in picking and greater yields in harvesting. Although Japan does produce single-origin teas, most Japanese teas are blended using tea from various gardens as well as tea from the previous year, ensuring that each type of tea is very similar from year to year. The blends typically aren't released until later in the year, into the autumn months.

The Japanese produce and drink primarily green tea, although due to recent interest in westernized coffee shops and cafes, they now consume some black tea as well. Matcha remains popular, and frequently flavors pastries, ice cream, and more.

Nepal

Tea is relatively new to Nepal. Although seedings were received in 1862 as a gift from China, it wasn't until the 1960s that tea was seriously grown. Today, tea is an up-and-coming enterprise — coupled with the tea industry's commitment to environmental conservation and concern for those who work in the tea gardens, an emphasis on maintaining high tea quality, and a push for improvements, including that of country infrastructure. The tea industry comprises mostly small independent farmers who are personally invested in their gardens, and more than half the workers in the industry are women.

Eastern Nepal, where the tea gardens are located, has a similar environment to Darjeeling. In the lower altitudes of this mountainous country, mostly CTC from the *assamica* tea variety is produced, largely for domestic consumption, although some is exported, primarily to India. On the higher slopes (3,000 to 7,000 feet) of the Himalayas, "hill tea" is produced. Most of this is organically grown orthodox (hand-rolled) tea, from the *sinensis* tea variety. More than 90 percent of orthodox tea is exported, largely to India, although Nepal also exports to China.

South Korea

Tea was probably initially brought to Korea by Buddhist monks returning from China in the 500s or 600s CE. The tea plants that grow wild at Mt. Jiri come from the original plants of the 800s when Kim Taeryom planted *C. sinensis* seeds (brought from China) in the Ssanggyesa Monastery. Some of today's plants are hundreds of years old.

In the 1900s, the Japanese established tea plantations in Boseong with seed from Japan, thus beginning commercial production in the country. Although the plantation was abandoned in 1945, it was restored in the 1950s, and nearly half of South Korea's tea production now comes from this area. DNA analysis demonstrates that these plants still genetically match Japanese tea (those in the rest of the country are more genetically diverse and probably come from China).

Today, subtropical, volcanic Jeju Island also boosts a rapidly growing tea industry, consisting mainly of large commercial operations that rely on automated systems. Korea produces primarily green tea.

Sri Lanka

The British brought tea *(sinensis* variety*)* to Sri Lanka (formerly Ceylon) in the early 1860s at a time when 94 percent of the country's cultivated land was planted in coffee. Commercialized in 1867, the tea industry is now the country's largest employer, and Sri Lanka is the world's fourth-largest tea exporter. Ceylon tea has been designated an "ozone friendly tea" and was given the Montreal Protocol implementer's award.

This mountainous island is well suited for tea, allowing year-round harvests and yielding a range of teas with unique qualities, including low-grown (under 2,000 feet in altitude), mid-grown (2,000–4,000 feet), and high-grown (above 4,000 feet) tea. Although some gardens still have the *sinensis* variety, most gardens now grow *C. sinensis* var. *assamica*. Full-bodied Ceylon teas range in quality and include premium high-grown teas. Ceylon also serves as the base for many blends, such as breakfast teas and earl grey.

Taiwan

Tea has been grown on the small island of Taiwan (formerly Formosa) since the early 1700s, although commercial ventures didn't begin until the 1800s when immigrants from China's Fujian Province brought both tea plants and production expertise. Taiwan's unique growing conditions are ideal for tea — black, green, and oolong teas are all produced here. About a hundred small tea companies grow tea in the mountainous regions to the north and northeast, producing fine oolong tea.

Turkey

Although tea was planted in Turkey in the late 1800s and again in the early 1900s, it wasn't until the late 1930s that the industry got off the ground, assisted by a 1940 act that protected farmers' rights and set up the state as a buyer. Today, Turkey is one of the world's largest tea producers, but most of its tea is consumed domestically as black tea, with production barely keeping up with demand. The tea industry is centered in Rize, near the Black Sea; more than half the country's output is produced by Çaykur (Tea Board), the country's oldest tea-producing company, established by the state in 1971.

Vietnam

Tea has been consumed in Vietnam for thousands of years. Today, the country is one of the world's largest exporters, but the tea is primarily lower-quality black tea sold wholesale. The industry has been plagued by problems that need addressing, especially if it hopes to better align with the demands of global consumers. Recommendations include producing higher-quality tea that's free of contaminants; increasing yield; moving to organic methods; sharing profits more equally; and improving branding, marketing, and distribution. Despite the challenges, Vietnam does produce a small amount of high-quality orthodox teas.

Europe

While Europe mostly lies outside tea-growing regions, experimental and pilot gardens have been planted here and there, including in Scotland. Georgia, however, has produced tea for many years — but it's also located closer to Asia. This small country is considered a transcontinental country, straddling eastern Europe and western Asia. It is nestled between Russia, Turkey, Armenia, and Azerbaijan, and it runs along the eastern shore of the Black Sea. Chinese tea shrubs have been cultivated in the region since the mid-1700s. During the Soviet Union years, tea gardens covered more than 150,000 acres, and Georgia supplied the Soviets with 95 percent of their black tea; however, the tea was produced for volume rather than quality. Although the gardens were abandoned following Georgia's independence in 1991, the plants kept growing. Today, Georgia produces black, green, and white tea harvested from these wild plants as well as from newly tended gardens — this time with an eye for quality.

Africa

Tea-producing countries in Africa include Kenya, Malawi, Rwanda, Tanzania, Zimbabwe, Mozambique, Uganda, and Burundi, although Kenya is by far the largest producer. African countries account for some 30 percent of global exports (more than 500,000 tons), with Kenya supplying around 70 percent of that.

Tea is not native to Africa but was brought here at the end of the nineteenth century by British colonial rulers who wanted to reduce their dependence on Chinese trade and establish more secure sources of tea. The soil and climate lent themselves well to tea, and in 1880, the first tea estate was planted, in Malawi. In 1903, the first African-grown teas became a part of British tea culture. Shortly afterward, Germans settled in Tanzania, followed by Belgium and French producers in Burundi and Rwanda.

Most of the tea produced in Africa comes from plants of India origin, the *assamica* variety, and is processed by the CTC method. This tea is frequently used for blending, including in many breakfast blends. Tea can be harvested year-round in those countries closest to the equator such as Kenya.

South Pacific

South Pacific countries produce mainly herbal teas, although several small tea gardens exist. Zealong is New Zealand's only commercial tea estate, founded in 1996 with 130 tea cuttings and located in the upper North Island, where the terroir is ideal for tea. Today, the estate has 1.2 million plants and produces black, green, and oolong tea.

The Americas

The Americas are known more for their herbal teas, but a limited amount of tea is produced in both North and South America.

United States

Although small tea gardens can be found in several states, the Charleston Tea Garden in South Carolina is the only larger-scale operation. Currently owned by the Bigelow Tea Company, the garden was established in 1987 by William Barclay Hall, who marketed the tea as "American Classic Tea." The company currently produces machine-harvested black and green tea.

South America

South America's mountainous regions — with volcanic soil, high altitude, and ideal rainfall — are well suited for tea. The Andes Mountains cut down through Ecuador and Colombia while the equator runs across northern Ecuador and southern Colombia. Around 70 years ago, Colombia imported tea seeds from Sri Lanka, hoping to boost their own export economy. Today, several gardens produce tea, including some orthodox selections. Ecuador also produces a small amount of tea, and, further south, Argentina and Peru produce black tea, a low-quality product largely intended for blending, instant tea, or the domestic market.

Chapter **17**

Embracing Age-Old Traditions and Ceremonies

Wherever tea is served, there's mostly likely a ritual. You may take a moment to select your tea, and then pause before deciding whether to brew in the cup or pull out a teapot. There's the pleasure in opening a bag or tin of tea and appreciating its aroma. If you've brewed a large leaf or oolong tea, there's the delight of finding unfurled intact leaf sets, complete with bud. And sharing a cup with a friend? It's community, support, love. Granted, these may be small things, but anything that enhances your experience can be a tradition.

As tea spread throughout the world, societies built their own rituals and claimed tea for their own. Today, these rich traditions continue to be celebrated and remain embedded in cultural practices. Here in this chapter, we begin in China, tea's birthplace, and then travel farther afield. We consider the specialized tea ware that developed, the many ways that people have their tea, tea ceremonies, and just what constitutes a full English tea. Along the way, we see who drinks, and who purchases, the most tea. Finally, we discuss the popular South American drink, mate. Technically an herbal tea, we include it here for its rich tradition.

Heading to China, Where It All Began

From that first cup of tea brewed back in the Stone Age, the Chinese have esteemed tea. By China's late Tang Dynasty (618–907 CE), tea production had spread, Chinese of all classes were drinking tea, and both tea and porcelain were valuable exports. Integrated into China's cultural history, tea appears in early manuscripts, which praise the characteristics of various teas. A vocabulary was established, expectations for each tea were born, and legends were handed down over generations. Tea became associated with the arts, fine ware, and mindful appreciation. High-quality tea held extreme value for its own sake, and as tribute to the emperor, reward to elites, political leverage, economics, and more. Today, the teas that China produces — often using age-old methods — are part of the country's intangible cultural heritage, and tea continues to be celebrated.

Tea ceremony

China's tea ceremony dates back at least to the eighth century when contemporaries Jiao Ran, a monk, and Lu Yü, a writer and tea master, wrote about tea. One of Jiao Ran's poems referenced the ceremony specifically while Lu Yü penned his comprehensive *Classic of Tea* on tea culture. However, the ceremony existed in various forms, with different regions of China perfecting their own practices. Today, the tea ceremony is still part of Chinese culture, whether held in an elaborate or simple setting. Guidelines advise how to make, serve, and experience the tea, but the focus is firmly on the tea itself, including which tea is chosen and the appearance of its leaf, aroma, color of liquid, and taste. Tiny cups are used because the tea is meant to be mindfully appreciated (see Figure 17-1 for examples of small Jian ware and clay cups).

TIP

The gongfu (or gongfu cha) tradition — brewing tea with skill — came from the practice of brewing expensive tea in a small Yixing teapot. Today, inexpensive tea sets are readily available online, and you can find many videos and books that explore the rich history and culture of tea in China.

The gaiwan

Meaning "lidded bowl," the *gaiwan* serves as both teapot and teacup. The vessel was developed during the Ming Dynasty (1368–1644) and remains popular. Tea leaves are put into the small bowl or cup and hot water added. After the leaves have brewed, the lid is used to hold the leaves back while the liquor is sipped. Because you use a high ratio of leaf to water, this is a good method for tasting tea. The leaves can also be infused multiple times, allowing comparison.

Alternately, after brewing the leaves in the *gaiwan*, the liquor can be poured into a second vessel, and from there, into smaller tasting cups, gongfu style (Figure 17-1).

FIGURE 17-1: Examples of teacups used in China, Japan, Korea, and India.

Photos by Jill Rheinheimer

WHO IN THE WORLD DRINKS THE MOST TEA?

Per person? That would be the Turks, at nearly nine pounds of tea per person per year! For that amount, we calculate that every single person needs to drink nearly four cups of tea daily. However, since babies and little kids won't be pulling their share, Turkish adults are drinking a lot of tea! Tea has a deep history in Turkey, first coming from China via the Silk Roads. The Turkish word for tea, *çay*, is based on Chinese *chá*. Today, tea, a sign of hospitality, is integral to Turkish life.

Investigating India

India is known for its black tea, chai, and complicated tea history. Despite producing some of the best-known, highest-quality, and most sought-after loose-leaf teas, you will often see people in India drinking from a cup that has a teabag hanging from the side. The influence of the British and their push for mass-produced lower-quality tea — which was easier to sell — is still seen today.

In the United States, we often equate India with chai, a spicy, sweet concoction frequently served in coffee shops and cafes (refer to Figure 17-1 for chai cups). But even this stems from colonial times when locals were often left with low-quality or unaffordable tea. If the tea was low quality, people had to mask its flavor. If expensive, they had to stretch it. Adding spices, milk, and sugar was a solution for either case.

WHO IN THE WORLD PURCHASES THE MOST TEA?

Tea purchasing trends change from year to year and often depend on extraneous factors, such as sanctions, wars, supply chain disruptions, political alliances, domestic tea production of the importing country (for instance, if they didn't produce enough tea for their own needs), and more. For years, Germany was known as being a major purchaser and blender of fine teas due to its historical and geographical significance when tea imports to Europe first began. Today, other countries such as Pakistan, Russia, and Middle Eastern countries import quite a lot. Believe it or not, the United States is always ranked among the top three!

Examining Tea Traditions Around the World

Many countries have developed rich traditions centered on tea.

Japan

We have to go way back to learn how tea traditions started in Japan — all the way back to the eighth or ninth century. It is thought that the Buddhist monk Eichū brought black tea leaves back from China and served them to the emperor. It wasn't until the late 15th and early 16th centuries that tea became popular in Japan and spread to all classes, quickly becoming an important part of Japanese culture (refer to Figure 17-1 for an example of rustic teacups used today).

TIP

The Japanese tea ceremony is called *Chanoyu, Sado,* or *Ocha.* Some of you may have seen this formal ceremony depicted in museums, at cultural centers, or in films. You can find many books and resources that give an in-depth look at the history and ways of the traditional Japanese tea ceremony. In contrast to the Chinese tradition, the ritual and artistic aspects take precedence over the tea itself. In China, it is almost more of a tasting than a ceremony. Any tea may be brewed, unlike the Japanese ceremony, which centers around matcha.

A few important pieces of equipment are needed to properly prepare matcha during the tea ceremony (refer to Figure 17-1):

>> A small white cloth, or *chakin,* is mainly used to wipe the tea bowl.

>> A whisk, *chasen,* is used to mix the powdered tea with the hot water; it is carved from a single piece of bamboo.

>> Tea scoops are generally made from a single piece of bamboo but can also be made from wood or even ivory. The *chashaku* is used to scoop tea from the tea caddy into the tea bowl.

>> The bowl used to make matcha is the *chawan.* Many styles and colors are available to choose from. Shallow bowls in which tea can cool faster are often used in summer, whereas deep bowls are used in winter. The best bowls are thrown by hand, and imperfections are often seen as beauty.

Korea

Tea was probably brought to Korea by Buddhist monks returning from China in the 500s or 600s CE. By the mid-700s, King Gyeongdoek popularized the brew;

Ch'ungdam, a Buddhist monk, initiated the Buddhist tea rite; and tea was being grown in the country. During the Goryeo (Koryo) Dynasty, tea culture was at its zenith. Rituals developed as drinking tea became an elaborate affair in the royal court and potters created elegant celadon tea ware. The tea ceremony, *darye*, was integral to both national and religious practices.

During the succeeding Joseon (Choson) Dynasty, Buddhism replaced Confucianism, white porcelain displaced celadon, and tea was largely confined to ritual purposes. By the late 1500s, most of the tea gardens had disappeared.

However, interest in tea renewed in the 20th century, and tea is again a popular beverage (refer to Figure 17-1 for an example of Korean teacups). Although the tea ceremony nearly disappeared in society at large, Buddhist monks continued the practice. Today, teahouses, temples, and cultural events demonstrate or guide people through the ritual, which may reflect either Buddhist or Confucian influence.

Britain (and the art of having tea)

As Americans, we're used to drinking tea anytime we like, and "having tea" generally means "I'll have a cup of tea, please," regardless what the clock says. However, the 1800s brought various tea traditions to Britain.

During the 1830s, **temperance tea parties** began. Held in the middle of the day — on race days, which typically involved alcohol — tea and snacks, and eventually sweets, were served. These parties targeted both men and women.

By the 1840s, **low** or **afternoon tea** became popularized, perhaps by Anna Maria the Duchess of Bedford. Enjoyed by the upper classes, low tea included tea and light snacks and was designed to tide people over until their second meal of the day, which, due to improved artificial lighting, was served late in the evening. "Low" referred either to the low tea tables that were used for this snack or to its serving time, later in the afternoon.

Meanwhile, **high tea,** or **meat tea,** was had by the working class. High tea included tea and a hardy meal; it was served on standard-height tables, in the evening, after working hours. This was the heaviest meal of the day.

Perhaps not to be outdone, or because they envied that more substantial meal (at least, *we* would prefer having something solid over light snacks), the upper classes co-opted the idea, adding meat, sweets, and fruit to the afternoon tea offerings. By the mid- to late-1800s, this tea was dominated by women and ranged from intimate (friends and family, mainly to converse) to extravagant (large gatherings entertained by music, dancing, and games). Tea accessories, servants, large houses, and sizable budgets were required.

Today, multiple versions of "tea" can be enjoyed, although in Britain, they're offered primarily to tourists (and scones didn't show up until the 1900s):

>> Cream tea: tea, scones, cream

>> Light tea: tea, scones, cream, sweets

>> Afternoon tea: tea, light snacks

>> Full tea: tea, scones, cream, sweets, savories (usually served on a three-tiered platter)

No matter how you have your tea, drinking from a lovely porcelain English teacup is never wrong (see Figure 17-2)!

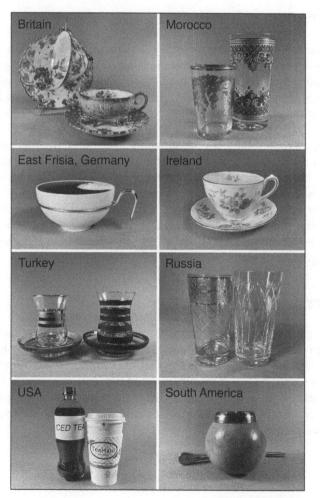

FIGURE 17-2:
Examples of teacups used in various countries.

Photos by Jill Rheinheimer

The Himalayas

Tea first arrived in Tibet during the 700s. Several centuries later, Tibet was exchanging war horses for China's black tea bricks, carried in by yak. Various grades of tea were imported — from actual tea to mostly twigs. Tea was consumed black, with milk, with milk and salt, or as butter tea.

For butter tea, a portion of a tea brick was crushed into a powder that was churned with yak butter, yak milk, and salt until it emulsified. Because yak butter had a high-fat content and a consistency closer to cheese, butter tea supplied much-needed nutrition to those living in the cold, rugged Himalayan mountains. The drink was often served on carved wood tea tables and is still enjoyed in some Himalayan regions, including Tibet, Bhutan, and Nepal.

Morocco

Tea was introduced to Morocco in the 1700s as trade between Asia, Africa, and Europe grew; by the 1800s, Morocco was importing China green gunpowder and young hyson teas. At the time, Moroccans drank mint leaves medicinally — and they soon put mint and tea together, creating a drink that's become synonymous with family and hospitality.

Today, Moroccan mint tea is commonly made with green gunpowder tea and a type of spearmint known as Moroccan mint, nana mint, curly mint, or Maghrebi mint. With less menthol than peppermint, nana mint has an earthier, sweeter flavor and is still grown primarily in the Mediterranean region. The tea is traditionally made in a silver teapot and then poured out while the teapot is held high above the glasses (see Chapter 10, Figure 10-7 for a teapot example). This "high pour" both cools and froths the tea. The sweetened brew is served in richly decorated glasses, as seen in Figure 17-2.

Germany

Although the Portuguese brought tea to the continent by the early 1600s, tea was slow to dislodge beer as Germany's favorite beverage. It didn't help that German physician Simon Paulli warned against the dangers of tea, contending that if you were more than forty years old, it would bring an early death! Eventually, however, other opinions prevailed. By the early 1700s, Germans began to drink more tea, especially in East Frisia, which borders the North Sea and the Dutch Republic, the major tea importer at the time.

Even today, East Frisians consume the most tea in Germany and have developed a unique brew: strong black tea poured over rock sugar, with a bit of heavy cream carefully added (refer to Figure 17-2). East Frisian tea is never stirred, which allows the three distinct flavors — strong tea, cream, sugar — to individually shine as the beverage is sipped.

Ireland

Tea was initially a luxury in Ireland, and it wasn't until the late 1700s that the lower economic classes could afford an inexpensive version. They masked its inferior quality by making a very strong brew and generously adding milk. By the 1830s, tea had become a mainstay. Following the Great Famine (1840s) and the subsequent prolonged poverty and agricultural depression, many people could not afford nutritious food — but tea continued to be cheap and plentiful. Conflating the consumption of tea (which, when drunk with milk, supplied much-needed calories) with societal failings, tea was blamed for causing laziness, addiction, neglect, and more. Eventually, finger-pointing ceased, and the drink was again enthusiastically embraced by all.

When World War II disrupted the tea trade, Ireland imported tea directly from India, where it was produced for only five to six months of the year and then stored for the other months. In the 1960s, tea from Africa became available. Produced year-round and processed by the then-new CTC (cut-tear-curl) method, this fresh hearty tea was mixed with the stored, lighter Indian tea, thereby beginning a rich tradition of blends that were unique to Ireland. Today, the Irish continue to drink a lot of tea (refer to Figure 17-2), second only to the Turks in per capita consumption.

Turkey

The Turks rank number one in tea consumption per capita, brewing their favorite beverage in a samovar, or *çaydanlik* (see Chapter 10, Figure 10-7), which has two stacked pots. Like the Russian samovar, the çaydanlik may derive from the portable cookers used in Mongolia and by Asiatic nomads. To make tea, water is boiled in the bottom pot and then poured over tea leaves (*çay*) in the top one, making a tea concentrate. When the tea is poured into glasses, it's topped off with water. The tea-to-water ratio can range from light to strong (called "rabbit's blood" due to its red color). Turkish tea is traditionally served with sugar cubes but never with milk.

Customarily, the tea is served in elegant tulip-shaped glasses, like those in Figure 17-2. Not only do they showcase the color of the tea, but the glasses pay homage to the importance of tulips in Turkish culture. Native to Turkey, tulips were cultivated especially for Sultan Suleiman I during the 1500s. By the early 1700s, or the Age of the Tulips, the flower symbolized wealth and status. Today, tulip motifs can be found in art, clothing, and so on.

Russia

After the Russia–China border was established in 1689, travel by trade caravan improved — although it took nearly a century to build an adequate road. Even with that road, the 11,000-mile journey from the Fujian tea gardens to Moscow entailed sixteen months, thousands of workers, and tens of thousands of camels. Russia imported both loose tea and tea bricks, but the bricks were more common because they were durable and better maintained flavor on the long journey — plus they could double as currency.

During the 1770s, the Russians developed the samovar (or self-boiler), which combined functionality with prestige. Fuel stuffed into a pipe running through the samovar heated the water held in the urn-shaped portion, while tea concentrate was kept warm in a small teapot atop the samovar (see Chapter 10, Figure 10-7). A small amount of concentrate was then poured into a teacup and diluted with hot water from the samovar.

Today's samovar blends may be made with Indian and/or Chinese black teas and are often slightly smoky, reminiscent of caravan campfires. Traditionally the tea was served black, often in crystal glasses (refer to Figure 17-2), and was sipped through a sugar cube held in the teeth. Now, honey or jam may sweeten the brew.

United States

The colonists — prior to brewing their tea in seawater — drank mainly bohea, a category of tea that was more black than green and included congou and souchong. Green tea (specifically singlo and hyson) was also brought over for that first harbor-wide tea party. Green tea didn't store as well as bohea, and several months before the Boston party, a Mr. Palmer mused that the British should send singlo to the colonies because it spoils faster than bohea, they had a lot of it, they risked losing it to spoilage, and they could sell it for a higher price in America. Well, they definitely lost it all to spoilage!

When Americans returned to tea, we drank both black and green tea until World War II, when we turned exclusively to tea from India. Today, we continue to drink mostly black tea, and more than three-quarters of that is iced. If we have a tea tradition, it's probably having an iced tea with a burger in a restaurant or on the go (refer to Figure 17-2)!

South America

With enough caffeine to rival coffee, mate (yerba mate), an herbal tea, has been enjoyed in South America for centuries. Shared in social gatherings, traded, included in ceremonies, used medicinally, and fermented, mate was embedded in the culture of many peoples. When the Spanish arrived on the continent in the 1600s, they were initially slow to recognize the many benefits of the drink and brutally suppressed its use. Economics eventually won out, however, and they were soon cultivating — and profiting from — the plant.

Mate never lost its popularity, and Argentina celebrates National Yerba Mate Day every November 30. Continuing a long tradition, mate is brewed in a hollow gourd (*chia*) and sipped through a strainer straw *(bombilla)*, as seen in Figure 17-2.

Chapter **18**

Insight into the Tea Industry

When you buy tea, your first thought may be this: Will I like it? However, you may also wonder about the environmental footprint of that tea, or whether workers were exploited during its production. As storms grow increasingly violent and droughts protracted, you may ponder the prospects for the tea plant, and even worry that tea won't be part of your future.

In this chapter, we delve deeper into the tea industry itself. Just how well are workers treated? Do tea certifications mean anything, or should we disregard them? We look at what determines tea's purity and quality, and then consider how and why growers seek different cultivars and the reasons behind tests that prove a tea's place of origin. We explore how both you and the tea industry can repurpose used tea leaves and tea waste, and, finally, we analyze the future of tea in an ever-changing world.

Looking at the Lives of Tea Workers

We wouldn't have tea if not for the thousands of workers in the tea industry. Although many have good jobs and fair wages, others live in appalling conditions.

Living and working conditions/wages

REMEMBER

The living and working conditions for tea workers usually differ by country or even region of country, and by the type of garden. It is a bit tricky to assess issues such as wages and working conditions because we first must understand the set standard for each country and region based on factors that may be unique to that area, such as average cost of living, health care, education, and so on. This is one reason why so many fairtrade organizations exist; groups like Fairtrade International help consumers understand the conditions in which their tea was produced. Not all tea gardens are bad when it comes to fair wages and living and working conditions — even some that aren't certified through organizations.

Working in Japan, China, and India

In Japan, for example, the government strictly regulates all wages, so it is unlikely that you will find a certified fairtrade Japanese tea since a higher standard of living already exists. Also, many gardens are family owned and operated, or even village owned, with collective processing facilities so that the workers are also profit sharers; this is also the case in some parts of China.

Speaking of China, the birthplace of tea, workers are often paid fair wages and are frequently revered for their work in the tea industry. Unfortunately, most of the work is seasonal, so although the wages may be fair, the work might be available for only three to four months of the year.

In India, overall, the tea industry is the country's second-largest employer. Most of these employees are women, 80 percent of whom pluck tea. Labor costs account for two-thirds of production costs. For India, as well as some other tea-growing countries, high production costs — coupled with low profit margins — mean that wages may be cut or not paid. On large plantations, wages often are not living wages and are frequently paid in-kind. Even when promised higher wages, workers often don't get them, depending on the harvest yield and the ever-changing market value of the tea. Unfortunately, like with many industries in almost every country, profits don't always make it to industry workers.

Working on large plantations

Employees of large plantations may live on or near the plantation. However, if no schools are nearby, a parent may have to walk long distances with their young children, consequently having fewer working hours. Children often end up working at the plantations, with few options for additional schooling or other jobs. If they do obtain an education, they generally leave the area.

Difficulties with medical care

For many workers, medical care may be lacking or inadequate, especially if no large hospitals are close by. Employees often don't have health insurance, so medical costs come out of wages. Disease, snake bites, a lack of drinking water, long workdays, repetitive tasks, and few human rights compound the problem. When possible, workers leave large estates to seek better wages and living conditions elsewhere, whether in a different tea garden or in a different job altogether.

The struggle of the small farmer

Small farmers in many areas also struggle. They may not produce enough tea, or their tea sells too low to make any money. Although they are independent, they may still depend on large plantations to get their product to the market. To mitigate risk, they may join a cooperative, but even then, many end up taking out high-interest loans that are difficult to pay back. Because their profit margin is so slight, any disruptions — environmental, transportation, yield, sales — imperil them.

The dangers of chemical exposure

As with any agricultural crop, weak plants have trouble fending off pests. Aging tea plants growing in depleted soil may necessitate herbicide and chemical fertilizer use. Workers are exposed to these toxins when they apply the herbicide or fertilizer, but the lingering residue is also harmful. Because tea plants and the soil retain many of the active ingredients, workers continue to be exposed whenever they work in the gardens, including when they harvest the leaves. (Unfortunately, these tea leaves do end up in your cup if not tested for contaminants by independent sources. Read more about this in the section "Looking at Tea Purity and Quality" later in this chapter.) In addition, unsecured containers pose threats to curious children or wildlife.

Reviewing Tea Certifications

TIP

Certifications can serve as protections — for workers in the tea industry, producers, consumers, wildlife, and the environment. Here are some certifications and what they mean:

>> **Organic.** To be certified organic, the producer must meet the regulations set by the United States Department of Agriculture (USDA). The United States works with international trade organizations and establishes organic equivalency agreements with other countries. That list currently includes the tea-producing countries of Japan, Korea, and Taiwan. Organic products that are imported to the United States from India must be certified by an agent accredited by the USDA. Organic standards prohibit certain substances; specify how pests, disease, and weeds are controlled; define how soil and crops can be fertilized; and so on.

>> **Fairtrade.** Fairtrade works toward improving the lives of those in the tea industry, including such things as providing a living wage, protecting human rights, improving living conditions, mitigating the effects of climate change, and helping small farmers find buyers. Fairtrade producers are paid a minimum price, specific to their tea, along with a premium. Farmers and tea workers must jointly decide how to spend the premium, whether for educational purposes or to improve farming techniques.

>> **Rainforest Alliance.** The Rainforest Alliance, which now includes the UTZ certification program, supports tea growers and their farming methods, especially in the face of climate change. Implementing new farming strategies requires both education and money. Therefore, to help growers follow through, the alliance establishes growers and buyers as partners. Farmers must follow sustainable practices and move toward giving workers a living wage, while buyers must fund the certification and pay above-market price for the tea. Worker protections are built into the certification process.

>> **Elephant friendly.** Elephants and tea gardens aren't always the best match. Elephants fall into irrigation ditches and wells, trample gardens, are electrocuted by fences and low-hanging lines, ingest unsecured chemicals, and lose access to their usual corridors. To address these problems and improve elephant-human relations, elephant-friendly standards were designed. In 2017, the Broader Impacts Group of the University of Montana and the Wildlife Friendly Enterprise Network implemented the first such certification program on behalf of the Asian elephant.

When you buy tea, you may pay more for those that are labeled with any of these certifications. However, your purchase plays a role in protecting the environment and wildlife — and helps improve the lives of tea growers and producers. Just keep in mind that "organic" doesn't necessarily mean that the tea is completely free of contaminants, as we discuss in the next section.

Looking at Tea Purity and Quality

When you buy tea leaves, you want them to be free of anything harmful, and you want a quality product.

Purity

REMEMBER

Although you may equate "organic" with "purity," the label doesn't guarantee that. The tea plants may be grown under organic guidelines, but the leaves can be contaminated during or after production. Testing the final product in a laboratory is the only way to know for certain that your tea is free of contaminants, which may include

>> Pesticides, herbicides, and heavy metals

>> Additives, such as artificial coloring, to enhance the perceived quality

>> Additives that are natural ingredients but shouldn't be there, such as sugar, glutinous rice flour, cashew nut husk, other herbals (including weeds and non-food plants), and tea leaves (when added to herbal tea)

>> Teabags that release microplastic and nanoplastic particles

REMEMBER

Be aware that not all teas are tested, and every country has its own requirements for purity. Buying organic tea may be a step in the right direction, however.

Quality

You can think of tea quality as a spectrum — from top-shelf down to the dregs. Unfortunately, well over half of all tea produced globally falls near the bottom of that range, hovering around "poorest quality." Only *half a percent* meets the "highest standards." The rest fall somewhere in-between.

Many factors affect tea quality:

>> Environment, including region of the world, amount of sunlight, humidity, temperature, rainfall, soil conditions, and altitude

>> The tea plant itself, including its variety, the age of the cultivar, and whether it's a clone or seedling

>> Agricultural practices

>> Processing, including

- Harvesting: the season and even the time of day that the leaves are harvested, method (by hand or machine), leaves chosen, and expertise

- Tea production: techniques used, expertise, and blending (where applicable)

- Post-production packaging, transportation, and storage

>> Brewing (even the best teas can be compromised with improper brewing)

To ensure you're getting top-quality tea, buy from someone you trust.

Developing New Cultivars

In a world already full of differing tea cultivars, farmers and researchers continue to develop new ones, seeking resiliency, especially as the environment grows less predictable and more unstable. Tea currently requires certain parameters, so how can we make tea plants better tolerate drought, heat, frost, and/or cold? Can the plants more effectively resist disease and handle stress? Maintaining genetic diversity is critical so that we can continue to develop new cultivars, especially if existing cultivars are wiped out due to disease, inability to handle challenging growing conditions, and so on.

Fingerprinting Tea

Fingerprinting can identify a person — and tea! But why does a tea leaf need to be fingerprinted? Using genetic markers to prove genetic identity can safeguard the reputation of high-quality tea. Fingerprinting can demonstrate that a tea was grown where the package says it was grown, or that it's single origin and not mixed with inferior tea or with tea from elsewhere. It prevents tea from being sold as something that it's not.

Therefore, tools to trace and authenticate tea are being developed. Unfortunately, this isn't easy because we still don't know the entire genomic sequence of *Camellia sinensis,* which is complicated by the plethora of differing cultivars; by tea that is processed in various ways; and by data that hasn't been standardized. Still, research is promising. For example, leaf components, such as minerals, may reflect the soil they were grown in, and catechins and lipids may point to geographic origin.

Traveling from the Garden to You

Unless you live near a tea garden, your tea must travel to you, whether by truck, train, ship, or airplane. Natural and human-induced disasters can disrupt this supply chain, often triggering higher transportation costs as well. During a drought, low water levels necessitate lighter cargos — or don't allow passage — down rivers. On the other hand, flooding also suspends travel. Wars, of course, can dramatically alter supply, transportation options, routes, and more. If a pallet of tea arrives by ocean freight, it must be lifted off the ship and onto a train car (and go through customs). Taken to a supply yard, it is then transported by truck to your local tea shop or supermarket. It's truly remarkable how many people help make sure that you get your favorite tea!

Noting the Environmental Impact of Tea

The carbon footprint of tea is negligible compared to some other common beverages and food — at least until you brew the leaves. Boiling water is very inefficient. But despite having a low carbon footprint, things can always improve. Tea producers might strategically apply organic fertilizers or use solar power for withering and drying the leaves.

The tea industry must also address waste, while simultaneously figuring out how to shelter vulnerable plants from an already changing and unpredictable environment.

Repurposing spent tea leaves

You may wonder what to do with your tea leaves after you've wrung as much drinkable tea as possible out of them. If the leaves are very tender, such as gyokuro or sencha, you can eat them, whether tossed into a salad, mixed with rice, or incorporated into a frittata! But even with unpalatable leaves, you have a couple of options.

The tea industry has the same dilemma — what do we do with all the tea waste? Researchers seek ways to turn waste into resource:

>> **Nutrients.** Tea leaves are rich in nitrogen, phosphorus, and potassium, the same nutrients that are in household fertilizers. So, make one last weak brew out of your leaves, water your houseplants with the liquid, and then work the leaves into garden soil. Large-scale composting of tea debris also puts this natural fertilizer to good use; the nutrients even seem to make iron more available to growing plants. Tea waste may be used as animal feed as well.

>> **Absorption and adsorption properties.** You can use tea leaves to dye or "age" fabric and paper (absorption). Tea can also adsorb toxins, allowing them to be removed. Potential commercial applications include cleaning up wastewater and making problematic dyes safer.

>> **Fuel.** Tea waste can be converted into usable energy (gasification, for instance), especially when combined with rice husks, or can be turned into biomass fuel, biochar (charcoal), or bio-oil.

>> **Fiber.** Because tea waste contains a lot of fiber, adding it to softwood pulp may offer another way to make paper and cardboard.

>> **Separate components.** Caffeine, of course, is extracted and used in other products, but what else can we pull out of tea waste? The waste retains all the things that make tea healthy, including its antioxidants. How can we best extract individual components and then put them to use?

Impact of climate change

You need a healthy ecosystem for sustainability, and in many tea-producing countries, things are out of whack. On the African continent, for instance, drought and floods have plagued Rwanda, and unstable rainfall patterns have growers in

Kenya concerned that the country may become unsuitable for tea. Erratic weather in Nilgiri, India, has forced farmers to replace tea with sturdier crops, while farther north, in Assam, the Brahmaputra River has too much silt, making it susceptible to erosion and flooding. In Sri Lanka, flooding and landslides have taken their toll, while years of tea production have degraded the soil.

Tea is sensitive to precipitation levels, so vacillations in rainfall are devastating, particularly when drought alternates with intense rainfall. In hot weather and during droughts, the leaves weaken and become susceptible to disease and pests. However, pesticides change the soil composition, are absorbed by the tea plant, and destroy helpful organisms along with the pests. Both pests and pesticides can reduce tea quality. Tea growers need smart irrigation, shade trees, enriched soil, drought-tolerant plants — or perhaps a different crop.

Contemplating the Future of Tea

Despite being the second-most consumed beverage in the world, the future of tea is uncertain. Climate change, cultural shifts, economic turmoil, and low profit margins all threaten the industry.

India is experiencing myriad problems that include antiquated machinery, ever-increasing production costs, subpar tea, poor working and living conditions for workers in the tea industry, and erratic weather. Assam and southern India experience repeated flooding, while drought and too-intense rainfall cycles allow pests to proliferate, reduce tea volume and quality, and destroy workers' homes. The country also must deal with stagnant prices and the fact that fewer Indians are drinking the tea that they produce. Even the Tocklai Tea Research Institute, the world's longest-operating tea research facility, has curtailed research and development while seeking funding.

In Darjeeling, there have been multiple employee strikes, workers are leaving the industry, the children of workers are pursuing other jobs rather than work in tea gardens, and the work force is aging. As for the gardens themselves, the plants are also aging and the soil is spent, which necessitates the use of chemicals. There is little room for expansion (and only tea is allowed to be grown), so plantation owners are investing less in the gardens as productivity declines. With the unpredictability of Darjeeling tea, buyers look to other countries for tea. To bring in more revenue, tea tourism is being pushed.

In neighboring Nepal, tea plants are younger, and the soil hasn't been overfarmed. Thus, the plants are more robust and have better natural resistance to pests. The country's growers are mostly small independent farmers who are personally invested. However, most of the tea is destined for India — but currently, India is actively discouraging the import of Nepali tea because it's been blended with and passed off as Darjeeling tea, or because it hasn't met India's standards. While some growers are seeking other buyers, many tea farmers are turning to other crops.

The Sri Lankan tea industry is in crisis. Although it's the fourth-largest tea producer in the world, its future is under threat. Years of tea production have degraded the soil, flooding and landslides continue to damage or destroy gardens, and workers are leaving the colonial-era large tea estates to seek better wages and living conditions.

Young people in China are increasingly turning to coffee, black tea, and ready-to-drink teas, even though the country is the world's top green tea producer. China does produce black tea, but now also imports Darjeeling tea to meet the demand. Still, the tea industry is robust and well poised to recover from setbacks. The Chinese drink a lot of tea, giving the country a solid foundation that enables the industry to mass-produce bulk tea for export and ensures a steady income. The thirst for tea, both internally and globally, allows the industry to expand and keeps workers in demand.

As in China, Japan is seeing a cultural shift in preferences. There's been a move to ready-to-drink and convenience products as tea producers try to retain the domestic market.

Countries on the African continent also struggle with the ramifications of climate change. Drought, floods, and unstable rainfall patterns are pounding the industry. Growers in Kenya, Africa's largest tea producer, look for ways to cut production costs, such as mechanical harvesting or more effective fertilizing methods.

Overall, the situation is dire in many tea-growing regions. Erratic climate events exacerbate many of the challenges that the industry faces — difficult working conditions, narrow profit margins, economic and political instability, and so on. Tea plants in some regions struggle to adapt to changing growing conditions. Growers and producers, however, are doing all they can to ensure that tea has a future. Whether researchers are developing resistant tea cultivars or tea stores are bringing exciting products to a new generation of consumers, the tea industry is determined to keep your teacup filled.

6
Let's Have Tea — In the Kitchen, at the Bar

Incorporate tea as a spice, a dry ingredient, or an infusion in your cooking and baking. Have fun with the recipes we include and get ready to eat more tea.

Grasp the relationship between flavors so that you can pair food and tea like a pro.

Understand the elements of a cocktail, dip into extraction chemistry, and apply your knowledge to make tea cocktails, reimagined with tea. Enjoy tea on a whole new level with the fabulous recipes we supply for some amazing cocktails.

Chapter **19**

Cooking and Baking with Tea

When I (Lisa) come into my tea store early in the day, I love to stand in front of my wall of more than 200 tins and take my time choosing the perfect tea to brew to start my day. After picking out my morning tea, brewing it in my favorite mug, and taking my first sip, I walk back to the wall — but this time I gaze more intently at it, studying my choices to decide which tea I am going to cook or bake with that day. Will I make a Darjeeling salad dressing, a classic earl grey chocolate cake, or maybe my son's favorite genmaicha seafood ramen? I don't just see my wall of tea as something to sell or drink, but also as a wall of ingredients for my next kitchen experiment.

In this chapter, I show you different ways in which you can use tea in your cooking and baking, and I provide you with some fun and easy recipes to get started.

Tea as a Spice

Have you ever used liquid smoke? Or maybe a rich beef stock to deepen the flavor of soup? Or even used a little extract to enhance the flavor of your whipped cream? Why not use tea to do all that?

"Spice" is defined as a noun: any of various aromatic vegetable products (such as pepper or nutmeg) used to season or flavor foods. Although tea is not a vegetable, it fits well into this definition.

In the 1400s, spices first made their way into Europe when Portuguese explorers brought them back from the Middle East, traveling by land and sea trade routes. These spices were used both in food dishes and in medicines. Then, in the very early years of the 1600s, the Dutch brought tea to Europe. In the beginning, tea, like spice, was often used in elixirs and soups served as medicines. Yes, you read it here — in soups! The use of spices and tea became more commonplace in the kitchens of the wealthier classes by the mid- to late 1600s. Although both spices and tea remained very expensive and were heavily taxed, tea quickly became a sought-after drink for the rich.

In China, its country of origin, tea was frequently blended with citrus and flowers. Similarly, as tea became more available in other regions of the world, it was often combined with spices, or it was blended with things that were locally available. In India, tea was blended with spices such as cardamom, ginger, and pepper, whereas in Europe, berries and other fruits commonly "spiced up" a plain cup of tea.

Tea, like popular spices, has many different flavor profiles depending on the type of tea it is. For example, a Japanese green tea has a strong umami or vegetal note whereas a dark black tea is a bit malty and rich. A pu-erh will give any dish an earthy, almost meaty, quality. The blended, scented, or aroma teas have their own unique flavors, depending on the ingredients and methods used to add flavor. All these teas are great for experiencing different flavors in the cup, so why not on your plate?

Tea as a Dry Ingredient

REMEMBER

TIP

If you want to use tea as a dry ingredient, you will most likely have to grind it down a bit. People don't want to get a big piece of tea leaf stuck in their teeth. In addition, you want the flavors throughout the dish, not just in a bite or two. You can grind tea in many ways:

>> You can make good use of that pestle and mortar you have sitting around.

>> You can very easily grind up tea using your fingers and hands.

DON'T WORRY; DINNER WON'T KEEP YOU UP AT NIGHT

Keep in mind that there will be a slight caffeine kick to your dishes if you add tea. The amount is normally quite low since the amount of tea used in most recipes is minimal. Also, adding oil and fat (like cream) seems to keep caffeine from doing its thing.

>> You can use a food processor or a spice grinder. Just keep in mind that the flavors can permeate the grinder and alter the flavor of other spices or teas that you might grind in the future. I know people who use a coffee grinder for their spices—but make sure you have never used it for coffee. Otherwise, everything will be served with a "hint of coffee."

>> I have even used a plastic bag and a rolling pin to crush up my tea leaves. Whatever does the trick!

At work, I use large commercial burr grinders when making my Eat More Tea tea spice blends, but I'm making kilos of each blend. At home, you need only a tablespoon at a time, at most.

The ground tea can be added to a recipe in the same way that you would add salt and pepper. A teaspoon of lapsang souchong tea, for example, will give an entire dish smokiness — no need to fire up the smoker or add liquid smoke. A small handful of slightly ground sencha leaves tossed into warm sushi rice will add a slight savory and vegetal note while also adding beautiful green flecks to the rice. I love to mix a little finely ground orange blossom oolong into my butter for shortbread.

You are probably familiar with matcha. This is an easy addition to a recipe because it is already in fine powder form, but watch out, not all matcha is the same (see Chapter 5).

Any type of dry tea leaves can also be combined with other spices, such as cumin, paprika, pepper, and salt, for example, to make an exciting dry rub.

Tea as an Infusion

Normally, when we brew tea, we pour hot water over the leaves, let it steep, strain out the leaves, and drink the liquid. Why not take that same brewed tea and use it as a stock to add flavor to rice or a sauce? Why only use water?

When I want to take a piece of cake to the next level, I like to add a dollop of whipped cream. When I want to *really* up my dessert game, I serve it with tea-infused whipped cream.

TIP

An infusion can be done with any liquid. When I want to extract the most flavor from tea into water, milk, cream, or whatever liquid my recipe calls for, I like to do a longer cold infusion. This allows for maximum flavor extraction without the bitterness that sometimes comes with heated extractions.

All this is probably best explained through some recipes. The ones in the next section are some of my favorite tea-infused recipes. From appetizers to main dishes and sauces to desserts, tea makes a great ingredient.

REMEMBER

Remember, however, to plan ahead when you make these! The preparation times don't include overnight infusions, brewing time, or cooling time.

Recipes: Snacks

TIP

I love to make these recipes for snacks or as appetizers to a meal. Remember to allow time for cooling or chilling.

Old-School Cheese Ball

One of the best things about a classic cheese ball is that it can be made ahead of time — and even frozen for up to a month — so you can easily have it on hand for your next dinner, cocktail party, or picnic.

Keemun, a Chinese-style black tea, will give this cheese ball a slight smokiness with a nutty quality. Approximately 2–3 heaping tablespoons of loose-leaf tea should yield about 1 tablespoon of ground tea.

PREP TIME: 15 MINUTES	COOK TIME: NONE	YIELD: 6–8 SERVINGS

INGREDIENTS:

16 ounces softened cream cheese

2 cups finely grated sharp cheddar (I do not recommend preshredded cheese)

2–3 chopped green onions, using the green part as well

1 tablespoon finely ground keemun black tea leaves (or your favorite black tea)

1 tablespoon hot sauce, like tabasco (optional)

⅔ cup finely chopped fresh parsley leaves

1 teaspoon garlic powder

1 teaspoon dried oregano

1 teaspoon onion powder

Black pepper to taste

½ cup finely chopped pecans

DIRECTIONS:

1 Place cream cheese in a mixing bowl and mix until smooth (either with a spoon or by using a mixer). Add cheese, green onion, ground tea, hot sauce, parsley, garlic powder, oregano, onion powder, and pepper and combine well.

2 Use a rubber spatula to get the mixture into one lump. Use your hands (I suggest lightly greasing them first with a bit of butter or oil) and form the mixture into a ball.

3 Place the pecans on a plate. Hold the cheese ball in one hand and use the other hand to scoop the pecans onto the outside of the ball, pressing them in gently and turning the ball to coat all sides.

4 Cover the cheese ball with plastic wrap and refrigerate for about 1 hour. Make sure to remove the cheese ball about 20 minutes before you are ready to serve.

PER SERVING: *Calories362 (From Fat 304); Fat 34g (Saturated 17g); Cholesterol 92mg; Sodium 408mg; Carbohydrate 5g (Dietary Fiber 1g); Protein 11g.*

Quick Candied Sweet and Salty "Chai" Nuts

Candied nuts are always a huge hit. Warm spices such as cinnamon are frequently used — so why not go for some of the best warm spices, all mixed together? Although I like to use Eat More Tea's Masala Spice Blend No. 3, adding cinnamon to your favorite chai blend will also do the trick.

PREP TIME: 20 MINUTES	COOK TIME: 20 MINUTES	YIELD: 8–10 SERVINGS

INGREDIENTS:

2 tablespoons loose leaf chai blend

⅛ cup boiling water (to brew the chai)

4 tablespoons brown sugar

1 ½ teaspoons cinnamon or masala chai spices

Pinch cayenne pepper (optional)

½ teaspoon sea salt

3 cups pecan halves (other nuts such as walnuts, almonds, or cashews also work well)

DIRECTIONS:

1 Line a baking sheet with parchment paper.

2 Brew the loose-leaf chai with the boiling water for 5–8 minutes. It should be a very strong brew. Strain the tea into a skillet and heat, using medium heat.

3 Add brown sugar, cinnamon or masala chai spices, pepper (if desired), and salt to the tea and cook until it bubbles, stirring the entire time.

4 Add the nuts and stir until nuts are coated. Continue stirring for 2–3 minutes until shiny, being careful not to let them burn.

5 Spread the nuts on your parchment-lined baking sheet to cool. Break up the nuts when cool. If they are stickier than you like, you can dust them with powdered sugar before storing in an airtight container.

PER SERVING: *Calories 219 (From Fat 192); Fat 21g (Saturated 2g); Cholesterol 0mg; Sodium 95mg; Carbohydrate 8g (Dietary Fiber 3g); Protein 3g.*

Sencha Quick Pickles

Pickling is one of the oldest forms of food preservation, and there is a reason why we still love pickles today — they're delicious! Japanese green teas, such as sencha, offer a light umami note to your pickles.

PREP TIME: 15 MINUTES	PICKLING TIME: 2 HOURS MINIMUM	YIELD: 6 SERVINGS

INGREDIENTS:

½ cup rice wine vinegar

2 teaspoons salt

1 tablespoon sugar

2 peeled and cracked garlic cloves

1 large English cucumber (or 5–6 mini cucumbers) sliced into spears or 1-inch slices on an angle

4 tablespoons sencha green tea leaves

1 cup water at 195°F (for brewing the tea)

DIRECTIONS:

1 Put vinegar, salt, sugar, and cracked garlic cloves in a bowl with the sliced cucumbers.

2 Brew the sencha at 195°F for about 2 minutes (you want a strong brew).

3 Strain the tea over the cucumber and other ingredients in the bowl, making sure that all the cucumbers are covered with liquid, and refrigerate until chilled. You can either serve them as quick pickles when cold or let them pickle longer for a stronger pickle flavor.

VARIATION: You can also pickle other veggies. Try garlic scapes or asparagus!

PER SERVING: *Calories 19 (From Fat 1); Fat 0g (Saturated 0g); Cholesterol 0mg; Sodium 626mg; Carbohydrate 4g (Dietary Fiber 0g); Protein 0g.*

Recipes: Mains

TIP

These are some of my favorite go-to recipes, whether hosting a tea-and-food pairing event at TeaHaus, inviting guests over, or simply having a family meal. Remember to plan ahead, however. Some recipes require time to chill. For those that include grilling, factor in extra time if you're using a charcoal grill.

Smoky Souchong Ribs with a Sweet and Smoky BBQ Sauce

I am not a big meat eater, but I do enjoy a summer BBQ with fall-off-the-bone baby back ribs. I especially like the flavor of smoky meat, but I don't own a smoker. Thank goodness I have plenty of smoky tea to use instead!

For the dry rub, I love to use Eat More Tea's Smoky Souchong Spice Blend No. 1, but you can use the ingredients listed here to make something similar.

PREP TIME: 30 MINUTES	COOK TIME: 3–4 HOURS	YIELD: 2–3 SERVINGS

INGREDIENTS:

2 tablespoons finely ground lapsang black tea

1 teaspoon garlic powder

1 teaspoon salt

1 teaspoon pepper

1 tablespoon onion powder

1 teaspoon chili powder

2 teaspoons cumin

1 rack (approximately 3 pounds total) of ribs (any type) with the membrane removed. Removing the membrane ensures fall-off-the-bone ribs. Often your butcher will have already removed it, but ask to make sure.

DIRECTIONS

1 Mix all dry ingredients to make the dry rub.

2 Generously season both sides of the ribs with the rub.

3 Cover your pan and the ribs with aluminum foil.

4 Bake the ribs at a low temp (275°F) for approximately 3–4 hours or until they are tender.

5 In the meantime, start the sauce. Put all ingredients (except the rib drippings since the ribs are still in the oven) in a saucepan. Mix well on low heat until the sugar is dissolved. Remove from the heat until you are ready to add the drippings.

BBQ sauce:

½ cup ketchup

1 tablespoon red wine or apple cider vinegar

2 tablespoons brown sugar (depending on how sweet you like your sauce)

Salt, to taste

Pepper, to taste

2–3 tablespoons of drippings from the ribs

6 When it's time to pull the ribs from the oven, carefully drain the drippings through a strainer directly into the prepared BBQ sauce (you should get 2–3 tablespoons depending on how fatty the ribs are). Whisk over medium heat until the fat is fully emulsified into the sauce.

7 Slather the ribs with the BBQ sauce and broil them on high (or throw on a hot grill) for a few minutes until the sauce is caramelized.

PER SERVING: *Calories 780 (From Fat 269); Fat 30g (Saturated 10g); Cholesterol 262mg; Sodium 1401mg; Carbohydrate 22g (Dietary Fiber 1g); Protein 101g.*

Genmaicha Ramen

This recipe is my son Andrew's favorite after-school meal. He makes it for himself and for his brother a couple times a week! It is super easy and can be made as basic or as fancy as you want by adding extra veggies, grilled chicken, pork belly, and so on. Andrew sometimes uses sencha, houjicha, or Greek mountain tea for the broth, but for this recipe, I used his favorite: genmaicha.

PREP TIME: 10 MINUTES	COOK TIME: 10 MINUTES	YIELD: 1–2 SERVINGS

INGREDIENTS

1 sheet of nori (optional)

1 package of ramen noodles (discard the seasoning packet; you need only the noodles)

1 teaspoon sesame oil (my son likes spicy sesame oil)

1 garlic clove, minced

Handful of baby spinach

Additional vegetables such as mushrooms, bok choy, or peppers (optional)

3 heaping teaspoons genmaicha green tea

2 cups water (to brew tea)

1 teaspoon soy sauce

1 egg, lightly beaten

5–6 medium raw shrimp or 5–6 bite-sized pieces of firm tofu

1–2 green onions, chopped, using the green part as well

DIRECTIONS

1 If using nori, line your ramen or soup bowl with the nori sheet.

2 Boil the ramen noodles as directed on the package. When done, strain them and put them in the bowl over the nori.

3 While the ramen is cooking, start your broth.

4 In a saucepan, put in the sesame oil until hot and then add the garlic and let cook for a minute or two, until fragrant.

5 Add the spinach and other veggies if you have them. Cook them until your desired texture is achieved. Hold off on adding the green onion.

6 Brew the genmaicha in water that's just under boiling for 2–3 minutes. Either strain out the leaves or leave them in for more flavor and texture. (Note, however, that the leaves can be a bit tough and slightly bitter.)

7 Add the 2 cups of brewed genmaicha and soy sauce to the veggie pan. Bring to a light boil.

8 Add the beaten egg and shrimp or tofu; stir together until the shrimp is fully cooked or tofu is hot all the way through.

9 Pour over the noodles and nori.

10 Sprinkle the green onion over the top and add salt to taste.

TIP: You can add hot chili oil, pickled ginger, sesame seeds, furikake, or other toppings to elevate this quick-and-easy ramen.

PER SERVING: *Calories 260 (From Fat 105); Fat 12g (Saturated 4g); Cholesterol 129mg; Sodium 934mg; Carbohydrate 28g (Dietary Fiber 1g); Protein 11g.*

Mint Green Tea Gazpacho

In the hot months, I love cold soups. They are healthy, easy, and so refreshing. This is my go-to recipe when it's too hot to turn on the oven or even the grill. I use Moroccan mint tea from TeaHaus (#949), but you can use any mint green tea — or just mint leaves. I recommend nana mint (a variety of spearmint) rather than peppermint if you can find it.

PREP TIME: 20 MINUTES	COOK TIME: NONE	YIELD: 4–6 SERVINGS

INGREDIENTS

1 English cucumber, divided

1 green bell pepper

2–3 pounds fresh ripe tomatoes, chopped (I try to remove as many seeds as I can, but it isn't necessary.)

1 small red onion

4 garlic cloves

2 tablespoons olive oil, plus some to drizzle

3 tablespoons red wine vinegar

½ cup strong brew of Moroccan mint green tea, cooled to room temperature

1–2 teaspoons sea salt

Cracked pepper, to taste

4–5 cherry tomatoes, halved, for garnish

Fresh nana mint, for garnish

DIRECTIONS

1 Chop a quarter of the cucumber into small pieces and set aside for garnish.

2 Put the remainder of the cucumber, bell pepper, tomatoes, onion, garlic, olive oil, vinegar, brewed tea, salt, and pepper into a blender and blend until smooth.

3 Chill in the refrigerator for at least 2 hours.

4 Garnish with remaining cucumber, halved cherry tomatoes, fresh nana mint (or spearmint) leaves, and a drizzle of olive oil.

PER SERVING: *Calories 96 (From Fat 63); Fat 7g (Saturated 1g); Cholesterol 0mg; Sodium 474mg; Carbohydrate 8g (Dietary Fiber 2g); Protein 1g.*

Grilled Chicken with Blackberry and Currant Black Tea-Infused Gastrique and Grilled Polenta

This recipe is from a very good friend and an amazing chef, Natalie Marble. She is great! Look her up: @nataliemarblecooks. You can make the polenta a day ahead of time (keep it refrigerated until you're ready to use it).

PREP TIME: 20 MINUTES	COOK TIME: 1 HOUR	YIELD: 4-6 SERVINGS

INGREDIENTS FOR CHICKEN AND GASTRIQUE

Gastrique:

4 cups strongly brewed black currant black tea

2 cups sugar

1 cup sherry vinegar

4 cups fresh blackberries

Salt, to taste

Pepper, to taste

Juice of 1 lemon

Chicken:

6 large skinless, boneless chicken thighs (using dark, fatty poultry is preferable, to stand up against the sauce)

Olive oil

Kosher salt

Freshly cracked black pepper

DIRECTIONS

1 To prepare the sauce, bring the tea to a boil in a saucepan, reduce it by half (approximately 20 minutes), and set aside.

2 Put the sugar into a clean, dry saucepan, and cook over medium heat without stirring. When the sugar at the sides of the pan begins to caramelize, stir with a wooden spoon or high-heat spatula to even out the color.

3 Remove the pan from the heat and carefully pour the sherry vinegar into the caramelized sugar.

4 Add the reduced tea and the blackberries.

5 Return to the heat and stir until well blended.

6 Bring to a simmer and reduce until the liquid starts to thicken up.

7 Season with salt and pepper to taste.

8 Finish with a little fresh-squeezed lemon juice to brighten it up.

9 To grill the chicken, preheat the grill to high.

10 Lightly brush the chicken with olive oil and season liberally with kosher salt and freshly cracked black pepper.

11 Grill, turning once, until cooked through (with an internal temperature of at least 165°) and well caramelized on the outside.

12 Slice chicken and serve on top of grilled polenta (recipe follows) with a spoonful of the blackberry gastrique.

INGREDIENTS FOR GRILLED POLENTA

2 ears of corn

3 cups strongly brewed blood orange black tea

¾ cup polenta

Salt, to taste

Pepper, to taste

½ cup parmigiano-reggiano, shredded

6 tablespoons unsalted butter

DIRECTIONS

1 Preheat grill to medium-high and grill the ears of corn until cooked through and well charred; cut kernels from cob.

2 To make the polenta, bring brewed tea to a boil in a large saucepan.

3 *Very* slowly stir in polenta, being careful to constantly stir so that polenta doesn't stick and scorch in corners of pan; season with salt and pepper to taste.

4 Reduce heat to a low simmer, stirring frequently to prevent sticking, until mixture is thick and cooked through, about 20–30 minutes.

5 Remove from heat and stir in parmigiano-reggiano, grilled corn kernels, and butter.

6 Pour polenta onto an oiled sheet pan and smooth out into an even layer of your desired thickness; refrigerate immediately.

7 When chilled and firm, cut polenta into desired shape.

8 Brush both sides with olive oil and grill until both sides are crispy with grill marks and polenta is heated through.

PER SERVING: *Calories 679 (From Fat 180); Fat 20g (Saturated 10g); Cholesterol 95mg; Sodium 849mg; Carbohydrate 106g (Dietary Fiber 7g); Protein 21g.*

Assam Honey-Glazed Salmon

PREP TIME: 15 MINUTES	COOK TIME: 10–15 MINUTES	YIELD: 4–6 SERVINGS

INGREDIENTS

Four 6-ounce portions of salmon

½ teaspoon salt

½ teaspoon pepper

Sauce:

3 tablespoons unsalted butter

2 tablespoons olive oil

6 cloves garlic, minced

½ cup honey (you can reduce it to ¼ cup if you prefer)

3 tablespoons *very* strongly brewed Assam black tea, it is best to brew 2 tablespoons of Assam loose tea in ⅓ cup boiling water for 5–8 minutes, strain, and then use 3 tablespoons of the brewed tea

2 tablespoons soy sauce

1 tablespoon sriracha sauce

2 tablespoons lemon juice

Handful of fresh chives, parsley, and/or cilantro, chopped, for garnish

DIRECTIONS

1 Dry the salmon with a paper towel and season with salt and pepper. Set aside and turn the oven on low broil with the rack in the middle position.

2 In an oven-safe pan large enough for the salmon pieces, melt the butter in with the olive oil. When melted, add the garlic and cook for about 30 seconds before adding the honey, brewed tea, soy sauce, sriracha, and lemon juice.

3 Cook the ingredients together over medium-high heat, stirring well for about 1 minute.

4 Add the salmon to the pan (skin-side down if your salmon filets aren't skinned).

5 Cook the salmon for about 3 minutes while continually basting the filets with the sauce (using a spoon).

6 Place the pan in the oven under the broiler for about 5–6 minutes, basting it twice, until the sauce is caramelized and the fish is cooked to your liking.

7 Garnish with the freshly chopped herbs.

PER SERVING: *Calories 347 (From Fat 157); Fat 17g (Saturated 5g); Cholesterol 78mg; Sodium 606mg; Carbohydrate 25g (Dietary Fiber 0g); Protein 23g.*

Tea-Smoked Chicken Wings

Smoking food doesn't always require an outdoor smoker or a fancy smoke infuser. You can use a large wok with a tall lid or a large stock pot with a lid, a steamer rack, and some aluminum foil. Much like using lapsang souchong tea for the Smoky Souchong Ribs (earlier in this chapter), this method gives your meal a smoky note without all the trouble of getting an actual smoker.

WARNING

It's best not to use a non-stick wok or pot because non-stick pans are not made for high-heat cooking methods.

This recipe calls for a classic Chinese green tea such as lung ching, but you can use any tea. Even an aroma tea — for example, oriental moon (#970) from TeaHaus — can add some exotic flavors such as cardamom, sandalwood, and licorice.

PREP TIME: 20 MINUTES (PLUS TIME TO MARINATE)	COOK TIME: 1 ½ HOURS	YIELD: 4 SERVINGS

INGREDIENTS

2 teaspoons Chinese five spice

½ teaspoon salt

½ teaspoon pepper

10–12 chicken wings or 6–8 drumsticks or a medium whole chicken (cooking times will vary depending on how large the chicken pieces are)

Handful of spring onion, chopped, including the green part

Fresh ginger, roughly chopped, about 1 tablespoon

"Smoker":

2 tablespoons lung ching green tea (or other tea)

2 tablespoons brown sugar

2 tablespoons white rice (not cooked)

DIRECTIONS

1 Combine the Chinese five spice with the salt and pepper.

2 Rub the chicken pieces with the seasoning and let them marinate with the rub in the refrigerator for a few hours or overnight in a sealable bag together with the spring onions and ginger. If you are using a whole chicken, stuff the cavity with the onions and ginger.

3 Place the chicken on a steam rack in a pot or wok with about an inch of water or until the water is just under the rack. Cover tightly and steam for about 30–40 minutes or until the chicken is done (internal temperature of 165°F). You may need to add more water if steam evaporates before the chicken is done.

4 Remove the chicken from the pot or wok along with 2 teaspoons of broth and set aside. Clean the pot or wok and rack so you can use it for the smoking.

5 Place a piece of aluminum foil on the bottom of the wok or pot.

6 Add the tea, sugar, and rice on top of the foil and put the rack over it.

(continued)

(continued)

Sauce:

1 tablespoon soy sauce

1 teaspoon oyster sauce (optional)

1 teaspoon honey

2 teaspoons broth left from steaming

7 After the chicken has cooled for about 5 minutes, combine the sauce ingredients and then brush the chicken with the sauce.

8 Place the pot over high heat. When smoke starts to appear, put in the rack and chicken. Cover it tightly so that no smoke can escape.

9 Let the chicken smoke for about 8–10 minutes (the longer the time, the smokier the flavor). Don't leave it unattended due to the high heat.

10 When the smoking process is done, make sure your exhaust fan is on or take the pot or wok outside to remove the lid so that you don't fill your kitchen with smoke and set off a smoke alarm.

11 Carefully put the chicken on a serving plate and let it rest for about 10 minutes. You can brush it with sesame oil to give it a glossy and beautiful finish before serving.

PER SERVING: *Calories 566 (From Fat 349); Fat 39g (Saturated 11g); Cholesterol 235mg; Sodium 669mg; Carbohydrate 2g (Dietary Fiber 0g); Protein 48g.*

Recipes: Sides

No meal is complete without some side dishes. Especially unique and delicious are those made with tea!

Earl Grey Rice

Sometimes "sides" can be a bit boring, but with one simple change, you can elevate them to something special. When I serve pork tenderloin or a simple roasted chicken, I always want the side to be a little less boring. I am not a fan of earl grey tea (to drink, that is) but I love to cook and bake with it — a lot! This simple recipe is always a hit. Here, I use my Victorian Earl Grey tea (TeaHaus #6969) because it has rosemary, a little lavender, and a touch of rose in it. You can use any earl grey or other black scented/aroma tea such as an orange black tea or a floral blend black tea.

PREP TIME: 15 MINUTES | **COOK TIME: 30 MINUTES** | **YIELD: 4–6 SERVINGS**

INGREDIENTS

2 cups brown rice

4 cups strongly brewed Victorian Earl Grey tea

½ onion, finely chopped

1 garlic clove, finely chopped

2 teaspoons olive oil

¼ cup dried apricots, sliced

½ cup slivered almonds, lightly toasted

Salt, to taste

Pepper, to taste

Rosemary or thyme, to taste, optional

DIRECTIONS

1 Make the rice, following the directions given on the bag but instead of water, use the strongly brewed tea.

2 While the rice is cooking, sauté the onion and garlic with the olive oil in a pan large enough to hold the rice.

3 Add the apricots and let them cook 2–3 minutes to soften a bit.

4 Add the cooked rice and stir in the toasted almonds.

5 Add salt and pepper to taste. You can also add herbs such as rosemary and thyme to fit the dish you are serving it with.

PER SERVING: *Calories 317 (From Fat 69); Fat 8g (Saturated 1g); Cholesterol 0mg; Sodium 161mg; Carbohydrate 56g (Dietary Fiber 4g); Protein 7g.*

Pu-erh Mushroom Sauce

Pu-erh is another one of those teas that I am not a big fan of as a drink, but I use it quite often in cooking. The richness of the tea gives many dishes more depth. When I convert classic dishes, such as French onion soup, into a vegetarian version, I often replace the beef stock with pu-erh.

I like to use mixed mushrooms for this recipe, but it doesn't really matter which mushrooms you use. To extract the most flavor from the tea, start infusing the half-and-half the night before you plan on making this recipe. If you forget, you can infuse it by heating the half-and-half with the tea leaves for about 10 minutes on low heat.

This gravy is amazing on a simply seasoned pork chop served with earl grey rice.

PREP TIME: 20 MINUTES (PLUS OVERNIGHT INFUSION)	COOK TIME: 20 MINUTES	YIELD: 4–6 SERVINGS

INGREDIENTS

1 cup half-and-half

2 tablespoons pu-erh tea

½ white onion, finely chopped

1 tablespoon unsalted butter

12 ounces mushrooms, washed and sliced

2 garlic cloves, minced

Salt, to taste

Pepper, to taste

1 teaspoon dried thyme

½ cup white wine

¼ cup heavy cream

½ cup parsley leaves, chopped, for garnish

DIRECTIONS

1 Infuse the half-and-half with the pu-erh tea overnight in the fridge.

2 Strain the tea leaves from the half-and-half; you may need to slightly heat the mixture so that it's easier to remove the leaves and retain more liquid. Set aside.

3 Sauté the onion in the butter until softened, about 5 minutes.

4 Add the mushrooms and cook until they have released their juices.

5 Add the garlic, salt, pepper, and thyme and continue to cook for about 1 minute. Use the wine to deglaze the pan, scraping the bottom to release all the flavor, until most of the liquid has evaporated.

6 Add the cream and pu-erh-infused half-and-half and simmer until thickened (5–10 minutes). Add more salt and pepper to taste if needed. Garnish with chopped parsley.

PER SERVING: *Calories 146 (From Fat 94); Fat 10g (Saturated 6g); Cholesterol 34mg; Sodium 416mg; Carbohydrate 7g (Dietary Fiber 1g); Protein 4g.*

Tea-Infused Acorn Squash with Hazelnuts, Brown Butter, and Thyme

This is another great recipe from my friend Natalie. She loves baked apple green and black tea (TeaHaus #908) because it is a perfect fall flavor to pair with the squash.

PREP TIME: 15 MINUTES	COOK TIME: 45 MINUTES	YIELD: 4 SERVINGS

INGREDIENTS

½ cup strongly brewed baked apple tea

¼ cup hazelnuts, roughly chopped

4 tablespoons unsalted butter

1–2 acorn squash, halved and seeded

1 tablespoon olive oil

1 tablespoon dark brown sugar

Kosher salt

1–2 star anise pods

½ teaspoon fresh lemon juice

Freshly ground black pepper

1 teaspoon fresh thyme leaves

DIRECTIONS

1 Brew the baked apple tea.

2 Preheat the oven to 425°F.

3 In a small sauté pan over medium heat, toast the hazelnuts until lightly browned and fragrant. Set aside and let cool.

4 In a small saucepan over medium heat, melt the butter, skimming the solids from the surface until the butter is clear. Turn the heat to low and cook until the butter turns a deep brown and smells intensely nutty. Remove from the heat and set aside.

5 Brush the squash halves with the olive oil and place them in a roasting pan, cut side down. Roast for 35–45 minutes or until caramelized and tender when pierced with a knife.

6 Cut the squash halves into thirds and transfer to a serving platter.

7 Return the brown butter to medium-high heat and add the hazelnuts and brown sugar; season with salt.

8 Stir in the star anise and cook until fragrant and the sugar is dissolved.

(continued)

(continued)

9 Add the tea a little at a time and continue to stir and cook until you have an emulsified, slightly thickened pan sauce.

10 Remove from the heat and stir in the lemon juice.

11 Pour over squash and season with a few grinds of fresh pepper and fresh thyme leaves.

PER SERVING: *Calories 228 (From Fat 174); Fat 19g (Saturated 8g); Cholesterol 31mg; Sodium 239mg; Carbohydrate 15g (Dietary Fiber 2g); Protein 2g.*

Darjeeling Salad Dressing

I prefer a first-flush Darjeeling for this recipe because of its brisk, slightly dry quality (see Chapter 4).

PREP TIME: 10 MINUTES	COOK TIME: NONE	YIELD: APPROXIMATELY 1 ½ CUPS

INGREDIENTS

1 tablespoon first-flush Darjeeling black tea

¼ cup boiling water (to brew tea)

2 teaspoons sugar

1 teaspoon onion powder

¼ cup red or white wine vinegar

½ cup olive oil

½ teaspoon salt

Cracked pepper, to taste

DIRECTIONS

1 Brew tea in boiling water for 2 minutes and strain. Allow to cool.

2 Whisk (or shake) together the brewed tea and the remaining ingredients.

PER SERVING: *Calories 42 (From Fat 41); Fat 5g (Saturated 1g); Cholesterol 0mg; Sodium 39mg; Carbohydrate 0g (Dietary Fiber 0g); Protein 0g.*

Tea-Infused Butter

As Julia Child said, "If you are afraid of butter, use cream." And what better use of cream than to make your own butter? Whether serving something savory or sweet, butter always makes it better — but have you tried tea-infused butter?

It doesn't really matter which tea you use to infuse your cream. The most important thing is to plan ahead. To get the most flavor, it is best to leave the tea leaves infusing in the heavy cream for 2–3 days in your refrigerator.

I suggest 2–3 tablespoons loose-leaf tea per pint of heavy cream. If I want a salty butter, I add ¼ teaspoon salt. For a neutral butter, I add only the tea, but if I want a dessert or sweet butter, I add a teaspoon of sugar or honey. I let it all infuse together for 2–3 days in the fridge. You may need to slightly heat the cream to strain the leaves but be sure to chill it again before churning.

My favorite teas for making butter are the following:

» Savory butters
  - Lapsang souchong black tea
  - Green gunpowder tea
  - Genmaicha green tea

» Neutral butters
  - Orange blossom oolong
  - Houjicha roasted green tea
  - Mint tea

» Sweet butters
  - Masala chai (or other spiced tea)
  - Vanilla black tea
  - Chili Chocolate (TeaHaus #6971) or other chocolatey tea

INGREDIENTS

Loose tea

Heavy cream

DIRECTIONS

1 After infusing with your tea of choice (generally 2–3 table-spoons of loose tea to a pint of cream works well), double strain the cream to make sure there aren't any tea leaves left. You may need to slightly heat the cream to strain the leaves but be sure to chill it again before whipping.

2 Use a stand mixer with a whisk attachment and whisk on high for approximately 10–20 minutes. You will start to see the liquid separate from the fat. Turn the mixer off and strain out the whey (liquid) through a fine mesh strainer. Put the cream back in the mixer and continue whisking until you have but-ter. You may need to strain out the liquid one or two more times. If you still see a lot of liquid, you can use a cheesecloth to squeeze out any excess liquid.

If you don't have a stand mixer, pour the cold strained cream into a jar with a lid. Throw in a clean marble or two, seal the jar, and start shaking. You will be at this for about 30–45 minutes so make sure that the cream doesn't get too warm from your hands and remember to pour out the sepa-rated liquid once the fat starts to separate. You may need to pour out the liquid three or four times throughout the shaking process.

You can roll the butter into a log with plastic wrap or simply put it into a bowl. You can keep it covered in the fridge for up to a month.

Hint: Shaking the cream by hand is a great activity to keep kids busy.

PER SERVING: *Calories 68 (From Fat 66); Fat 7g (Saturated 5g); Cholesterol 27mg; Sodium 8mg; Carbohydrate 1g (Dietary Fiber 0g); Protein 0g.*

Tea-Infused Cream

If a recipe calls for milk, half-and-half, or heavy cream, a simple tea infusion as described earlier for butter can be used to add more flavor.

A pint of tea-infused heavy cream can easily be whipped for a beautiful tea-infused whipped cream. Simply whip until stiff; if you want to add some sweetness, add 1–2 teaspoons of sugar. Imagine a simple chocolate cake topped with earl grey whipped cream, or a fruit salad with jasmine cream on top. Infusing heavy cream with tea is a simple way to elevate any recipe.

A savory cream can add flavor to any cream-based sauce for an added wow!

Recipes: Desserts

TIP

No meal is complete without dessert. However, these recipes may well tempt you to skip the meal and go straight to dessert! When you make these recipes, do remember to allow time for infusions, cooling, and so on.

Fruit Paradise Tea Sabayon with Fresh Fruit

Here is another great recipe from Natalie. She uses TeaHaus paradise fruit tea (#1435) and fresh berries, but any fruit tea blend would work well. The TeaHaus passionfruit tea (#1637) is also excellent for this recipe, stellar with tropical fruits such as mango and pineapple. For a warmer flavor, try a spiced chai or a vanilla rooibos and serve with spiced cooked apples or plums.

PREP TIME: 45 MINUTES	COOK TIME: 20 MINUTES	YIELD: 6 SERVINGS

INGREDIENTS

Sabayon:

⅓ cup brewed paradise fruit tea (2 tablespoons tea brewed in ⅓ cup boiling water for 10–20 minutes)

4 large egg yolks

¼ cup sugar

¼ cup heavy cream

Fruit:

6 cups fresh seasonal fruit of your choice, cut into wedges or bite-sized pieces, if necessary

1 vanilla bean, split lengthwise and seeds scraped

Sugar, to taste

DIRECTIONS

1 Strain the brewed tea and let it cool completely.

2 Place the fruit in a bowl with vanilla bean seeds and sugar and slightly mash to create some juices. Leave to macerate and gently mix every 10 minutes for about a half-hour. Set aside.

3 To make the sabayon, in a large metal bowl, whisk together the egg yolks and sugar; add the brewed tea and whisk well.

4 Set the bowl over a saucepan of gently simmering water and whisk constantly until the mixture is very thick and glossy, about 4–5 minutes. (It should hold its shape when spooned onto a plate.)

5 Transfer the mixture to a clean bowl set in a larger bowl of ice water and whisk until the mixture feels cold.

(continued)

(continued)

6 In a separate bowl, beat the heavy cream to soft peaks. Gently fold the whipped cream into the chilled egg mixture.

7 To serve, arrange the fruit in bowls; spoon the sabayon on top and serve immediately.

PER SERVING: *Calories 167 (From Fat 62); Fat 7g (Saturated 3g); Cholesterol 153mg; Sodium 11mg; Carbohydrate 26g (Dietary Fiber 3g); Protein 2g.*

Winter Magic Rooibos Poached Pears with Vanilla Black Tea-Infused Crème Anglaise

I have a thing for pears in the early fall. They are so lovely with a dash of warm spices. Apples also work well with this recipe. My winter magic rooibos (TeaHaus #1320) has a slight sandalwood note that pairs perfectly with pears, but you can use any rooibos. Plan ahead so you can infuse your half-and-half overnight.

PREP TIME: 10 MINUTES (PLUS OVERNIGHT INFUSION)	COOK TIME: 30 MINUTES	YIELD: 4 SERVINGS

INGREDIENTS

2 cups strongly brewed winter magic rooibos (6 tablespoons tea brewed in 2 cups boiling water for 10–20 minutes)

4 pears, cut in half and cored

⅛ cup sugar

Crème anglaise:

2 cups half-and-half infused overnight in the refrigerator with vanilla black tea

1 vanilla bean cut lengthwise (optional)

½ cup sugar

4 egg yolks

DIRECTIONS

1 Before you start, place a fine strainer over a bowl and place the bowl in an ice bath. Set it aside to use in step 7.

2 Brew the loose tea and strain it into a saucepan over the pears and sugar. Let the pears sit in the tea as it cools, setting the pan aside while you prepare the sauce.

3 To make the crème anglaise, strain the tea from the half and half you infused the night before. Combine the half and half and the vanilla bean in a large saucepan. Cook over medium-low heat for about 5 minutes or until small bubbles appear around the rim. Be careful not to scald it.

4 In a medium bowl, whisk the sugar and egg yolks just until combined. You can use a stand mixer, but this also works well by hand.

5 Pour in half of the hot half-and-half in a thin stream into the egg and sugar mixture while whisking.

6 Return the mixture to the saucepan and cook over moderate heat, stirring constantly with a wooden spoon, until the sauce has thickened slightly, 4–5 minutes.

(continued)

(continued)

7 Immediately strain the sauce into the bowl in the cold-water bath to stop the cooking. If you used a vanilla bean, scrape the vanilla seeds into the sauce.

8 Refrigerate the sauce so that it cools while you continue with the pears.

Back to the pears:

9 Place the saucepan with the tea and pears over medium-high heat. Bring the pears to a slight boil until tender. Depending on the ripeness of your pears, this can take 15–20 minutes.

10 Strain the pears but save the sauce to make a syrup later if you want.

11 Place the pears in a serving dish, 1–2 pears per person, and pour some of the cooled sauce anglaise over them and serve.

TIP: If you saved the tea, you can add ¼ cup more sugar and cook it over medium-high heat until it reduces to a thin syrup. You can use this syrup in cocktails (see Chapter 21), to flavor yogurt, or over pancakes.

PER SERVING: *Calories 538 (From Fat 168); Fat 19g (Saturated 10g); Cholesterol 255mg; Sodium 61mg; Carbohydrate 91g (Dietary Fiber 7g); Protein 7g.*

Flourless Orange Hazelnut Chocolate Cake

This simple cake is so rich and elegant — yet it's also as simple as blending a few ingredients and pouring them into a pan. Because I love hazelnuts and chocolate, and because I love chocolate with citrus, I figured I could put them all together for a perfect cake flavor combination. You can substitute the hazelnut with almond. A marzipan black tea (TeaHaus #952) also works well.

PREP TIME: 20 MINUTES (PLUS 2 HOURS FOR ORANGES)	COOK TIME: 1 HOUR	YIELD: 6–8 SERVINGS

INGREDIENTS

2 small oranges, washed well

1 tablespoon lemon zest

2 cups strongly brewed Hazel's chocolate tea from TeaHaus (#1638) (6 heaping tablespoons brewed in 2 cups of boiling water for 3 minutes)

6 eggs

1 ¼ teaspoons baking powder

½ teaspoon baking soda

1 cup sugar

2 cups hazelnut meal (also known as hazelnut flour)

½ cup cocoa powder (unsweetened)

¼ teaspoon cardamom

Powdered sugar for dusting

DIRECTIONS

1 Wash and cut the oranges in half and remove any seeds. Place the oranges and the lemon zest into a large saucepan. Strain the tea over the oranges and zest and let the mixture simmer until the oranges are soft. This could take up to 2 hours if the peel is thick.

2 Preheat your oven to 350°F and spray or grease an 8-inch round cake pan.

3 Strain the oranges and zest, keeping the liquid if you would like to make a syrup for later.

4 Place the oranges and zest into a blender or food processor with the sharp blade and pulse until smooth. Add the rest of the ingredients (except the powdered sugar) one by one, quickly pulsing between each addition, and then pulse until well blended, scraping down the sides once or twice.

5 Pour the mixture into the pan and bake for 45 minutes to 1 hour, or until a toothpick inserted comes out clean.

6 Let the cake cool, dust with powdered sugar, and serve.

TIP: If you save the tea, you can make a lovely hazelnut citrus tea syrup. Place the tea in a saucepan with ½ cup sugar and leave on a low boil until it is reduced to a thin syrup. You can use this syrup on almost anything.

PER SERVING: *Calories 355 (From Fat 167); Fat 19g (Saturated 3g); Cholesterol 159mg; Sodium 55mg; Carbohydrate 42g (Dietary Fiber 7g); Protein 12g.*

Super Simple Tea-Infused Truffles

I can't tell you how many times I needed an easy dessert to take somewhere. These truffles are simple and delicious. By adding tea, you are upping your impressive game big time! I use my TeaHaus cream earl grey (#6974) for this recipe, but almost any tea will work. I often use my favorites: houjicha or sencha. You truly can use any tea you want!

PREP TIME: 10 MINUTES (PLUS OVERNIGHT INFUSION)	COOK TIME: NONE	YIELD: 10–12 SERVINGS

INGREDIENTS

8 ounces good-quality semi-sweet chocolate, cut into pieces (I love Trader Joe's or Aldi's chocolate when I make these at home)

1 tablespoon unsalted butter

½ cup heavy cream that has been infusing overnight with 2 tablespoons tea

1 tablespoon cocoa powder (unsweetened) combined with 1 tablespoon powdered sugar, for dusting

DIRECTIONS

1 Put the chocolate pieces and butter in a microwave-safe bowl.

2 Slightly heat the cream with the tea to make it easier to strain. Strain it over the chocolate and butter. Press down on the tea leaves with a spoon to get all the cream out that you can.

3 Place the bowl in the microwave at 50 percent power for 2 minutes. Remove the bowl and stir. Keep doing this until the mixture is completely melted and smooth.

4 When the chocolate is melted and blended perfectly with the cream and butter, place a piece of plastic wrap directly over the surface and refrigerate until it is firm enough to scoop into a ball.

5 Scoop bite-sized balls and roll them in your hand. If they get too warm, place them back into the refrigerator until cold again. It can get a little messy.

6 Roll the balls in the cocoa/powdered sugar mixture.

TIP: You can keep the truffles in the refrigerator for about 2 weeks or in the freezer for a few months in an airtight container. You can pull them out and let them come to room temperature whenever you have guests swing by.

PER SERVING: Calories 137 (From Fat 93); Fat 10g (Saturated 6g); Cholesterol 16mg; Sodium 6mg; Carbohydrate 13g (Dietary Fiber 1g); Protein 1g.

Chapter **20**

Tea and Food Pairing

When we hear of wine-and-food pairings, we often envision fancy meals with expert sommelier picks and well-curated menus, but really we are "pairing" food and drinks all the time. Think about it — would you grab an icy cold beer when swiping a cookie off that hot baking sheet, just out of the oven? Would you want a tall glass of milk with your hot dog at a baseball game? We won't judge you if you do, but we're guessing you made a food pairing decision that was based on your personal taste as well as on a general sense of what goes with what.

In this chapter, you see how tea is akin to wine, learn how to pair the perfect cup of tea with your favorite foods, and discover how to curate a menu to impress.

Noting the Similarities to Wine

REMEMBER

It doesn't take a trained palate or an expert to figure out what *you* like. However, knowing more about food and drinks opens the door to new flavors and culinary experiences. We all taste food and drinks differently, but there are some notable characteristics that can be broken down, enabling us to better pair certain things.

In the past, chefs and sommeliers paired wine by simply grouping it. We've all heard this: Red wine goes with rich foods and meat, whereas white wine goes with vegetables or fish. But, over time, winemaking became more complex as have our palates. Grape varieties are now more sophisticated, farming has advanced, and a lot more science is involved in the entire process. No longer is wine made by simply picking the grapes and stomping on them in a barrel like Lucy did (great *I Love Lucy* episode, by the way).

As mentioned in Chapter 10, the term "sommelier" comes from the French and dates to the 1300s. The sommelier was charged with carrying his lord's luggage, picking his wine, and so on — much like the concept of head butler in the United Kingdom. The title slowly became associated only with those who chose the wine. It wasn't until the mid-1900s that official training and certification courses became available, first in Europe and then in the United States.

WAIT! Before we go on, you might be thinking that a *Wine For Dummies* chapter accidentally got added to this tea book. No, everything we just said relates to tea as well, with one difference: Tea is even more complex than wine. (Shhhhh . . . don't tell the wine authors that we said that.)

And one last thing before we turn to tea. Just like the many types of grapes used to make wine, many varieties of *Camellia sinensis* plants are used to produce tea. Each variety will impart its unique characteristics to the tea.

Getting Scientific: How Our Senses Come into Play

Flavor is a science! Several universities offer degrees such as "Food and Flavor Chemist" or "Food Science." It is a very complex science that involves both our mouth and our nose.

Using a tasting wheel

TIP

I'm sure you've seen something similar to the illustration in Figure 20-1 before. These tasting wheels are often used to help us pick words to best describe what we are tasting. We can use these words to better describe our experience with flavor, thus making it easier to pair things together. Sometimes "like" qualities go well together, but, often, extreme opposites add depth and bring out more nuances and flavor profiles.

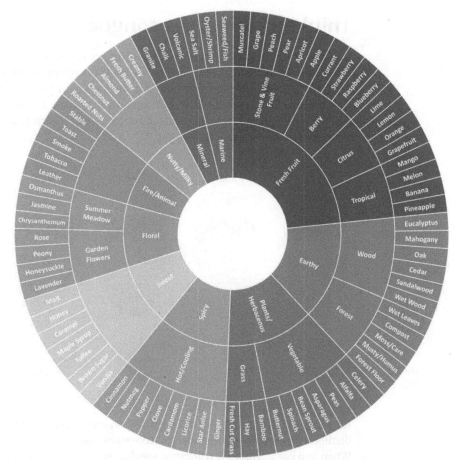

FIGURE 20-1:
TeaHaus tasting
wheel.

Source: Illustration by Lisa McDonald

One of my favorite pu-erh teas was described by a customer this way: "You know when you are shopping and you get close to the belt section in the men's department? That's what this tea tastes like, but in a good way." A sommelier would simply say the tea had notes of leather (but in a good way). Another pu-erh was described by a customer as tasting like "old wet dirt — but in a good way." A slightly better term might be "forest floor." Teas can be herbaceous, fruity, nutty, floral, and so on, and having words to describe them is helpful when pairing them with food. (Although, admittedly, sometimes the best way to describe a tea is simply, "it's just good.")

Thinking about the tongue

In addition to using a tasting wheel, it's also nice to see where flavor lands on the tongue because that makes it easy to see what tea flavor profiles might pair best with which foods (see Figure 20-2). However, there is one more sense that scientists are making a case for. Yes, our tongues may have a sixth sense. Now, that doesn't mean our mouths can see dead people; it just means that our mouths have more senses than originally thought.

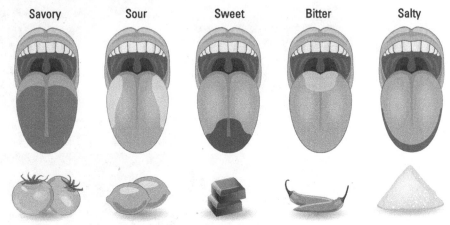

Savory   Sour   Sweet   Bitter   Salty

FIGURE 20-2:
Tongue map.

Although the five main types of taste (savory, sour, sweet, bitter, and salty) can be distinguished by triggering specific receptors, the sixth sense is more of a feel. When you eat a lemon, it triggers a specific area on your tongue; you can distinguish it from other flavors, you register it as "sour," and you identify it as "lemon." The fat receptors (which scientists have known about for years), however, are triggered by fatty acid — but a specific flavor cannot be distinguished. Because the flavor is indistinguishable, the sensation is more of a feel. This is where the term "mouthfeel" when describing flavor often comes from. The word for this sense is, in itself, a mouthful: "oleogustus," which is taken from Latin, meaning "a taste for fat."

The Japanese word *kokumi*, best translated as "rich taste" or "delicious," also describes a sixth sense. It is often used to explain mouth fullness or roundness of flavor. Its origin comes more from glutamyl peptides that occur naturally in things such as bread or other fermented foods. The term is still often used to describe the mouthfeel that you get from triggering the fatty acid receptors; it's also considered a possible sixth sense.

Because savory or umami flavors are sensed on most of our tongue (refer to the tongue map, Figure 20-2), bolder teas are often best to pair with more savory meals. A strong ginger black tea or a mint tea will hit all the parts of the tongue. Therefore, instead of mint jelly, try serving a strong Moroccan mint tea with lamb chops or an herbaceous falafel. Try brewing an orange ginger black tea with a traditional Indian dish, like biryani or samosas. Because both the food and teas are bold, the flavors will enhance each other as opposed to one over-whelming the other.

Sweet is sensed on the tip of the tongue, so a more bitter tea, which is sensed in the back of the tongue, might be a nice way to pull sweetness into your mouth, ensuring that all the taste buds are aroused.

One of my favorite pairings seems — to some — to be counterintuitive. I *love* to drink a grassy green tea that has a slight creamy note (remember *kokumi*), a tea such as gyokuro, with a very dark, bitter piece of chocolate. The bitterness of the chocolate is sensed in the back of the tongue; therefore, placing the chocolate on your tongue while you sip the strong umami tea, which is sensed around the front and broader part of the tongue, soothes the bitterness of the chocolate as it goes down.

Often sour, such as a squeeze of lemon, is used in a more bitter black tea, as is sugar. All three elements are sensed on a different part of the tongue so bringing these flavors together intensifies the sensation of taste in the mouth. By adding different flavors, we can trigger more receptors at once, which helps round out the overall flavor.

Adding milk or cream to tea has always been a point of contention among tea drinkers. Setting aside all tradition and personal preference, let's look at what adding it to tea does to our taste buds.

There are so many other "milks" around these days that we need a "Types of Milk For Dummies" book, but here I am talking about good ol' cow's milk. Skim milk or "fat free" cream won't do much to the taste other than water it down a bit because there is a lack of those fatty acids that are needed to trigger the fat receptors.

Both whole milk and half-and-half have a savory or umami quality that is great for dulling the bitterness of a strong, bold black tea. For example, an Assam tea is often characterized as being malty ("malty" being a term that's often used to describe a sweet, nutty richness). This quality can be rounded out with fat, thus triggering more receptors and giving you more mouth fullness. Because the changes that occur when adding milk (or other things like lemon), you may need to reconsider the pairing to food since the tea itself has a different flavor profile. Adding fatty acids can bring out more flavor while dampening some of the unwanted ones. I joke that the Brits need to add milk to their tea because they make it so bitter. There is some truth to that if we look at the science behind taste.

Perfectly Pairing Tea with Food

In the East, tea has been served with proper meals as far back as we can study, whereas in the West, tea has been mainly served alone or with a light snack, so to say. We think of a cup of tea as something to have with a dainty sandwich or a sweet biscuit. Of course, in the United States, iced tea has long been a summer beverage as well as a drink commonly ordered with a meal, much like pop (or soda, for those of you outside the Midwest) or ice water. In fact, the United States consumes close to 4 billion gallons of tea per year! That's right, we have been pairing tea with food for a long time — maybe just without thinking about it. A large portion of this tea is consumed in the form of "ready to drink" beverages that you grab at the supermarket or gas station along with a bag of chips. Hey, right there is a tea and food pairing.

But let's get a little more refined than a gas station cooler and grab-and-go snack rack, shall we? And now, as a tea sommelier, I (Lisa) will be your guide as we continue.

Matching tea with different foods

Thinking of flavors in a more concrete way guides us as we consider what foods are complementary. For example, a light white tea that offers a slightly dry note along with a fruity finish pairs well with steamed asparagus. However, if you add some hollandaise sauce to that asparagus, I would go with a crisp, bolder first-flush Darjeeling, not a white tea.

If I am making a beautiful sushi platter or serving lightly steamed fish, I would most likely pair it with a Japanese sencha, because the umami or savory note of the tea has an almost seaweed-like quality that pairs perfectly with fresh fish and rice. If I were to broil that same fish with some salt and pepper, however, I would make a pot of a Chinese-style green tea that might be described as having a sweeter and hay-like note. The tea would counter the toastiness and slight saltiness from the seasoning and broiling of the fish.

A strong black tea, like an Assam or breakfast blend, may pair better with a steak while a milky tea may pair best with a sweet dessert. A nutty or more earthy oolong or a slightly smoky Chinese black tea can stand up to a heartier red meat dish, because there are enough layers of flavor in the tea to stimulate more areas of your palate. These teas also can pair well with a creamier dessert, such as crème brûlée or a sabayon. Due to its subtle profile, a white tea may pair best with some fresh fruit or simple cheese and crackers.

Other teas such as rooibos, herbal, and fruit blends can be fun to pair with specific foods as well. A nutty, sweet tobacco-like rooibos is great with a vanilla sauce over an apple cake. I almost always make a big pitcher of iced fruit tea to accompany my summer cookouts, and who doesn't want someone to make them a cup of chamomile that's served with a honey biscuit?

When pairing teas with food, you have so many teas and so many different options. In the end it is about personal preference. As with wine, sommeliers can only give suggestions and present guidelines to help navigate the immensity of flavor options in tea. My best advice? Don't get caught up in the what-goes-with-what aspect of tea and food pairing. Drink what you like with your food and enjoy!

REMEMBER

Putting together a menu

Often, picking a menu starts with the weather. A summer barbeque with friends calls for a couple of favorite iced teas. Hearty soup and crusty bread on a cold Sunday evening, however, beckon a hot, slightly smoky oolong.

For example, brewing a darker oolong to serve with a thick butternut squash soup is ideal. The sweetness of the squash is tamed by the woody, dry, yet smooth tea, which doesn't give into the sweet as a sweeter tea might. The contrast is an important part of pairing. The Assam honey glazed salmon recipe from Chapter 19 would be great with a contrasting, grassy sencha. Going back to that barbeque, a strawberry mint black tea or a bitter lemon fruit tea would offer light refreshment that can stand up to a burger with all the fixings, a hotdog with spicy mustard, or smoky souchong ribs (see recipe, Chapter 19).

Before planning what tea to serve, dissect your food menu. Take each course on its own and think about the purpose of the pairing. Do you want to add contrast to the dish or do you prefer to pull out a specific flavor element? Most importantly, you should trust your tastebuds, experiment, and have fun!

TIP

IN THIS CHAPTER

» Looking into the deep history of tea in alcohol

» Understanding what makes a cocktail

» Exploring the various ways to incorporate tea into cocktails

» Diving into tea cocktail recipes

Chapter **21**

Tea Mixology

There is *nothing* twenty-first century about using tea in boozy drinks! Sure, tea cocktails may be an up-and-coming rage, but back in the day, 17th-century sailors employed by the British East India Company were thrilled to discover that India possessed a greatly desirable beverage: punch. Containing both tea and booze, punch quickly became a staple when aboard. The drink also demonstrates the versatility of tea as a cocktail ingredient — centuries before the word "cocktail" was ever used to describe a boozy beverage.

The definition of a cocktail has changed over time. Historically speaking, the word initially specified a particular kind of mixed drink; the first published definition occurred in 1806 in the *Balance and Columbian Repository* newspaper (Hudson, New York): "*a stimulating liquor, composed of spirits of any kind, sugar, water, and bitters.*" In contemporary English, and in this book, we understand "cocktail" as a mixed drink made either from mixed spirits or from spirits mixed with other ingredients, such as juice, syrups, tonics — or even tea.

However, a cocktail aspires to be more than a drink made of disparate ingredients; it transcends its blend of alcohol, acid, sweetener, bitter, and dilution. The finished product becomes greater than the sum of its parts. Thus, tea — with its nearly endless varieties and flavor profiles — can play a wonderful and unexpected role in adding layers, balance, and harmony to cocktails, creating new sensory experiences along the way.

From ancient techniques to modern methods, in this chapter we briefly explore how tea has been consumed with alcohol throughout the ages. We delve into cocktail ingredients so that you understand how tea can work with, and elevate, the individual components. Then, our recipes get you started, just in time for cocktail hour, *tea-cocktail* hour, that is!

PUNCH, AND THE HISTORY OF TEA IN MIXED DRINKS

Much of the booze-soaked history behind the creation of many mixed drinks has been lost to time (and the hazy memories of those who may have had a few too many). Similar to the mysteries and folklore that surround the origin of what we consider "classic cocktails" — like a martini, manhattan, or margarita — punch has a past buried in the murky depths of sailor stories.

Punch first entered the English lexicon in the early to mid-1600s, when the East India company sent sailors, soldiers, and merchants to India and southeast Asia to collect goods for the spice trade. They were introduced to a drink with many names, or at least many misspellings: *paanstch, paunch, bolleponge, palepuntz,* or *boule-ponge* (the latter three roughly meaning "bowl-of-punch"). Though the names were different, the general ingredients remained the same: spirit, citrus, sugar, water, and spice. Unsurprisingly, it is believed that the word "punch" (and all the other ones listed) was derived from the Hindi word *panch,* which means "five." Aside from the water itself, most of the ingredients were native to the area. The spirit was typically batavia-arrack, a beverage similar to rum; it is distilled from palm flower sap, sugar cane, Indonesian red rice, or a combination of those. Sugar cane and fruit from the genus *Citrus* are also native to that part of the world. Most importantly, the spice trade drove colonial traffic through the region, and many of the spices, like nutmeg and cloves, were originally exclusively found in the "Spice Islands" of Indonesia.

One thing that isn't clear, though, is whether the inhabitants were already consuming this beverage when the colonists arrived, or whether it was created for the new visitors or some of the sailors invented it with ingredients they had available to them locally.

Speaking of locally available items, tea was quite a large piece of the spice trade. Back in Europe, both tea and spices were highly valued and seen as status symbols. Punches would be served at parties and social gatherings along with tea, and it was only a matter of time before they were mixed together. There is some evidence this practice began in the late 1600s; it was in 1732, in Philadelphia, that we see one of the first examples of tea in a mixed drink. The Philadelphia Fish House Punch (see the recipe later in this chapter) incorporated black tea with rum and brandy to make tipple that was reportedly very popular with the likes of George Washington, among others.

Later, in 1862, it was cemented in history when Jerry Thomas wrote *The Bartenders Guide,* the first American book dedicated to mixed drinks. The very first chapter is about punch, and one of the very first things he mentions is that you should use tea instead of water for your punch recipes. Tea would go on to be featured in many punch recipes throughout the years.

Unfortunately, punch fell out of style, and tea wasn't nearly utilized to its potential for quite some time. Only in the last 20–25 years has the properly made cocktail seen a renaissance, and bartenders since have been creating new and wild flavor combinations using tea as a cocktail ingredient.

Deconstructing Cocktails

Tea can be incorporated into almost any cocktail ingredient, or the brewed tea itself can be an ingredient. Although right about now you may be inspired to start pulling out your cocktail glasses, it's very helpful to begin with some basics: identifying common cocktail ingredients and understanding a little extraction chemistry.

TIP

Sure, you can simply follow our recipes without knowing a thing about the science — we provide easy-to-follow directions to make some really awesome cocktails! However, if you grasp the chemistry and rationale behind the recipes, you can readily apply this knowledge to create your very own unique concoctions.

Essential cocktail ingredients

Modern cocktails remain steeped in that 17th-century punch, which had five ingredients: alcohol, water, bitter (tea or spice), sweet, and sour. Although tea served as the bitter component of punch, its possibilities extend far past that. But wherever tea fits into the cocktail (rest assured, the "Putting Tea into Cocktails" section explores tea's potential), your drink ideally balances these components:

>> **Alcohol.** For cocktails, spirits are usually the alcohol of choice (for example, gin, vodka, whiskey, rum, or tequila), but this doesn't rule out other forms. Wine, beer, cider, or mead, for instance, can definitely step in.

>> **Acidulant.** An acidulant adds sourness to the cocktail. There are numerous options:

- Citric acid, in the form of citrus juice, is the most commonly used acidulant. Examples include lemon, lime, orange, grapefruit, or yuzu juice.

- Malic acid is another common acidulant. It's associated with tart fruits like Granny Smith apples, tart cherries, grapes, and tomatoes.

- Acetic acid is the basis of vinegar and its sourness. The "shrub" cocktail, in particular, uses vinegar to its advantage.

>> **Sweetener.** This is obviously the component that lends sweetness to the drink. There are many kinds of sugars, such as cane sugar, beet sugar, raw (or demerara) sugar, and light and dark brown sugar. Other forms of sweetener include honey, maple syrup, corn syrup, agave nectar, and molasses.

>> **Dilution.** The dilution is often overlooked as an "ingredient" because, in a cocktail, it usually comes from water or from the ice that melts while shaking or stirring a cocktail. However, dilution is quite important to the drink's balance.

Do remember that you aren't limited to still water for dilution. Sparkling water can add bubbles. Alternately, you can use infused water (tea!), flavored soda, milk/cream, or fruit or vegetable juices.

>> **Bitter.** The bitter may be the most neglected ingredient for cocktails. Although bitterness doesn't always appeal to everyone, it is one of the most important components for a balanced cocktail. When used in the correct proportion, bitter is often the flavor profile that bridges the gap between all the other ingredients; it really brings everything together.

Bitterness is most often found in plant-derived compounds such as phenols and polyphenols, including flavonoids and catechins, and caffeine — all of which are found in tea. The most common bittering agent in cocktails is the aptly named "bitters," which is typically a concentrated extraction or decoction of different plant materials, mostly in the form of roots, bark, flowers, dried citrus peels, and other botanicals.

Note that ingredients can play multiple roles in a cocktail. The cola–based Cuba Libre cocktail is a fine example. Inspect the ingredients list of your favorite brand of cola and you will find water (dilutant); sugar or corn syrup (sweetener); citric acid (acidulant); and "natural flavors," which are typically extracts made from vanilla, cinnamon, nutmeg, and the peel of lemons, limes, and oranges, which are bitter. There's only one missing ingredient for cola to transform into a cocktail. Just add rum to your cola, and voilà, you have a Cuba Libre cocktail!

Extraction chemistry

As you get deeper into this topic and delve into the myriad preparations and uses for tea, it's sometimes difficult to know what some of the scientific jargon really means. Two main components of cocktail chemistry are extraction and solvent.

Extraction

TECHNICAL STUFF

Extracting just means removing something by effort or force. In our context, extraction refers to the process by which bioactive, medicinal, and flavorful portions of plant tissues are separated by means of selective solvents or mechanical separation. Basically, extraction is a general term that refers to taking chemical compounds from one substance and transferring them into another medium. This can be accomplished by infusion, decoction, distillation, tincture, and tisane, defined as follows:

>> **Infusion.** Plant material is soaked or steeped in a liquid so that chemical compounds are removed from the plant and are transferred into the soaking or steeping liquid. Brewing a cup of tea or coffee is an infusion. However, the liquid need not be exclusively water — you can infuse oil with garlic and herbs, or you can infuse milk with the flavor of your favorite breakfast cereal.

Sometimes the terminology can get confusing. In the culinary world, when "extract" is used as a noun, it usually refers to a concentrated infusion. Which begs the following question: What is the main difference between what you'd normally call an "infusion" versus what's called an "extract"? It's the concentration of the solute (the substance being dissolved).

The length of time, type of solvent (see the next section), and temperature of your infusion will dictate what types of compounds and flavors you will extract.

>> **Decoction.** For decoction, plant material is boiled in a liquid to dissolve the chemical compounds. A decoction, then, is essentially a hot infusion. So, what's the difference between a hot infusion and a decoction?

- An infusion typically refers to an extraction in which we use leaves or flowers, and we don't boil them for long amounts of time.

- A decoction usually refers to an extraction in which we use roots, bark, or rhizomes, and we boil them for an extended length of time. (Bark, roots, and rhizomes tend to be denser than leaves and flowers and, therefore, require more heat to dissolve the desired chemical compounds.)

>> **Distillation.** Compounds are separated with heat. Distillation can come after, or be part of, decoction or infusion. The goal of distillation is to further separate the chemical compounds using their different boiling points.

>> **Tincture.** A tincture is basically an infusion, but the solvent is ethanol (the kind of alcohol found in beer, wine, and spirits), and the solute is highly concentrated. Tinctures are often also referred to as "extracts"; the most common variety is likely vanilla extract.

>> **Tisane.** Another type of infusion, a tisane includes soaking or steeping multiple forms of plant material, such as leaves, flowers, fruit, and spices, in liquid to extract their chemical compounds.

Solvent

A solvent is usually a liquid that can dissolve another substance (the solute) to form a solution. Solvents are generally classified as either polar (partially charged; can dissolve other polar compounds) or non-polar (equally charged so it can't dissolve polar compounds). Water, a polar solvent, is known as the universal solvent because it can dissolve a greater number of chemical compounds than any other known solvent. Other common solvents are alcohol (keep reading!) and fats (like vegetable oils).

Putting Tea into Cocktails

So, now that you have all the ingredients and terminology down, how do you add tea to your cocktail repertoire?

Choosing the method

Sometimes you can simply add brewed tea (see Philadelphia Fish House Punch) or matcha (see Matcha Batida) to your cocktail. Most of the time, however, we perform these steps:

1. **Extract the chemical compounds from the tea leaves in some manner.**

2. **Transfer those compounds into another medium (such as a sweetener or spirits), thereby making an infusion.**

3. **Use the infusion as a cocktail ingredient.**

Making cocktails, like baking, involves a little chemistry! But basically, you're just transferring the flavors and complexity of tea into something that's easier to use as a cocktail ingredient. This process also allows you to better control the tea's intensity. A bonus? These infusions can be stored and used for multiple cocktails.

REMEMBER

Keep two things in mind:

>> Tea will infuse its flavor into just about any liquid medium you put it in.

>> Many different kinds of teas are available, each with myriad flavor profiles.

The possibilities, then, are truly endless! So how do you start? You can approach your tea infusion from a couple different angles: thinking of the types of tea or considering the cocktail.

Start with the tea

You can begin by choosing the flavor of tea you want to extract. For instance, you may have an earl grey tea that you would love to try in a cocktail. You first need to decide how intense you want that flavor to be, which will help you determine what type of extraction to make. After you've made your extraction, you can decide how you want to use it in a cocktail.

Something to consider is that different solvents extract at different rates. To make a syrup, you will most likely extract at room temperature into water, which is typically the slowest extraction. Straight tea and syrups are also generally the least intense, adding more nuanced flavors. Alcohol is a more powerful solvent, so the more alcohol in the mix, the more extraction you will have, and thereby, you increase the intensity of the flavors. Using alcohol at 80–100 proof (40–50% alcohol, by volume) means you're using both water and alcohol as a solvent, so you will get even more flavor, and more quickly. The higher the proof of the spirit, the faster and more intense your extraction will be.

Therefore, expect the intensity to rank as follows:

>> **Least intense.** Extractions into water. Examples include

- Syrups

- Straight tea

>> **Medium intensity.** Extractions into medium-proof spirits (80–100 proof). Examples include

- Infused spirits

- Liqueurs

>> **Most intense.** Extractions into high-proof spirits (greater than 120 proof). Examples include

- Tinctures

- Bitters

Start with the cocktail

Alternately, you can first choose a cocktail that you want to infuse with tea. In this method, you will need to decide which ingredient is the best medium to convey that flavor, and then make the infusion. For example, if you like an old fashioned, you can either infuse the whiskey with tea, make a simple syrup with tea, or make the bitters with tea. You can also make ice out of brewed tea so that when it slowly melts, the tea flavor grows throughout the drinking experience.

Types of tea infusions

With multiple types of infusions possible (see "Extraction Chemistry," earlier, for specifics) and thousands of tea choices, your cocktail potential is practically unlimited! Here are some characteristics of the various infusions that we use in our recipes.

Tea syrups

A syrup is a thick, sweet liquid. You can use a syrup as a sauce (chocolate syrup on ice cream or maple syrup on pancakes), but cooks and bartenders also commonly use syrups to increase sweetness, and so you'll see syrups in many recipes. In the cocktail world, the most common syrup is called simple syrup, which is essentially equal parts water and sugar. The type of sugar you use to make simple syrup will alter the flavor of your syrup, but the recipe remains basically the same: one part sugar to one part water.

TIP

You can give even more flavor to your syrup by adding fruit juice or a small amount of extract (like vanilla or almond extract). But more interesting yet: Bring new flavors to the table by adding tea to your simple syrup. The water already needs to be hot to dissolve the sugar, so why not add some tea into the mix? You can use just about any tea to make a syrup. Just brew the tea about twice as strong as you normally would, and when it's done brewing, pour the hot tea over an equal volume of sugar, stirring to dissolve the sugar. Let the syrup cool and use it in your favorite drinks!

Tea-infused spirits

Alcohol is a powerful solvent, so be careful when making infusions with something as flavorful as tea. Some flavors extract faster than others, and the percentage of alcohol will affect the speed of your infusion. Spirits that are 80 to 100 proof (40% to 50% alcohol) work the best for infusions like this.

TIP

Tea leaves from *Camellia sinensis* often extract very quickly and can be very tannic and overly bitter when over-extracted (think of what tea tastes like after you steep it in boiling water for too long). Stick to lower volumes of tea leaves and shorter infusions. Allowing two to three tablespoons of tea leaves to infuse in 750 milliliters of spirits for two hours at room temperature is usually all it takes, but taste it; if you like your flavor to be more intense, let it infuse a little longer.

Fruit and herbal teas typically don't have any *Camellia sinensis* leaves so they can be infused for longer periods of time without significant risk of over-extraction. Infusion times can range from two to twenty-four hours at room temperature. Although you can get by with less tea for longer infusions, you'll want to use two to five tablespoons of tea for 750 milliliters of spirits.

Tea tinctures and bitters

TIP

As mentioned earlier, a tincture is really just an intensified infusion. When making a cocktail with an infused spirit, you'd normally use one to two ounces of that spirit because you don't want the flavor to be too strong. However, when adding a tincture or bitters to a drink, you add only a few dashes (⅛ to ¼ of a teaspoon) so that the flavors can be dialed up. The premise is still the same — soak the alcohol with the tea — but for a tincture, double or triple the amount of tea. Generally speaking, this is going to overpower the flavor of the spirit, so it's best to use a neutral spirit for this application, such as vodka, moonshine, or unaged brandy. A higher alcohol content will also bring out more flavor: 100 proof will work fine, but 120 to 151 proof will make even more intense flavors.

Bitters are often complex blends of herbs, spices, bark, and roots. They help balance the sweet, sour, and strong (alcohol) characters from the other cocktail ingredients. Think of using bitters like how you would use salt for food — they can highlight the existing flavors, and they also add a bit of their own character.

Although bitters and tinctures are both examples of intense extractions into alcohol, the difference in terminology basically boils down to the fact that bitters are bitter in character, and they are almost always a blend of multiple botanical ingredients. Most bitters recipes call for gentian, quassia, quinine, and bitter orange peel, among other botanicals.

Recipes for Tea Syrups, Infusions, Tinctures, and Bitters

REMEMBER

Making tea infusions is very easy, and they are the basis of many of our cocktail recipes (see "Tea Cocktail Recipes"). However, keep in mind that infusing can take anywhere from a few hours to a few days, so be sure to plan ahead. The great thing about these infusions is that they keep for at least several weeks (when stored properly), so they're ready to go whenever you're in the mood for a great cocktail!

TIP

Lisa always keeps a strong fruit tea syrup in the fridge to add to her favorite sparkling wine when friends swing by. Tea syrups are great for nonalcoholic drinks as well. Flavored waters (sparkling or still) are very popular and can be found on grocery shelves everywhere, but you can easily make your own. To save money and always have it available, keep a few tea syrups in your fridge. Lisa's kids, for instance, love to pour a little passionfruit or blood orange fruit tea syrup into carbonated water. It's better than juice, healthier than soda pop, and fancier than plain water.

Please note that although we often give specific tea recommendations in our recipes, you can substitute a similar tea.

Awesome Assam Tea Syrup

ACTIVE TIME: 3 MINUTES	INACTIVE TIME: 16–24 HOURS	YIELD: 2 CUPS

INGREDIENTS

8 ounces filtered water

3 heaping teaspoons Assam black tea

8 ounces (by weight) brown sugar

DIRECTIONS

1 Boil the water and brew the tea for 3–4 minutes; do not strain.

2 Add the sugar to the hot tea in a mixing bowl or glass jar. Stir until sugar is dissolved.

3 Allow to come to room temperature and then place in the refrigerator for a few hours but preferably overnight.

4 Strain through a tea strainer or coffee filter.

5 Refrigerated, tea syrup will keep well for about a month.

VARIATION: You could use just about any strong, flavored tea. If you want a more straightforward tea flavor, try using cane sugar instead of brown sugar.

Jasmine Honey Syrup

ACTIVE TIME: 3 MINUTES	INACTIVE TIME: 16–24 HOURS	YIELD: 1.75 CUPS

INGREDIENTS

8 ounces filtered water

3 heaping teaspoons jasmine green tea

¾ cup honey

DIRECTIONS

1 Boil the water and brew the tea for 2–3 minutes; do not strain.

2 Add the honey to the tea in a mixing bowl or glass jar. Stir until honey is dissolved.

3 Allow to come to room temperature and then place in the refrigerator for a few hours but preferably overnight.

4 Strain through a tea strainer or coffee filter.

5 Refrigerated, honey syrup will keep well for about two weeks.

VARIATION: You could use just about any heavily scented or flavored tea, like an earl grey, lapsang souchong, or an orange blossom oolong; this recipe also works incredibly well with herbal teas such as mint tea.

Sencha Agave Syrup

ACTIVE TIME: 3 MINUTES	INACTIVE TIME: 16–24 HOURS	YIELD: 1.75 CUPS

INGREDIENTS

8 ounces filtered water

3 heaping teaspoons sencha green tea

¾ cup agave

DIRECTIONS

1 Boil the water and brew the tea for 1–3 minutes; do not strain.

2 Add the agave to the tea in a mixing bowl or glass jar. Stir until agave is dissolved.

3 Allow to come to room temperature and then place in the refrigerator for a few hours but preferably overnight.

4 Strain through a tea strainer or coffee filter.

5 Refrigerated, agave syrup will keep well for about a month.

VARIATION: Although most green teas work great with agave, just about any fruit tea (or green tea and fruit blend) will do a wonderful job. Brew fruit teas for a few extra minutes before adding the agave.

TeaHaus Peaches and Cream Syrup

ACTIVE TIME: 3 MINUTES	INACTIVE TIME: 16–24 HOURS	YIELD: 2 CUPS

INGREDIENTS

8 ounces filtered water

3 heaping teaspoons TeaHaus #931 peaches and cream green tea

8 ounces (by weight) demerara sugar (or 1 cup + 2 tablespoons by volume)

DIRECTIONS

1 Boil the water and brew the tea for 3–4 minutes; do not strain.

2 Add the sugar to the tea in a mixing bowl or glass jar. Stir until sugar is dissolved.

3 Allow to come to room temperature and then place in the refrigerator for a few hours but preferably overnight.

4 Strain through a tea strainer or coffee filter.

5 Refrigerated, this syrup will keep well for about a month.

VARIATION: TeaHaus #1444 sensual affair (summer romance) fruit tea blend (with raspberries, strawberries, rose hips, and vanilla) makes an amazing syrup following the same method.

Campfire Whiskey Infusion

ACTIVE TIME: 2 MINUTES	INACTIVE TIME: 2–8 HOURS	YIELD: 750 ML

INGREDIENTS

2–5 tablespoons lapsang souchong black tea

750 milliliters whiskey (preferably rye whiskey)

DIRECTIONS

1 Add tea to bottle or jar (more tea if stronger flavor is preferred).

2 Pour spirit over the tea and infuse for 2–8 hours (closer to 2 hours for lighter character, closer to 8 hours for considerably more smoke and a bit of black tea bitterness).

3 Double strain to remove tea; put spirit back into original (or new) bottle.

4 It's useable after it is strained, but this infusion is better after about a week in a cool dark place.

VARIATION: Other full-bodied teas will work just as well (the TeaHaus #1390 maple walnut rooibos is excellent). Alternatively, you could infuse other spirits, such as tequila, rum, or cognac.

Coconut Green Tea Rum Infusion

ACTIVE TIME: 2 MINUTES	INACTIVE TIME: 2–12 HOURS	YIELD: 750 ML

INGREDIENTS

2–5 tablespoons TeaHaus #974 coconut green tea

750 milliliters rum (preferably a light or silver rum)

DIRECTIONS

1 Add tea to bottle or jar (more tea if stronger flavor is preferred).

2 Pour spirit over the tea and infuse for 2–12 hours (closer to 2 hours for lighter character, closer to 12 hours for bigger green tea and coconut character).

3 Double strain to remove tea; put spirit back into original (or new) bottle.

4 It's useable after it is strained, but this infusion is better after about a week in a cool, dark place.

VARIATION: Fruit and herbal teas also work great with rum, but any clear spirit will go nicely with this infusion.

Elderflower White Tea Vodka Infusion

ACTIVE TIME: 2 MINUTES	INACTIVE TIME: 2–4 HOURS	YIELD: 750 ML

INGREDIENTS

2–5 tablespoons TeaHaus #1038 elderflower white tea

750 milliliters vodka (preferably 80 to 100 proof)

DIRECTIONS

1 Add tea to bottle or jar (more tea if stronger flavor is preferred).

2 Pour spirit over the tea and infuse for 2–4 hours (closer to 2 hours for lighter character, closer to 4 hours for more floral notes).

3 Double strain to remove tea; put spirit back into original (or new) bottle.

4 It's useable after it is strained, but this infusion is better after about a week in a cool dark place.

VARIATION: Replace the elderflower white tea with just about any floral tea, and/or replace the vodka with any clear spirit.

Strawberry Mint Lavender Ice Cubes

ACTIVE TIME: 2 MINUTES	INACTIVE TIME: 3–4 HOURS	YIELD: 750 ML

INGREDIENTS

16 ounces filtered water (to brew tea)

4 heaping teaspoons TeaHaus #6970 strawberry mint lavender black tea

DIRECTIONS

1 Brew 2 cups of very strong tea.

2 Strain and allow to come to room temperature.

3 Put tea into clean ice cube trays.

4 Place in freezer and allow 3–4 hours to freeze completely.

VARIATION: Replace TeaHaus strawberry mint lavender tea with just about any tea.

Bitter Lemon Tincture

Note that neutral or rectified alcohol is any spirit distilled to a minimum of 190 proof and without added flavor.

ACTIVE TIME: 2 MINUTES	INACTIVE TIME: 336 HOURS	YIELD: 1.75 CUPS

INGREDIENTS

2 cups 100-proof neutral alcohol

8 teaspoons TeaHaus #1432 bitter lemon fruit tea

DIRECTIONS

1 Add tea and alcohol to a jar or mixing vessel.

2 Allow to infuse for two weeks.

3 Strain through tea strainer or coffee filter.

4 Bottled and stored in a cool dry place, tincture will last up to a year.

VARIATION: Other fruit and herbal teas work great as tinctures; try the TeaHaus #1390 maple walnut rooibos.

Chai Bitters

ACTIVE TIME: 15 MINUTES	INACTIVE TIME: 672 HOURS	YIELD: 2 CUPS

INGREDIENTS

3 heaping tablespoons chai blend (any loose-leaf chai blend will work)

2 cups 100-proof neutral alcohol (such as vodka)

2 tablespoons simple syrup

DIRECTIONS

1 Add tea and alcohol to a jar or mixing vessel.

2 Store in a cool dry place and allow to infuse for 3 weeks, shaking every day.

3 Strain thoroughly, using a cheesecloth or coffee filter.

4 Add simple syrup and allow bitters to rest for another week.

VARIATION: If you would prefer this to be more bitter, consider adding a teaspoon of gentian root or 1–2 teaspoons of cinchona bark.

Earl Grey Bitters

ACTIVE TIME: 20 MINUTES	INACTIVE TIME: 672 HOURS	YIELD: 2 CUPS

INGREDIENTS

2 heaping tablespoons earl grey tea

2 cups 100-proof neutral alcohol (such as vodka)

Zest of an orange

Zest of a lemon

2 tablespoons simple syrup

DIRECTIONS

1 Add tea and alcohol to a jar or mixing vessel.

2 Store in a cool dry place and allow to infuse for 2 weeks, shaking every day.

3 Add the zest of the orange and lemon (note: zest only); infuse for another week.

4 Strain thoroughly, using a cheesecloth or coffee filter.

5 Add simple syrup and allow bitters to rest for another week.

VARIATION: If you would prefer this to be more bitter, consider adding 1–2 teaspoons of cinchona bark. A teaspoon of fresh ginger added at the same time as the zest is a welcome addition.

Tea Cocktail Recipes

Now that you've made your tea infusion, here's where we put everything together! So, mix up a drink for you and a friend and then kick back and enjoy. (By the way, we're confident that your tea-infused cocktail will be pretty awesome!)

Assam Old Fashioned

INGREDIENTS

2 ounces bourbon or rye

0.5 ounce awesome Assam syrup (see recipe earlier)

2–3 dashes Angostura bitters

DIRECTIONS

Add all ingredients to a mixing glass with ice and stir. Strain into a rocks glass filled with ice and garnish with orange zest and a brandied cherry.

The brown sugar and black tea make this a deeper, darker, more nuanced old fashioned.

Bright and Shiny

INGREDIENTS

1.5 ounces coconut green tea rum Infusion (see recipe earlier)

Spicy ginger beer

Lime wedge

DIRECTIONS

Add infused rum to a collins glass filled with ice. Top with ginger beer. Garnish with the lime wedge, which should be squeezed into the cocktail before drinking.

This is a variation of a cocktail called Dark and Stormy, which is traditionally made with dark rum. Our infusion is made with unaged rum, and the addition of green tea and coconut creates a lighter, brighter cocktail, hence the name.

Campfire Manhattan

INGREDIENTS

2 ounces campfire whiskey infusion (see recipe earlier)

1 ounce sweet vermouth

2–3 dashes Angostura bitters

DIRECTIONS

Add all ingredients to a mixing glass with ice and stir. Strain into a chilled coupe and garnish with a brandied cherry.

The smoke from the lapsang souchong tea adds depth to the classic Manhattan.

Chai Negroni

INGREDIENTS

1 ounce gin

1 ounce Campari (or something similar)

1 ounce sweet vermouth

5 dashes chai bitters (see recipe earlier)

DIRECTIONS

Add all ingredients to mixing glass with ice and stir. Pour into chilled coupe or martini glass and garnish with an orange peel.

Earl Grey Champagne Cocktail

INGREDIENTS

1 sugar cube

2–3 dashes of earl grey bitters (see recipe earlier)

5 ounces dry champagne

DIRECTIONS

Put the sugar cube into the champagne flute and soak it with the bitters. Add champagne and garnish with lemon zest.

Fancy Gin and Tonic

INGREDIENTS

Handful of strawberry mint lavender ice cubes (see recipe earlier)

1.5 ounces gin

Tonic water

DIRECTIONS

Add the infused ice cubes to a Collins glass, pour in the gin, and top with tonic water. Garnish with a sprig of mint, a lime wheel, and/or dehydrated fruit.

As the ice begins to melt, the flavor of the cocktail will gradually taste more and more like the tea.

Jasmine Bees Knees

INGREDIENTS

1.5 ounces gin

0.75 ounce fresh lemon juice

0.5 ounce jasmine honey syrup (see recipe earlier)

DIRECTIONS

Add all ingredients to a shaker with ice and shake thoroughly. Strain into a chilled coupe and garnish with a lemon twist.

Jasmine, honey, and lemon are a natural combination. You can accentuate those flavors by choosing a floral gin, such as Hendrick's, The Botanist, or Mammoth Distilling Northern Gin.

Matcha Batida

Cachaca, a distilled spirit made from sugar cane juice, is produced in Brazil.

INGREDIENTS

2 ounces cachaca

1.5 ounces sweetened coconut cream

½ ounce lime fresh lime juice

¾ cup ice

½ teaspoon matcha (culinary matcha or powdered green tea would be fine)

DIRECTIONS

Place all ingredients into a blender and blend until smooth. Pour into large rocks glass or tiki mug and garnish with lime.

You can add any type of fruit or fruit syrup; passionfruit and pineapple are quite popular and taste great with the matcha.

Maple Walnut Whiskey Sour

INGREDIENTS

1.5 ounces maple walnut rooibos-infused whiskey (just like the campfire whiskey infusion recipe earlier, but with maple walnut rooibos from TeaHaus)

0.75 ounce fresh lemon juice

0.5 ounce simple syrup

DIRECTIONS

Add all ingredients to a shaker with ice and shake thoroughly. Strain into a rocks glass with ice and garnish with a dash of bitters and a brandied cherry.

Paloma Amarga

INGREDIENTS

1.75 ounces tequila or mezcal

0.75 ounce fresh lime juice

3 dashes bitter lemon tincture (see recipe earlier)

3 ounces grapefruit soda

DIRECTIONS

Add tequila, lime juice, and tincture to a shaker filled with ice and shake. Strain into a Collins glass filled with ice and top with grapefruit soda.

The bitterness of the tincture, paired with the fresh lime juice, cuts through some of the sweetness of the grapefruit soda. A tiny pinch of salt helps, too.

Peaches and Cream Bellini

INGREDIENTS

1 ounce TeaHaus peaches and cream syrup (see recipe earlier)

4 ounces dry sparkling white wine (such as prosecco, cava, or Brut Champagne)

DIRECTIONS

Add the syrup to a Champagne flute and top with sparkling wine. Garnish with a slice of peach.

Philadelphia Fish House Punch (for 10–12 people)

INGREDIENTS

Zest of 3 lemons

¾ cup sugar

16 ounces boiling water (to brew tea)

3 heaping teaspoons Ceylon black tea

¾ cup fresh lemon juice

16 ounces rum (preferably Jamaican)

4 ounces cognac

2 ounces peach brandy

DIRECTIONS

1 Add lemon zest and sugar to a mixing bowl. Rub zest and sugar together to allow the sugar to draw out the oils. Let rest for at least 15 minutes.

2 Brew the tea leaves in the boiling water for 2–3 minutes; strain and pour the hot tea over the sugar-zest combination to completely dissolve the sugar.

3 Let tea and sugar solution cool a bit and then add the other ingredients.

4 Chill with a large chunk of ice. (You can fill a plastic food container or old whipped topping container with water and freeze it the night before. Larger ice chunks keep the punch colder with slower dilution.)

5 Serve with smaller ice cubes in individual punch glasses, garnished with lemon wheels and freshly grated nutmeg. Alternately, if it's cold outside, you can skip the ice and serve the drink warm; stud the lemon wheels with cloves.

Pu-erh Bloody Mary

INGREDIENTS

1.5 ounces pu-erh-infused vodka, made the same way as elderflower white tea vodka infusion but with pu-erh tea (see recipe earlier)

4 ounces bloody Mary mix

DIRECTIONS

Add ingredients to a Collins or pint glass full of ice and garnish to your heart's content with whatever you like best in your bloody Mary. Might we suggest pickled vegetables, lemon, black pepper, and olives?

The fermented pu-erh adds earthiness and plays well with the savory and spicy bloody Mary.

Sencha Margarita

INGREDIENTS

2 ounces tequila or mezcal

0.75 ounce fresh lime juice

0.75 ounce sencha agave syrup (see recipe earlier)

DIRECTIONS

Add all ingredients to a shaker with ice and shake thoroughly. Strain into a chilled coupe and garnish with a lime wedge.

The herbal and grassy flavors from the sencha layer in nicely with tequila and especially mezcal.

Tropical Hot Toddy

INGREDIENTS

2 ounces whiskey (preferably on the lighter side, such as an Irish whiskey or Canadian whisky)

0.5 ounce honey syrup (made like the jasmine honey syrup, see recipe earlier, but without tea)

6 ounces hot brewed TeaHaus #988 pineapple mango black tea

DIRECTIONS

Add whiskey and honey syrup to a toddy glass or coffee mug; pour the hot tea over it. Garnish with a lemon wheel; a cinnamon stick and/or star anise are a nice touch as well.

White Martini

INGREDIENTS

2 ounces elderflower white tea vodka infusion (see recipe earlier)

1 ounce dry vermouth

1–2 dashes orange bitters

DIRECTIONS

Add all ingredients to a mixing glass with ice and stir. Strain into a chilled coupe and garnish with a lemon twist.

Let's face it, a lot of vodka is boring. With the right proportion of vermouth and the addition of elderflower white tea, this vodka martini pops.

7

The Part of Tens

Try our suggestions to salvage that tea that you just don't like! From brewing tips to using it around the house, we offer plenty of ideas.

Examine common tea myths that you're sure to come across and untangle truth from fiction.

Chapter **22**

Ten Plus Things to Do with Tea That You Don't Like

How many times have you read a description of something and thought "this sounds amazing," but when you get it home and try it, you realize it's not at all what you had hoped? This happens to the best of us and to the best of teas. What one person finds to be a perfect brew, another may simply not enjoy. Here are some ideas for what to do with a tea you just do not like.

Try to Brew It Differently

Often, people say that black tea is bitter, or they don't like green tea, or white tea is flavorless. Because everyone has different tastes, this can be true of any tea, to any one person. However, sometimes it's just a question of how tea is brewed and served. Almost every day at TeaHaus, someone comes in and mentions that they don't care for green tea. We always ask how they brew it. Most of the time, they say they had it at a restaurant or even a coffee shop. If this is the case, the problem is that the tea often isn't being brewed properly. If you have a tea like that at home, before you throw it out try brewing it at a lower water temperature, or with more or fewer leaves, or for less or more time. Experiment a bit before you give up.

Embellish It

Say you have a "boring" black tea at home, and you don't drink it very often. Try adding something to it. For example, a simple, bold, and inexpensive black tea is perfect for a masala chai, which can be created by adding spices like cinnamon, cloves, ginger, and pepper. Other ways to embellish your tea include adding milk and sugar, fruit, herbs, and so on, or even blending it with another tea. You can turn "meh" tea into a favorite.

Chill It

Not all teas are best served hot. For example, some fruit teas are quite tart, whereas others can be a bit cloying when hot. But served over ice? They might be a perfect treat! Sometimes the fruit and herbs in blends come out more when iced. Flavors change quite a bit with simple changes to things, like serving temps. You can also freeze the tea to make ice pops or as ice cubes for a punch, lemonade, or iced tea.

Combine It with Something Else

Almost everyone has heard of an Arnold Palmer — a drink made famous by the golfer of the same name. Mr. Palmer would ask his wife, Winnie, to make him this iced tea and lemonade mix after a long hot day on the green. So many other combinations can make a tea something special. A hot cider blended with a strong spiced tea makes a lovely fall drink, or perhaps some iced TeaHaus coconut green tea with a little pineapple juice, or even just add a little sparkling water to a strong brew. The possibilities are endless.

Combine It with Something Alcoholic

Here you can have a lot of fun. We talk about this at length in Chapter 21, but tea is terrific with alcohol! Make a tea syrup to add to mixed drinks or sparkling wine (you simply use tea instead of water when you make a simple syrup). Or try infusing gin, vodka, or your favorite spirit with tea. These are easy ways to take a not-so-great tea to another level.

Use It as a Spice

Who says tea is just for drinking? Eat More Tea is a business dedicated to using tea in all types of culinary applications. Almost anything that calls for liquid can be made with tea instead. Try infusing cream with tea to make butter or whipped cream. Maybe grind up a little lapsang souchong to add a smokiness to your dinner or toss in some sencha leaves to your rice to add color. Be creative!

Get Crafty with It

Have you ever ruined your favorite white T-shirt because you spilled a black tea or something like a hibiscus fruit tea blend on it? Have no fear, tea makes a great liquid to tie-dye with — so you can make it look like it was intentional (see Figure 22-1)! You can also make things look old by "antiquing" them with tea.

You can also use tea leaves in candles, papermaking, or even in the base of a vase to help hold a candle steady, as shown in Figure 22-1.

FIGURE 22-1: Using tea leaves to tie-dye, to hold a candle, and for relaxing.

Photos by Lisa McDonald

Put It to Work Around the House

Stinky fridges can be the worst. A box of baking soda can often do the trick, but next time try setting a bowl of tea leaves or hanging a few unbrewed teabags in the fridge. Now we always recommend that you store tea *away* from strong smells like spices because the leaves can take the smells on, which is bad for a tea you like — but this property provides a perfect use for a tea you don't like!

You can also use highly aromatic teas, especially floral ones like rose or lavender, as potpourri sachets in your drawers and closets.

Brewed tea leaves make great compost and can help lock in moisture around the base of your plants.

Put It to Work for You

The large-leaf teas, once brewed and completely unfurled, feel lovely when placed — still warm — under your eyes or between your brows (refer to Figure 22-1). The warm moisture is relaxing, and as it dries, you can feel it slightly tighten the area.

If you cut yourself and don't have any gauze, a slightly dampened teabag may help stop the bleeding. You may also consider biting on a teabag after a tooth extraction. The astringency in the tea may help cause blood vessels to shrink, thus easing the bleeding.

Some teas, especially herbals, have vibrant colors, so adding a little hibiscus tea, for example, to a lip balm may add a nice pink hue. Some lotions and lip balms often use tea as well.

Offer It on Social Media

Tea lovers can find many online forums that are great for trading and sharing teas. Who knows, what one person thinks is bad another may love.

Gift It

If you buy a two-ounce bag of tea, take it home, brew a cup, have a sip, and decide you don't like it — gift it. Unless your friend has a gram scale, they will never know. You can put it into a nice tin or divvy it up into small bags for lots of friends to receive. Tea is a wonderful hostess gift!

Chapter **23**

More Than Ten Myths about Tea

Tea is awash with myths, sometimes perpetuated by people who should know better. Because we want you to fully savor the tea you love the most, let's examine some common misconceptions.

Price Equals Quality

The answer to whether price equals quality is the same if the question were being asked of wine — so, not necessarily. Many, many things determine the price of any given wine. On occasion, the story behind a wine is worth more than the grapes used to make it. The same can go for tea. For example, you may be willing to pay far more for a tea — regardless of the tea's quality — when you hear that the leaves were carefully plucked by hand by elderly women in a small, remote garden.

In addition, the price of tea can be influenced by disparate factors such as weather, the quantity produced, politics, shipping, and packaging. Sometimes the most beautiful and expensive tin is filled with the cheapest of teas.

The amount of labor required to produce a specific tea will also influence the price. A handpicked, hand-rolled tea will often be more expensive than a machine-harvested tea, but that doesn't necessarily mean the quality of the actual tea leaf itself is better or worse. For example, we have three jasmine teas at TeaHaus. The least expensive is so priced because the tea itself is of lesser quality (machine picked and processed). However, it has more jasmine flavor than our other two jasmine teas. The most expensive jasmine is our pearl. It is the most labor-intensive tea to produce because it is hand-rolled into perfect balls, but the leaf itself is not as high quality as our middle-priced jasmine curls. Its price reflects its high production cost. None of these teas are of "bad" quality, but they each offer a different story and experience.

WARNING

Buyer beware, though, of fancy packaging and highly marketed trendy tea. You are often paying more for the story than for the tea, which is sometimes okay, too.

Rinse the Tea Leaves

If you've ever been on the tea Subreddit, you've probably read a lot of posts about awakening your leaves, decaffeinating your tea, or even washing contaminants off your tea by rinsing the leaves. Though these may be grounded in historical or cultural practices, there is no need to rinse your tea before brewing a cup, and there are no benefits from rinsing the leaves. You may notice that with some teas — especially those that are tightly rolled — the second infusion is stronger than the first, but there is no reason to throw out the first brew as a rinse.

You Can Wash Caffeine Out

Unfortunately, this is a classic old wives' tale. In some cultures, the first quick brew is tossed out, and the second infusion is thought to be decaffeinated. However, to remove any significant amount of caffeine, the leaves must be brewed for a longer amount of time in boiling water. This would mean that the second brew would not be very drinkable. Remember, if you're tossing the caffeine, you are most likely also tossing all the things that make tea taste good — and good for you.

Tea Has More Caffeine than Coffee

Kinda. It's complicated. The amount of caffeine in a single tea leaf is greater than that in a coffee bean. However, a brewed cup of coffee will have up to five times the amount of caffeine than a cup of tea. The reason for this has more to do with how the beverage is prepared than how much caffeine naturally occurs in the plant.

Never Rinse the Teapot

The idea of never rinsing your teapot may come from the use of Chinese unglazed teapots. These porous clay pots absorb whatever's in them, so if the liquid is tea, that's great. In fact, that's why some people dedicate clay teapots to one type of tea. You want that flavor to permeate the pot and affect each brewing. But if you clean that pot with soapy water, you'll have soapy-tasting tea.

If you're not using a porous clay pot, you *don't* want tea residue to flavor your next tea — especially if you're changing it up. For example, if you brew a white tea in an unwashed pot that was previously used for a smoky Chinese tea or a grassy Japanese tea, you'll ruin the subtlety of your delicate tea. The whole point of using an inert teapot is to get the full flavor of your tea. This is best accomplished if the pot has been thoroughly cleaned.

Experts Always Know What They're Tasting

Never be intimidated by experts. They can't always tell what they're drinking. In one experiment, tea was served in various cups — which differed only in shape and size — to a dozen tea experts, who were then questioned about the tea. Only two of them figured out that every cup held the exact same tea.

And remember this as well: Whatever you taste is unique to you. Don't worry about expert opinions when it comes to picking the tea you like.

Green Tea Is the Healthiest

This myth seems to never go away. As a result, we often get customers who come in and ask, with a sigh, which green tea they should drink. They may even explain that they don't much care for green tea but it's supposed to be "better" for them.

Please, just drink the tea that you enjoy the most, whether black or green or whatever! All tea comes from the same plant. Yes, the polyphenols in black tea are in a different form from those in green tea, but all polyphenols are antioxidants, and research is increasingly showing that all types of tea are potentially beneficial.

Earl Grey Origin Story

Although earl grey tea — with its distinctive bergamot flavor—is one of the most well-known and beloved tea blends, the origin of the tea and its name is less certain. Charles Grey, the second Earl Grey, is often cited as the source of the tea. It's said that he was given such a tea and that he then requested that British tea merchants supply it. While it *is* true that his Reform Act lowered the cost of tea, Charles was born in 1764 and died in 1845 — whereas the first evidence that linked "Earl Grey" with "tea" was an advertisement in 1884. This would be during the third Earl Grey's lifetime (Henry George, 1802–1894).

However, there *were* earlier ads touting a pricy "celebrated grey mixture" of tea that had been "rewarded with the most distinguished patronage." Merchants named "Grey" abounded in the 1800s, so the tea could refer to one of them. But who was the patron? Or was that just an advertising ploy? And what was the "mixture"? According to the Oxford English Dictionary, these ads don't mention bergamot at all.

Researchers know that bergamot was added to tea as early as 1824 — but to cover up low-quality tea. One company was brought to court in 1837 for misleading consumers by selling the secretly doctored tea as a higher-quality product. It's possible that the bergamot element caught on and evolved into that "celebrated Grey mixture," but we aren't certain. Unless, of course, we can believe early-20th-century ads — such as those by Jackson's of Piccadilly, which claimed that earl grey tea was introduced in 1836 "to meet the wishes of a former Earl Grey." Which *could* be Charles or Henry George!

Tea Is Bitter

Because tea can have a tannic and sometimes astringent finish, people often jump to the word "bitter." Often, the bitterness is due to brewing the tea improperly. Bitterness is sensed on the back of the tongue, so it is often the flavor that lingers in the mouth. The level of bitterness varies greatly between types of tea, so knowing the best brewing method — time and water temperature — can help minimize this flavor profile. Keep in mind that something may taste bitter to one person but not to another.

Tea Expires

Although many teas are best enjoyed within a year, your tea can sit in your pantry for a *really* long time, especially if you've kept it safe from moisture, light, and strong aromas. Of course, if you see mold or something questionable, throw it into your compost! But for the most part — and especially for black tea — old tea is definitely drinkable. Some teas, like pu-erh or even sencha, *improve* with age! Sometimes, however, you'll find that your tea just doesn't taste as good as when it was fresh. It may seem weak or lackluster. If it was flavored, that flavor may have faded too much. To help remedy this, try using more tea leaves (but don't change your water temperature or brew time). Experiment a bit; you may need substantially more leaves. If the taste still isn't to your liking, check out Chapter 22, which offers a bunch of ideas for salvaging your tea.

Pinky Should Be Raised

Unless you're doing a parody, no. Keep that pinky down. But then, you may well ask, how did this whole raised pinky thing become a thing?

There are numerous possibilities. A practical explanation may simply be that those tiny, decorative teacup handles made the cup difficult to hold.

Some of the more popular historical explanations are

>> The syphilis finger. It is said that in the courts of King Louis XIV in Paris, syphilis was rife, and the disease often made the fingers stiff. It may also have been a way to indicate that you currently had the disease and, therefore, were "refraining." Servants saw the rich nobles drink with their pinkies up and went home to show their families, and, thus, it became associated with the upper class.

>> Spice finger. In medieval times, the wealthy could afford spices and would reserve the use of their pinkies to dip into the spices. Again, this was seen by people in the lower classes, who wanted to emulate the rich.

- Rumors had it that Anne Boleyn may have had a sixth finger, a pinky, on one hand, which couldn't bend. Everyone wanted to be like Anne. This has been proven not to be true.

- Dirty servant hands. Some historians talk about how nobility handled glasses and cups with as few of their digits as possible to avoid touching something their dirty servants had touched.

- Back in the days of knighthood, it was said that the elite ate with three fingers while the commoners ate with five. The ring finger and the pinky were considered "fingers of courtesy" because they covered the mouth as food was shoved in.

Though the real reason for having one's pinky up while drinking tea is unclear, it's hard not to think of all the tales behind it when you see someone pose for a picture with their pinky sticking up.

The Brits Drink the Most Tea

Nope! Despite what we see in the movies or on our favorite BBC show, the Brits don't get to wear the tea-drinking crown. That honor goes to the Turks, with the United States coming in at a close second or third!

Glossary

Adenosine: A neuromodulator that helps induce sleep.

Afternoon tea: Tea served with light snacks; originally a British tradition. *See also* **full tea.**

Alkaloid: A chemical that contains nitrogen, is found mostly in plants, and affects us physiologically; caffeine is an alkaloid.

Amino acid: A simple organic compound that is the building block of proteins.

Antioxidant: An agent that reacts with and removes oxidants.

Aroma wheel: *See* **tasting wheel.**

Assam: A major tea-producing region of India; Assam tea is known for its malty character.

Astringent: Dry mouthfeel.

Ayurvedic tea: In the Ayurvedic system of medicine, teas meant to counterbalance the doshas.

Bancha: Japanese green tea produced from the second harvest.

Bioavailability: How much of a specific polyphenol is absorbed and has an active effect in the body.

Bitters: Complex blend of herbs, spices, bark, and roots.

Black tea: Fully oxidized tea leaves.

Blend: A mixture of teas or a tea with inclusions.

Breakfast tea: Tea blend that is robust, hearty, and releases caffeine quickly; often had with milk and sugar.

Brew: The act of steeping tea leaves in hot water, and the liquor that results from this steeping.

Brew basket: Fine mesh strainer that separates tea leaves from liquid.

Butter tea: In the Himalayas, crushed tea frothed with yak butter, yak milk, and salt.

Caffeine: A psychoactive stimulant with a bitter taste that is found naturally in tea leaves; in tea, it appears to work synergistically with L-theanine to provide a "calm alertness."

Caffeine free: Herbal tea that never contained caffeine.

Camellia sinensis* var. *assamica: Tea variety native to Assam; used primarily to produce black tea, although it can be used to make any type of tea. *See also **Camellia sinensis* var. *sinensis.***

Camellia sinensis* var. *sinensis: Tea variety native to China; used primarily to produce green, white, and oolong teas, although it can be used to make any type of tea. *See also **Camellia sinensis* var. *assamica.***

Carbon dioxide (CO_2) decaffeination: A method to remove caffeine from tea leaves, using carbon dioxide as the solvent that binds to caffeine molecules. This method retains more flavor and polyphenols than other decaffeinating processes.

Catechin: A simple polyphenol that is the most common flavanol in tea.

Ceylon: Tea produced in Sri Lanka, formerly known as Ceylon.

Chai: *See **masala chai.***

Chinese green tea: Usually, green tea in which leaf oxidation is stopped by pan frying.

Chlorophyll: The green pigment in leaves that absorbs light.

Clone: A genetically identical plant. In tea, clones are grown from cuttings of the desired plant.

Cocktail: Mixed drink that contains alcohol, acidulant, sweetener, bitter, and dilution.

Complex polyphenol: Polyphenol that has been converted during tea leaf oxidation into a theaflavin or thearubigin.

Crush-tear-curl: *See **CTC.***

CTC: Tea leaves that have been cut by machine into uniform, small pieces (cut-tear-curl or crush-tear-curl), as opposed to orthodox tea.

Culinary matcha: Second-harvest tea leaves that have been ground into a fine powder; used for culinary purposes. *See also **matcha** and **powdered green tea.***

Cultivar: A variety of *Camellia sinensis* that has been selectively bred.

Cut-tear-curl: *See **CTC.***

Darjeeling: A major tea-producing region of India; the tea is known as the Champagne of tea and has a characteristic astringency.

Decaffeinated: Tea leaves in which most of the caffeine has been removed.

Decoction: A hot infusion, but using roots, bark, or rhizomes, which are boiled for an extended time.

Distill: Separate compounds with heat.

Dragon well: *See* **lung ching.**

Earl grey: A blend of tea and bergamot oil.

East Frisian tea: Strong black tea poured over rock sugar, with heavy cream added, but not stirred in. A specialty of East Frisia, Germany.

EGCG: A simple polyphenol (and the most abundant catechin) found in tea leaves and heavily studied for its potential health benefits. EGCG stands for epigallocatechin-3-gallate.

Elephant friendly: A certification program to protect elephants in tea-growing regions.

Extract: Remove something from one substance and transfer it into another medium.

Fairtrade: Program that pays a minimum price, specific to the tea, to producers.

Famous teas: A list of the finest teas produced in China and Taiwan.

Fannings: Tiny bits of tea leaf; along with tea dust, often used in teabags.

Fermented tea: Tea leaves that have been microbially fermented.

Filter: Anything used to separate tea leaves from the liquid; may be a brew basket, an integrated web in the spout of a teapot, a paper teabag, and so on.

Fingerprinting: Tracing and authenticating tea by examining genetic markers, leaf components, and so on.

First flush: The first harvest in early spring; term used mostly for Darjeeling and Assam teas.

Flavonol: A type of polyphenol.

Flowery: Buds or leaf tips.

Flush: Harvest season; term used mostly for Darjeeling and Assam teas. *See also* **first flush** and **second flush.**

Formosa: Tea produced in Taiwan, formerly known as Formosa.

Frost tea: Tea produced from lightly frozen tea leaves.

Fruit tea: Herbal tea consisting of fruit along with spices, flowers, and/or other herbals.

Fujian Province: A major tea-producing region in China.

Full tea: Tea served with scones, sweets, and savories, usually served on a three-tiered platter; originally a British tradition. *See also* **afternoon tea.**

Gaiwan: A lidded bowl in which tea is both brewed and consumed.

Genmaicha: Blend of Japanese green tea and roasted rice.

Golden: Young leaves.

Gongfu: A way of brewing tea; tea is brewed in a small teapot, poured into a pitcher or second teapot, and then poured into tasting cups.

Green tea: Tea that is less oxidized than black tea.

Gunpowder: A type of Chinese black or green tea; the leaves are rolled into pearls.

Herbal tea: An infusion made with leaves, flowers, and/or other parts of non-tea plants.

High mountain: Tea grown at or above 3,300 feet in elevation.

Hojicha: Roasted Japanese green tea.

Honeybush: An herbal tea made from the honeybush plant; produced in South Africa.

Infuser mug: Mug that includes a removeable brew basket and cover/coaster.

Infusion: Soaking or steeping plant material in a liquid to transfer the flavor of the material into the liquid.

Iron goddess of mercy: *See* **Tieguanyin.**

Japanese green tea: Usually, green tea in which leaf oxidation is stopped with steam.

Jasmine tea: Traditionally, a Chinese scented tea made by layering jasmine flowers with tea leaves to allow the leaves to absorb the jasmine aroma and flavor.

Keemun: A type of Chinese black tea that heavily reflects its terroir.

Kukicha: Japanese tea composed of twigs and leaf stems.

Lapsang souchong: A Chinese black tea known for its intense smokiness. The oldest of the black teas, it was first produced in 1568.

Liquor: Brewed tea or herbal tea.

Leaf set: The bud and first one or two leaves of the tea plant.

L-theanine: An amino acid that is found only in tea, one kind of mushroom, and guayusa. L-theanine, or theanine, appears to improve cognition, helps calm the nervous system, and increases feelings of well-being. It seems to work synergistically with caffeine.

Lung ching: Chinese green tea that tops the "famous teas" list.

Masala chai: A sweetened, spicy, milky tea that originated in India; "masala" refers to a blend of spices; *chai* means "tea."

Matcha: Shaded, deveined tea leaves that have been ground into a fine powder that is whisked into hot water. *See also* **culinary matcha** and **powdered green tea.**

Mate: A caffeinated herbal tea, traditionally sipped out of a gourd.

Moroccan mint tea: A sweetened mint tea commonly made with green gunpowder and nana mint; traditionally served in decorated glasses.

Mouthfeel: The sensation in the mouth when fat receptors are triggered by fatty acid.

Oolong tea: Tea that has undergone a lengthy and involved production process and has an oxidation level between that of black and green tea.

Orange pekoe: The leaf used to produce the tea; orange pekoe is the first leaf down from the bud on a tea plant.

Organic: Agricultural production standards set by the USDA.

Orthodox: Tea leaves that have been oxidized by bruising and have been kept whole or broken into pieces, as opposed to CTC.

Oxidant: An agent that can remove electrons (oxidize).

Oxidation: When leaf cell walls break, oxygen enters and reacts with the cell contents (oxidizes). To produce green tea, this process is stopped quickly. To produce black tea, the leaves are allowed to fully oxidize.

Oxidative stress: Too many unstable molecules or oxidants; oxidative stress can damage the body.

Pai mu tan: Chinese white tea that includes the bud and two young leaves.

Pairing: Putting tea and food together to enhance the flavor of both.

Pekoe: The leaf used to produce the tea; pekoe is the second leaf down from the bud on a tea plant.

Phenol: *See* **polyphenol.**

Phytochemical: A chemical, such as caffeine, made by plants.

Pluck: Pick tea leaves by hand.

Polyphenol: A micronutrient found in plants that potentially functions as an antioxidant. *See also* **complex polyphenol.**

Powdered green tea: Ground green tea leaves; used for lattes and other applications to obtain green tea flavor. *See also* **matcha** and **culinary matcha.**

Psychoactive stimulant: Substance that affects the mind (psychoactive) and increases physiological activity (stimulant); caffeine is one example.

Pu-erh: Microbially fermented tea; traditionally produced in Yunnan Province, China.

Purity: A measure of whether a tea contains residue of pesticides, herbicides, or heavy metals; additives that shouldn't be there; microplastics; and so on.

Purple tea: Tea produced from a genetic variant of *Camellia sinensis* that has purple leaves.

Rainforest Alliance: Partnership of growers and buyers.

Rock tea: Oolong teas produced in China's Wuyi Mountains from centuries-old tea plants and from clones of ancient plants.

Rooibos: An herbal tea made from the rooibos plant; produced in the Western Cape of South Africa.

Samovar: Method of brewing tea in Russia. An urn heats the water while a small teapot, set on the samovar, holds a tea concentrate.

Scented tea: Tea leaves that have absorbed the aroma and flavor of fresh flowers or aromatic fruit; a Chinese specialty tea.

Second flush: The second harvest, in later spring; term used mostly for Darjeeling and Assam teas.

Sediment: The small, dark particles that settle to the bottom of a cup of tea; results when tannins, a type of polyphenol, bind with proteins.

Sencha: Japanese green tea; constitutes around two-thirds of the tea produced in Japan.

SFTGFOP: Special finest tippy golden flowery orange pekoe; descriptors used primarily for tea produced in India.

Shading: Placing a cover over tea plants so that the leaves produce more chlorophyll and retain more L-theanine. Used in Japan to produce premium teas.

Silver needle: Chinese white tea comprising only the unfurled buds; its name derives from the minute silvery hairs on the buds.

Simple polyphenol: *See* **polyphenol.**

Single estate: Tea that comes from one tea garden and isn't blended with any other tea.

Single origin: *See* **single estate.**

Solvent: A liquid (usually) that can dissolve another substance to form a solution.

Sommelier: Someone trained in tasting and curating wine or tea.

Sparrow beak: Hand-plucked leaf set.

Stimulant: Substance that increases the level of physiological activity; caffeine is one example.

Tasting wheel: A chart that provides words to describe flavors.

Tea master: Someone trained in tasting and curating tea; the title requires years of training and knowledge.

Tea quality: Determined by environment, the tea plant, agricultural practices, tea processing, and brewing technique.

Tea syrup: A syrup made with sugar and tea.

Terroir: Environment in which tea is grown; contributes to the tea's character.

Theaflavin: Complex polyphenol that gives black tea its orange and red pigments, bright taste, and briskness.

Theanine: *See* **L-theanine.**

Thearubigin: Complex polyphenol that gives black tea its brown pigments, mellowness, and depth of flavor.

Tieguanyin: Oolong teas, originally produced in Fujian Province. May range from green to roasted.

Tincture: Infusion using ethanol as the solvent; highly concentrated.

Tippy: Leaf tips.

Tisane: *See* **herbal tea.**

Turkish tea: Traditionally made in a *çaydanlik*, a type of samovar, and served in tulip-shaped glasses.

Umami: The savory taste of food. In tea, umami describes the taste of L-theanine and glutamic acid.

Vegetal: Flavor reminiscent of vegetables.

Volatile: Substance that evaporates; contributes flavor, aroma, and complexity to tea.

White peony: *See* **pai mu tan.**

White tea: Tea leaves that have been withered but not oxidized; the least-processed type of tea.

Wild-grown: Tea plant that is native to an area and grows without cultivation, tea plant that grows in a forest, or tea plant that is minimally pruned.

Wilting: *See* **withering.**

Withering: Letting tea leaves dry, either naturally or with a fan.

Wulong tea: *See* **oolong tea.**

Yellow tea: Tea leaves that undergo micro-fermentation, which converts polyphenols into theaflavins and turns the leaves yellow; produced in southern China.

Yerba mate: *See* **mate.**

Yunnan: Complex black teas from China's Yunnan Province.

Yunnan Province: A major tea-producing region in China.

Index

A

accessories
  brewing baskets, 110
  coasters, 111
  cozies and warmers, 111
  cups, 14–15
  infuser mugs, 109
  measuring spoons and scales, 109
  novelty filters, 111
  strainers, 15, 110
  tea pets, 111–112
  tea tins, 109
  tea trays, 111
  teacups, 105–108
  teapots
    metal, 103–104
    pottery, 100–103
    shape, 105
    size, 104–105
  timers, 109
  water kettles, 14, 109
adenosine, 118, 297
ADHD (attention deficit/hyperactivity disorder), 126
Africa, 193, 216
afternoon tea, 200, 201, 297
aldehydes, 99
alkaloids, 116, 129, 297
already-boiled water, 18
Americas, 193–194, 205
amino acids
  arginine, 165
  defined, 297
  flavor and, 129
  glutamate, 120
  L-theanine, 120–122, 165

anthocyanin, 81
antioxidants, 157. *See also* epigallocatechin-3-gallate
  defined, 297
  polyphenols
    black tea, 144–147
    factors determining levels of, 147
    green tea, 143–144, 146, 148
    overview, 142–143
    tea sediment and, 145
arginine, 165
aroma wheel. *See* tasting wheel
ascorbic acid, 150–151
ashwagandha, 172
Asia
  China, 187–188
  India, 188–189
  Indonesia, 189
  Japan, 189–190
  Nepal, 190
  South Korea, 191
  Sri Lanka, 191
  Taiwan, 191–192
  Turkey, 192
  Vietnam, 192
Asian ginseng, 179
Assam Honey-Glazed Salmon, 232
Assam Old Fashioned, 277
Assam region, 188–189, 297
Assam teas, 10, 46–47
astragalus, 177
astringency, 10, 297
attention deficit/hyperactivity disorder (ADHD), 126

Awesome Assam Tea Syrup, 266
ayurvedic teas, 86–87, 297

B

bai mu dan, 72, 301, 303
baihao yinzhen, 71, 302
bancha, 58, 297
barley tea, 89, 178
basket filter, 21
Benifuki cultivar, 48
benzaldehyde, 98
Biluochun tea, 55–56
bioavailability, 150–151, 171, 297
Bitter Lemon Tincture, 274
bitters
  Bitter Lemon Tincture, 274
  Chai Bitters, 275
  in cocktails, 260
  defined, 297
  Earl Grey Bitters, 276
  tinctures and, 265
black tea
  caffeine, 43
  Ceylon, 10, 47
  Chinese
    gunpowder tea, 43–44
    keemun, 44
    lapsang souchong, 44–45
    Yunnan, 44–45
  choosing, 10
  classic blends
    breakfast teas, 49–50
    Earl Grey, 50
    masala chai, 51
    overview, 48–49

black tea (continued)
  defined, 297
  flavor profiles, 42
  Indian, 10, 35, 46–47, 189
  Japanese, 48
  making, 42
  overview, 41–42
  oxidation, 42
  Sri Lankan, 47
  wild-grown, 48
blackberry leaves, 170, 172
blended teas, 36–37, 297
blooming tea, 80–81
bohea, 45, 204
boiling water, 17
breakfast teas
  defined, 297
  English, 49
  Irish, 50
  overview, 10
  Russian, 50
  Scottish, 50
brew baskets, 110, 298
brewing process
  basket filter, 21
  best water to use, 18
  caffeine and, 124–125
  cups, 14–15
  defined, 297
  iced tea, 22–23
  measuring tea leaves, 16
  rebrewing leaves, 22
  strainers, 15
  sun tea, 22
  tempering the pot, 22
  timing guidelines, 18–20
  visually gauging water
    temperature, 16–17
  water kettles, 14
Bright and Shiny cocktail, 277

Britain
  afternoon tea, 200, 201, 297
  cream tea, 201
  full tea, 201, 300
  high tea, 200
  light tea, 201
  temperance tea parties, 200
bubble tea, 24
butter tea, 202, 298
buying tea, 11–12

C

caffeine
  ADHD and, 126
  benefits of, 118–119
  black tea, 43
  "calm alertness," 8
  cognition and, 163
  CTC tea and, 11
  decaffeinating tea, 133–138
  defined, 116–117, 298
  drawbacks of, 119
  factors determing how much
    per cup, 122–125
  genetics and, 99–100
  green tea, 131
  green teas, 54
  headaches and, 126–127
  herbal teas, 84
  how it works, 117–118
  L-theanine and, 120–122
  matcha, 130
  migraines and, 126–127
  misconceptions and myths
    about, 126–131
  as natural pesticide, 117
  oolong tea, 65
  overview, 115
  polyphenols and, 155
  pu-erh, 130

  Stone Age, 116
  in tea vs. coffee, 121–122
  tea vs. coffee, 293
  washing out, 292
  water temperature and, 125
  white tea, 70, 130
caffeine free, 9, 11, 298. See also
    decaffeinated tea
caffeine-to-theanine ratio,
    123–124
"calm alertness," 8, 122
Camellia sinensis
  CTC tea, 34–35
  defined, 1
  flavoring, 36–38
  flush, 35
  gardens, 27–28
  harvesting, 29–30
  orange pekoe, 33–34
  orthodox tea, 34
  overview, 25
  processing steps, 30–33
  SFTGFOP, 35
  single-estate teas, 36
  sparrow beak, 36
  terroir, 27
  varieties, 26
Camellia sinensis var. assamica,
    26, 122, 188, 298
Camellia sinensis var. sinensis, 26,
    122, 188, 298
Campfire Manhattan, 278
cancer, 158
cape tea, 85–86, 175, 300
carbon dioxide (CO_2)
    decaffeination,
    135–136, 298
carbonated iced tea, 24
cardiovascular disease, 159
Cassia cinnamon, 173
cast iron teapots, 103

catechins, 143–144, 146–148, 298. *See also* epigallocatechin-3-gallate

çaydanlik, 203

ceramic teapots, 101

certifications
  elephant friendly, 211
  fairtrade, 210
  organic, 210
  Rainforest Alliance, 210

Ceylon cinnamon, 173

Ceylon tea, 10, 47, 298

chai, 10, 51, 298, 301

Chai Bitters, 275

Chai Negroni, 278

chamomile, 178, 182

Chanoyu tea ceremony, 199

chasen, 199

chashaku, 199

chawan, 199

chemical exposure, 209

chili pepper, 89

chilled tea, 288

China
  future of tea industry, 216
  living and working conditions/ wages, 208
  overview, 187–188
  tea traditions and ceremonies, 196–197

Chinese black tea
  gunpowder tea, 43–44
  keemun, 44
  lapsang souchong, 44–45
  Yunnan, 44–45

Chinese green tea
  Biluochun, 55–56
  defined, 298
  green teas, 55–57
  gunpowder tea, 56–57
  huangshan maofeng, 57
  jasmine, 57
  lung ching, 57
  overview, 11
  palace needle, 57
  scented teas, 57

Chinese white tea
  pai mu tan, 72
  silver needle, 71

Chinese Yixing earthenware teapots, 101–103

chlorophyll, 58, 145, 298

Choson Dynasty, 200

cinnamon, 173

cistus incanus, 178

citric acid, 150–151

classic black tea blends
  breakfast teas, 49–50
  Earl Grey, 50
  masala chai, 51
  overview, 48–49

Classic of Tea (Lu), 196

climate change, 214–215

clones, 27, 122, 298

CO_2 (carbon dioxide) decaffeination, 135–136, 298

coasters, 111

cocktails
  bitters and, 260
  defined, 298
  extracting process, 260–262
  methodology, 262–263
  overview, 259–260
  recipes
    Assam Old Fashioned, 277
    Bright and Shiny, 277
    Campfire Manhattan, 278
    Chai Negroni, 278
    Earl Grey Champagne Cocktail, 278
    Fancy Gin and Tonic, 279
    Jasmine Bees Knees, 279
    Maple Walnut Whiskey Sour, 280
    Matcha Batida, 279
    Paloma Amarga, 280
    Peaches and Cream Bellini, 280
    Philadelphia Fish House Punch, 281
    Pu-Erh Bloody Mary, 282
    Sencha Margarita, 282
    Tropical Hot Toddy, 283
    White Martini, 283

Coconut Green Tea Rum Infusion, 271

cognition
  caffeine and, 118
  dementia and, 163
  guarana and, 174
  theanine, 120

complex polyphenols, 144, 146, 298. *See also* polyphenols

cooking with tea
  dessert recipes, 243–248
  main recipes, 226–234
  side recipes, 235–242
  snack recipes, 223–225
  spice, 219–220
  tea as dry ingredient, 220–221
  tea as infusion, 221–222

cornflowers, 173

cortisol, 165

COVID-19 pandemic, 210

cozies and warmers, 111

crab eye bubbles, 17

craft projects, 289

cream tea, 201

CTC tea. *See* cut-tear-curl tea

culinary matcha, 61, 298

cultivars, 26, 48, 58, 186, 212, 298

cups, 14–15

Curcuma longa L. plant, 180

curcumin, 180–181

cut-tear-curl (CTC) tea
  caffeine and, 11, 123
  defined, 298
  orthodox tea vs., 34–35
  oxidation and, 145

D

da hong pao, 68

dan cong, 66

dandelion, 178

Darjeeling region, 215–216, 298

Darjeeling Salad Dressing, 239

Darjeeling tea, 35, 46–47, 189

decaffeinated tea
  carbon dioxide decaffeinating method, 135–136
  defined, 299
  organic solvent decaffeinating method, 134–135
  overview, 133
  problems with
    cost, 137–138
    degradation of tea leaves, 136–137
    low demand for, 138
    not completely caffeine-free, 138
  utilizing extracted caffeine, 136
  water decaffeinating method, 135

decoction, 261, 299

dementia, 163

dessert recipes
  Flourless Orange Hazelnut Chocolate Cake, 247
  Fruit Paradise Tea Sabayon with Fresh Fruit, 243–244
  Super Simple Tea-Infused Truffles, 248
  Winter Magic Rooibos Poached Pears with Vanilla Black Tea-Infused Crème Anglaise, 245–246

diabetes, 159

disease prevention
  cancer, 158
  cardiovascular disease, 159
  diabetes, 159
  osteoporosis, 159
  overview, 157–158

distillation, 261, 299

dong ding, 66

dongfang meiren, 66–67

Dongting biluochun, 55–56

doshas, 86–87

dragon well, 57, 299, 301

E

Earl Grey Bitters, 276

Earl Grey Champagne Cocktail, 278

Earl Grey Rice, 235

Earl Grey tea, 10, 50, 299

East Frisian tea, 299

echinacea, 178

EGCG. See epigallocatechin-3-gallate

elderberries, 178

Elderflower White Tea Vodka Infusion, 272

elderly, health benefits of tea for
  cognition and dementia, 163
  life span, 164
  motor function and muscle strength, 163–164
  overview, 162–163

electric kettles, 109

elephant friendly certification, 211, 299

elevation
  Ceylon teas, 47
  high-elevation vs. low-elevation tea, 27
  high-mountain tea, 67

ellagitannins, 145

embellishing tea, 288

English breakfast tea, 15, 49–50

environment, 27, 303

environmental impact of tea, 213–215
  climate change and, 214–215
  overview, 213–214
  repurposing leaves, 214

epigallocatechin-3-gallate (EGCG), 148
  cancer and, 158
  cardiovascular disease and, 159
  defined, 299
  effect on brain activity, 146
  lab analysis, 154
  overview, 143–144

equipment. See accessories

ethyl acetate, 134–135

European tea growing, 192–193

extracting process, 260–262, 299

F

fairtrade, 208, 210, 299

famous teas
  biluochun, 55–56
  dan cong, 66
  defined, 299
  dong ding, 66
  huangshan maofeng, 57
  keemun, 44
  li shan, 67
  lung ching, 57
  silver needle, 71

Fancy Gin and Tonic, 279

fannings, 123, 137, 299

fermented tea
  defined, 299
  pu-erh, 75–77
  yellow tea, 77

filtered water, 18

filters
  brewing baskets, 21, 110
  defined, 299
  novelty, 111
  paper, 111
  strainers, 15
fingerprinting tea, 213, 299
Finum brewing basket, 110
fireweed, 173
first flush, 35, 46, 189, 299
fish eye bubbles, 17
flavanols, 143–144, 146–148, 163
flavonoids, 143–144, 299
flavor
  brewing process and, 287–288
  caffeine and, 129–130
  flavor profiles
    green teas, 54
    oolong tea, 65
    white tea, 70
flavoring tea
  blending, 36–37
  oils and extracts, 37–38
  scented process, 38
Flourless Orange Hazelnut Chocolate Cake, 247
flower herbal teas, 88–89, 299
flowering tea, 80–81
flower-scented teas, 38
flush
  defined, 299
  first flush, 35, 46, 189, 299
  second flush, 35, 46, 189, 302
food-tea pairing. See pairing
Formosa, 191, 299
free radicals, 157, 160–161
frost tea, 78, 299
frozen black tea, 78–79
Fruit Paradise Tea Sabayon with Fresh Fruit, 243–244

fruit tea
  defined, 299
  health benefits, 173–174
  overview, 11, 86
Fujian Province
  da hong pao, 68
  defined, 299
  dong ding, 66
  milk oolong, 80
  pai mu tan, 72
  tieguanyin, 68
  white teas, 71–72
full tea, 201, 300

G

GABA teas, 79
gaiwan, 197, 300
gardens, tea, 27–28
gateway teas, 10
genmaicha, 58, 300
Genmaicha Ramen, 228
Georgian tea, 62, 192–193
Germany
  as major tea purchaser, 198
  traditions and ceremonies, 202–203
  training programs, 92
ginger, 179
ginkgo, 179
ginseng, 179
glass teapots, 101
glycyrrhizin, 175
golden leaves
  defined, 300
  SFTGFOP, 35
goldenrod, 179
gongfu (gongfu cha) tradition, 196, 300
Goryeo Dynasty, 200
Greek mountain (shepherd's tea, ironwort), 174
green snail, 55–56

green tea
  brewing temperature, 18
  caffeine, 54, 131
  Chinese
    Biluochun, 55–56
    gunpowder tea, 56–57
    huangshan maofeng, 57
    jasmine, 57
    lung ching, 57
    palace needle, 57
    scented teas, 57
  defined, 300
  flavor profiles, 54
  Georgian, 62
  Japanese
    bancha, 58
    genmaicha, 58
    gyokuro, 58
    hojicha, 59–60
    kabusecha, 62
    kamairicha, 60
    kukicha, 60
    matcha, 60–62
    matcha genmaicha, 58
    sencha, 62
    tencha, 60–62
  making, 54
  overview, 11, 53
Grey, Charles, 296
Grilled Chicken with Blackberry and Currant Black Tea-Infused Gastrique and Grilled Polenta, 230–231
guangdong, 66
guarana, 84, 174
guayusa, 84
gunpowder tea, 43–44, 56–57, 300
gyokuro, 58

H

hand harvesting, 29
handles, teacup, 107

harvesting tea, 29–30. *See also* flush

headaches, 126–127

health benefits

  antioxidants, 141–148

  disease prevention

    cancer, 158

    cardiovascular disease, 159

    diabetes, 159

    osteoporosis, 159

    overview, 157–158

  for elderly

    cognition and dementia, 163

    life span, 164

    motor function and muscle strength, 163–164

    overview, 162–163

  health claims vs., 149–156

  herbal tea

    ashwagandha, 172

    astragalus, 177

    barley, 178

    blackberry leaves, 172

    chamomile, 178

    cinnamon, 173

    cistus incanus, 178

    cornflowers, 173

    dandelion, 178

    echinacea, 178

    elderberries, 178

    fireweed, 173

    fruit, 173–174

    ginger, 179

    ginkgo, 179

    ginseng, 179

    goldenrod, 179

    Greek mountain, 174

    guarana, 174

    health claims, 168–171

    hibiscus, 174

    honeybush, 175

    Japanese mulberry leaves, 175

    lavender, 179

    lemon balm, 179

    lemongrass, 179–180

    licorice, 175

    mate, 176

    milk thistle, 180

    mint, 180

    moringa, 176

    nettle, 176

    overview, 167

    rooibos, 176

    rose hips, 177

    turmeric, 180–181

    valerian, 180

    wellness teas, 181–182

  immune system, 160

  neurological, 160–161

  overview, 9

  pain management, 161

  social, 164–165

  stress relief, 164–165

  topical treatments, 161

  weight control, 162

health claims

  overview, 149–152

  research

    lab analysis, 154–155

    natural product libraries, 155–156

    observational studies, 153–154

    reliability of, 152–153

    synthetic compound libraries, 155–156

  wellness teas, 181–182

heat retention, teacups, 107

heating water, 16–17. *See also* water temperature

heme iron, 162

herbal tea, 11

  ayurvedic, 86–87

  caffeinated, 84

  defined, 300

  flowers, 88–89

  fruit, 86

  health benefits

    ashwagandha, 172

    astragalus, 177

    barley, 178

    blackberry leaves, 172

    chamomile, 178

    cinnamon, 173

    cistus incanus, 178

    cornflowers, 173

    dandelion, 178

    echinacea, 178

    elderberries, 178

    fireweed, 173

    fruit, 173–174

    ginger, 179

    ginkgo, 179

    ginseng, 179

    goldenrod, 179

    Greek mountain, 174

    guarana, 174

    health claims, 168–171

    hibiscus, 174

    honeybush, 175

    Japanese mulberry leaves, 175

    lavender, 179

    lemon balm, 179

    lemongrass, 179–180

    licorice, 175

    mate, 176

    milk thistle, 180

    mint, 180

    moringa, 176

    nettle, 176

    overview, 167

    rooibos, 176

    rose hips, 177

    turmeric, 180–181

    valerian, 180

    wellness teas, 181–182

herbal blends, 88
honeybush, 85–86
leaves, 89
overview, 83–84
rooibos, 85
seeds, 89
spices, 89
hibiscus, 88, 174
high tea, 200
high-mountain tea, 67, 300
Himalayas
butter tea, 202
Darjeeling, 189
Nepal, 190
hohin (houhin), 101
hojicha (houjicha), 59–60, 300
honeybush, 85–86, 175, 300
huangshan maofeng, 57
Hubei province, 57

I

iced tea
American consumption of,
41, 205
brewing guidelines, 22–23
carbonated, 24
Ilex paraguariensis, 84
immune system, 160
India
Assam, 188–189
Darjeeling, 189
future of tea industry, 215
living and working conditions/
wages, 208
Southern India, 189
traditions and ceremonies, 198
Indian black tea
Assam, 10, 46–47
Darjeeling, 35, 46–47, 189
Indian white teas, 73–74
Indonesia, 189
infuser mugs, 109, 300

infusions. *See also* cooking
with tea
defined, 261, 300
overview, 221–222
syrups
Awesome Assam Tea
Syrup, 266
Jasmine Honey Syrup, 267
overview, 264
Sencha Agave Syrup, 268
TeaHaus Peaches and Cream
Syrup, 269
tea-infused spirits
Campfire Whiskey
Infusion, 270
Coconut Green Tea Rum
Infusion, 271
Elderflower White Tea Vodka
Infusion, 272
overview, 264
tinctures and bitters
Bitter Lemon Tincture, 274
Chai Bitters, 275
Earl Grey Bitters, 276
overview, 265
Strawberry Mint Lavender Ice
Cubes, 273
instant tea, 24
Ireland
Irish breakfast tea, 50
traditions and ceremonies, 203
iron, 162
iron Buddha, 68, 300, 303
iron goddess of mercy, 68,
300, 303
ironwort, 174
isoamyl acetate, 98

J

jade dew, 58
Japan
future of tea industry, 216
living and working conditions/
wages, 208

overview, 189–190
traditions and ceremonies, 199
Japanese black tea, 48, 78–79
Japanese green tea
bancha, 58
defined, 300
genmaicha, 58
gyokuro, 58
hojicha, 59–60
kabusecha, 62
kamairicha, 60
kukicha, 60
matcha, 60–62
matcha genmaicha, 58
old tree bancha, 80
sencha, 62
tencha, 60–62
Japanese mulberry leaves, 175
Jasmine Bees Knees, 279
Jasmine Honey Syrup, 267
jasmine tea, 57, 300
Jian ware cup, 107
Jiao Ran, 196
Joseon Dynasty, 200
jun chiyabari oolong, 67–68

K

kabusecha, 62
kaempferol, 163
kamairicha, 60
kapha tea, 87
Katagi, Takatomo, 78
keemun, 44, 300
kettles, 14, 109
kid-friendly options, 9, 11
Köhler, Hermann, 26
kokumi, 252–253
Korea, 199–200
Koryo Dynasty, 200
kuki hojicha, 58
kukicha, 60, 300
kyusu teapots, 101

L

lab analysis, 154–155
Lamiaceae famiy, 180
lapsang souchong, 44–45, 300
lavender, 179
leaf herbal tea, 89
leaf sets, 15, 300
lemon, 23
lemon balm, 179
lemongrass, 179–180
licorice, 89, 175
life span, 164
light tea, 201
linalool, 45
Lipton, Thomas, 47
liquor, 300. *See also* cocktails
living and working conditions/ wages
  China, 208
  India, 208
  Japan, 208
  on large plantations, 209
  medical care, 209
  small farmers, 209
long jing (lung ching), 57, 299, 301
loose-leaf tea
  amount needed for brewing, 12
  storing, 12
  teabags vs., 10
low tea, 200, 201, 297
L-theanine
  caffeine and, 120–122
  caffeine-to-theanine ratio, 123–124
  defined, 300, 303
  Gyokuro, 58
  stress relief and, 165
Lu Yu, 196

M

main recipes
  Assam Honey-Glazed Salmon, 232
  Genmaicha Ramen, 228
  Grilled Chicken with Blackberry and Currant Black Tea-Infused Gastrique and Grilled Polenta, 230–231
  Mint Green Tea Gazpacho, 229
  Smoky Souchong Ribs with a Sweet and Smoky BBQ Sauce, 226–227
  Tea-Smoked Chicken Wings, 233–234
Malawi antlers, 74
Maple Walnut Whiskey Sour, 280
masala chai, 10, 51, 298, 301
matcha
  caffeine, 130
  defined, 301
  koicha, 61
  stress management and, 165
  tencha and, 60
  usucha, 61
Matcha Batida, 279
matcha genmaicha, 58
mate (maté), 84, 176, 301, 304
measuring spoons and scales, 109
measuring tea leaves, 16
meat tea, 200
mechanical harvesting, 29–30
Medicinal Plants (Köhler), 26
metal storage tins, 12
metal teapots
  cast iron, 103
  samovar, 103
  silver, 104
  stainless steel, 103

methylene chloride, 134
migraines, 126–127
milk and sugar, 23
milk thistle, 180
milky oolong, 80
Ming Dynasty, 108, 197
Mint Green Tea Gazpacho, 229
mint tea, 180, 202
"monkey-picked tea," 68
moringa, 176
Moroccan mint tea, 103, 202, 301
motor function, 163–164
mountain tea, 85–86, 175, 300
mouthfeel, 301
muscle strength, 163–164
myricetin, 163
myths about tea
  bitterness, 294–295
  Brits drink the most tea, 296
  caffeine
    tea vs. coffee, 293
    washing out, 292
  Earl Grey tea, 294
  "expert" tasters, 293
  Green tea, 293–294
  never rinse teapot, 293
  price equals quality, 291–292
  raised pinky, 295–296
  rinsing tea leaves, 292
  tea expires, 295

N

Nagatani Souen, 62
National Yerba Mate Day, 205
natural product libraries, 155–156
Nepal, 190, 215–216
nettle, 176

neurological health benefits, 160–161

Nilgiri frost tea, 78

non-heme iron, 162

novelty filters, 111

O

observational studies, 153–154

ocean green needle, 57

Ocha, 199

oils and extracts, 37–38

old tree bancha tea, 80

Old-School Cheese Ball, 223

oolong tea
  caffeine, 65
  dan cong, 66
  defined, 301
  dong ding, 66
  dongfang meiren, 66–67
  flavor profiles, 65
  high-mountain, 67
  jun chiyabari, 67–68
  making, 64
  origin of name, 65
  overview, 63–64
  taifu, 68
  tieguanyin, 68
  wuyi rock tea, 68

orange pekoe, 33–34, 301

organic certification, 210, 301

organic solvents, decaffeinating tea with, 134–135

oriental beauty, 66–67

orthodox tea, 34, 301

osteoporosis, 159

oxidants, 157, 301

oxidation
  black tea, 42
  defined, 301
  Japanese green teas, 55

oxidative stress, 157–158, 301

P

pai mu tan, 72, 301, 303

pain management, 161

pairing
  choosing menu, 255
  defined, 301
  matching tea with foods, 254–255
  overview, 249–250
  tasting wheel, 250–251
  tongue map, 252–253

palace needle, 57

Paloma Amarga, 280

Paulli, Simon, 202

Peaches and Cream Bellini, 280

pearl strand bubbles, 17

pekoe, 34, 301

peppercorns, 89

pH level, 18

phenols. See polyphenols

Philadelphia Fish House Punch, 281

phoenix, 66

phytochemicals, 117, 141–148, 301. See also polyphenols

pitta tea, 87

plantations, tea
  living and working conditions/ wages on, 209
  South Korea, 191

plucking, 186, 188, 301

polyphenols
  bioavailability, 150–151
  black tea, 144–145, 146–147
  caffeine and, 121–122, 155
  catechins, 143–144, 146–148
  defined, 301
  factors determining levels of, 147
  flavonoids, 143–144
  flavor and, 129

green tea, 143–144, 146, 148
  overview, 142–143
  tea sediment and, 145
  theaflavins, 144, 146
  thearubigins, 144–146, 148

porcelain teapots, 101

porosity, teacup, 106–107

pottery teapots
  ceramics, 101
  Chinese Yixing earthenware, 101–103
  glass, 101
  overview, 100–103
  porcelain, 101
  traditional Japanese pottery, 101

powdered green tea, 61, 302. See also matcha

processing steps, 30–33

propylthiouracil (PROP), 99–100

proteases, 160

psychoactive stimulant, 115, 302. See also caffeine

pu-erh, 75–77, 123, 124, 130, 302

Pu-Erh Bloody Mary, 282

Pu-erh Mushroom Sauce, 236

purity of tea, 211, 302

purple tea, 81, 302

Q

qihong, 44, 300

Qing Dynasty, 56, 64

quality of tea, 212, 303

quercetin, 163

Quick Candied Sweet and Salty "Chai" Nuts, 224

quinine, 99–100

R

Rainforest Alliance certification, 210, 302

raw pu-erh, 75–77

rebrewing leaves, 22

recipes

Bitter Lemon Tincture, 274

Chai Bitters, 275

cocktails

Assam Old Fashioned, 277

Bright and Shiny, 277

Campfire Manhattan, 278

Chai Negroni, 278

Earl Grey Champagne Cocktail, 278

Fancy Gin and Tonic, 279

Jasmine Bees Knees, 279

Maple Walnut Whiskey Sour, 280

Matcha Batida, 279

Paloma Amarga, 280

Peaches and Cream Bellini, 280

Philadelphia Fish House Punch, 281

Pu-Erh Bloody Mary, 282

Sencha Margarita, 282

Tropical Hot Toddy, 283

White Martini, 283

Coconut Green Tea Rum Infusion, 271

dessert

Flourless Orange Hazelnut Chocolate Cake, 247

Fruit Paradise Tea Sabayon with Fresh Fruit, 243–244

Super Simple Tea-Infused Truffles, 248

Winter Magic Rooibos Poached Pears with Vanilla Black Tea-Infused Crème Anglaise, 245–246

Earl Grey Bitters, 276

Elderflower White Tea Vodka Infusion, 272

main dish

Assam Honey-Glazed Salmon, 232

Genmaicha Ramen, 228

Grilled Chicken with Blackberry and Currant Black Tea-Infused Gastrique and Grilled Polenta, 230–231

Mint Green Tea Gazpacho, 229

Smoky Souchong Ribs with a Sweet and Smoky BBQ Sauce, 226–227

Tea-Smoked Chicken Wings, 233–234

side

Darjeeling Salad Dressing, 239

Earl Grey Rice, 235

Pu-erh Mushroom Sauce, 236

Tea-Infused Acorn Squash with Hazelnuts, Brown Butter, and Thyme, 237–238

Tea-Infused Butter, 240–241

Tea-Infused Cream, 242

snack

Old-School Cheese Ball, 223

Quick Candied Sweet and Salty "Chai" Nuts, 224

Sencha Quick Pickles, 225

Strawberry Mint Lavender Ice Cubes, 273

syrups

Awesome Assam Tea Syrup, 266

Jasmine Honey Syrup, 267

Sencha Agave Syrup, 268

TeaHaus Peaches and Cream Syrup, 269

"red tea," 43. See also Chinese black tea

repurposing leaves, 214

research

herbal teas, 169–171

lab analysis, 154–155

natural product libraries, 155–156

observational studies, 153–154

reliability of, 152–153

synthetic compound libraries, 155–156

ripe pu-erh, 75–77

roasted barley tea, 89

rock tea, 68, 302

rooibos, 11, 85, 176, 302

room deodorizer, 289–290

rose hips, 170, 177

Runge, Friedlieb Ferdinand, 116

Russia

breakfast blends, 50

traditions and ceremonies, 204

S

Sado, 199

samovars, 103, 204, 302

Satemwa Tea Estate, 74

scented tea, 38, 57, 302

Scottish breakfast blends, 50

"sealed yellowing," 77

second flush, 35, 46, 189, 302

sediment, 145, 302

seed teas, 89

sencha, 62, 302

Sencha Agave Syrup, 268

Sencha Margarita, 282

Sencha Quick Pickles, 225

SFTGFOP, 35, 302

shading, 58, 123, 302

shepherd's tea, 174

shiboridashi, 101

shopping for tea, 11–12

shrimp eye bubbles, 17

side recipes
  Darjeeling Salad Dressing, 239
  Earl Grey Rice, 235
  Pu-erh Mushroom Sauce, 236
  Tea-Infused Acorn Squash with Hazelnuts, Brown Butter, and Thyme, 237–238
  Tea-Infused Butter, 240–241
  Tea-Infused Cream, 242
silver needle, 71, 302
silver teapots, 104
silymarin, 180
simple polyphenol. *See* polyphenols
single estate (single origin) tea, 36, 302
Smoky Souchong Ribs with a Sweet and Smoky BBQ Sauce, 226–227
snack recipes
  Old-School Cheese Ball, 223
  Quick Candied Sweet and Salty "Chai" Nuts, 224
  Sencha Quick Pickles, 225
social health benefits, 164–165
Solidago spp, 179
solvents, 134–135, 262–263, 302
sommelier, 249–250, 303. *See also* tasting tea
South America, 205
South Indian white tea, 73–74
South Korea, 191
South Pacific, 193
Southern India, 189
sparrow beak, 36, 303
spice, tea as, 219–220, 289
spice finger, 296
spice herbal blends, 89
Sri Lanka, 47, 191, 216
stainless steel teapots, 103
standing water, 18
stem tea, 60, 300

stimulants, 303. *See also* caffeine
stinging nettle, 176
stoneware teacups, 107
stovetop kettles, 109
strainers, 15, 110
Strawberry Mint Lavender Ice Cubes, 273
stress relief, 164–165
strictinin, 145
sun tea, 22
Super Simple Tea-Infused Truffles, 248
Swiss water method, decaffeinating tea, 135
synthetic compound libraries, 155–156
syphilis finger, 296
syrups
  Awesome Assam Tea Syrup, 266
  Jasmine Honey Syrup, 267
  overview, 264
  Sencha Agave Syrup, 268
  TeaHaus Peaches and Cream Syrup, 269

T

Taeryom, Kim, 191
taifu oolong, 68
Taiwan, 67, 191–192
tamaryokucha, 60
Tang Dynasty, 196
tannins, 145
tasting tea
  brewing, 94–95
  describing tea, 96–99
  examining leaf, 94
  genetics and flavor perception, 99–100
  over-the-top descriptions, 93
  overview, 91

  sipping, 95
  smelling leaves and tea, 95
  tea professionals, 92–93
  tongue map, 96
  tasting wheel, 98, 99, 250–251, 303
tea balls, 110
tea bricks, 77
tea industry
  certifications
    elephant friendly, 211
    fairtrade, 210
    organic, 210
    Rainforest Alliance, 210
  chemical exposure, 209
  developing new cultivars, 212
  environmental impact of tea
    climate change and, 214–215
    overview, 213–214
    repurposing leaves, 214
  fingerprinting tea, 213
  future of, 215–216
  impact of COVID-19 pandemic on, 210
  living and working conditions/wages
    China, 208
    India, 208
    Japan, 208
    on large plantations, 209
    medical care, 209
    small farmers, 209
  overview, 207
  purity, 211
  quality, 212
  transporting tea, 213
tea lattes, 24
tea lights, 22
tea master, 93, 303

tea mixology
  cocktails
    extracting process, 260–262
    methodology, 262–263
    overview, 259–260
    recipes, 277–283
  infusions
    syrups, 264, 265–269
    tea-infused spirits, 264,
      270–272
    tinctures and bitters, 265,
      273–276
  overview, 257–258
tea pets, 111–112
tea plant. *See Camellia sinensis*
tea syrups. *See* syrups
tea tins, 109
tea trays, 111
tea warmers, 22
teabags, 10
tea-candle-lit warmers, 111
teacups
  aroma and, 106
  color, 107
  convenience, 107
  gaiwan, 108
  handle, 107
  heat retention, 107
  material, 106
  overview, 105–106
  porosity, 106–107
  sizes, 106
  teacups, 108
  from various countries, 201
TeaHaus Peaches and Cream
  Syrup, 269
Tea-Infused Acorn Squash with
  Hazelnuts, Brown Butter,
  and Thyme, 237–238
Tea-Infused Butter, 240–241
Tea-Infused Cream, 242

tea-infused spirits
  Campfire Whiskey
    Infusion, 270
  Coconut Green Tea Rum
    Infusion, 271
  Elderflower White Tea Vodka
    Infusion, 272
  overview, 264
tea-infused syrups, 24
teapots
  metal
    cast iron, 103
    samovar, 103
    silver, 104
    stainless steel, 103
  pottery
    ceramics, 101
    Chinese Yixing earthenware,
      101–103
    glass, 101
    overview, 100–103
    porcelain, 101
    traditional Japanese
      pottery, 101
  shape, 105
  sizes, 104–105
tea-producing regions
  Africa, 193
  Americas, 193–194
  Asia
    China, 187–188
    India, 188–189
    Indonesia, 189
    Japan, 189–190
    Nepal, 190
    South Korea, 191
    Sri Lanka, 191
    Taiwan, 191–192
    Turkey, 192
    Vietnam, 192
  Europe, 192–193

  overview, 185–187
  South Pacific, 193
  Tea-Smoked Chicken Wings,
    233–234
temperance tea parties, 200
tempering the pot, 22
tencha, 60–62
terroir, 27, 303
tetsubin, 103
theaflavins, 144, 146, 303
theanine. *See* L-theanine
thearubigins, 144–146,
  148, 303
ti kuan yin, 68, 300, 303
tieguanyin, 68, 300, 303
timers, 109
timing guidelines, 18–20
tinctures
  defined, 261, 303
  overview, 265
  Strawberry Mint Lavender Ice
    Cubes, 273
tippy, 35, 303
tisane, 261. *See also* herbal tea
Tixing teapot, 101–103
Tocklai Tea Research
  Institute, 215
tongue map, 96, 252–253
topical treatments, 161
traditions and ceremonies
  Britain, 200–201
  China
    gaiwan, 197
    gongfu tradition, 196
    tea ceremony, 196
  Germany, 202–203
  Himalayas, 202
  India, 198
  Ireland, 203
  Japan, 199
  Korea, 199–200

Morocco, 202
overview, 195–196
Russia, 204
South America, 205
Turkey, 203–204
United States, 204–205
transporting tea, 213
trimethylxanthine, 116–117.
　　See also caffeine
Tropical Hot Toddy, 283
tung ting, 66
Turkish tea, 192, 198,
　　203–204, 303
turmeric, 180–181
twig tea, 60, 300

U
umami, 253, 303
United States, 204–205

V
valerian, 180
vata dosha, 87
vegetal flavor, 54, 303
Vietnam, 192
vitamin C, 150–151
volatiles, 129, 303

W
"washing out" caffeine, 128
water

already-boiled, 18
boiling, 17
dissolved oxygen in, 18
dissolved solids in, 18
filtered, 18
standing, 18
water kettles, 14, 109
water method, decaffeinating
　　tea, 135
water temperature
boiling, 17
brewing guide, 20
caffeine and, 125
crab eyes, 17
fish eyes, 17
gauging visually, 16–17
green tea, 18, 58, 65
pearl strands, 17
shrimp eyes, 17
white tea, 18, 70, 130
weight control, 162
wellness teas, 181–182
White Martini, 283
white peony, 72, 301, 303
white tea
brewing temperature, 18
caffeine, 70, 130
Chinese
　　pai mu tan, 72
　　silver needle, 71
defined, 303
flavor profiles, 70

Indian, 73–74
making, 69–70
Malawi antlers, 74
overview, 69
water temperature and,
　　130
wild-grown tea, 48, 304
wilting, 42, 64
winter cherry tea, 172
Winter Magic Rooibos Poached
　　Pears with Vanilla Black
　　Tea-Infused Crème
　　Anglaise, 245–246
withering, 42, 64, 304
wulong tea. *See* oolong tea
wuyi rock tea, 68

Y
Yellow Mountain fur peak, 57
yellow tea, 77, 304
yerba mate, 84, 176,
　　301, 304
Yunnan Province, 45,
　　75, 304
Yunnan tea, 44–45, 304

Z
Zhejiang Province, 57
Zhu Quan, 38

About the Authors

Lisa McDonald spent her youth drinking a cup of tea here and there with her Welsh grandma but never "got into it" until after college when a backpacking trip to Europe became a fifteen-year stay in Germany and Sweden. She began teaching at the University of Tübingen and at the Deutsch-Amerikanisches Institut. After a couple of years, she began doing consulting work in the field of intercultural communications and started her own business. Because she had to travel so often, she made it a point to visit all the local tea shops that she could. And because Germany is one of the largest tea-purchasing countries and was where most of her work was done, there were a lot of tea shops to visit. Tea quickly went from a drink to an obsession.

Lisa was lucky to be hired to help design a tea sommelier-training program for a German company that wanted a more international base. She ended up being trained in tea while helping design a more accessible course. She was awarded the title European Tea Sommelier. After meeting her husband, a Ukrainian American engineer from Ann Arbor, Michigan, in Germany, the two got married and moved to Sweden. She continued her consulting work, traveling and tasting teas wherever she went. She was asked by several tea stores and large tea companies to run tea trainings as well as help with intercultural issues that would often arrive when groups/companies from more than one country tried to work together.

After a few years in Sweden where she gave birth to their first son, it was time to head back to the United States. After only a few months, Lisa decided to jump back into tea and open her own shop in Ann Arbor, Michigan. In December 2007, she gave birth to her second son, and later that week, she opened TeaHaus with more than 200 loose-leaf teas, tea merchandise, and gifts and a specific focus on education (TeaHaus.com). Since the opening, TeaHaus has expanded into a cafe/restaurant where almost everything on the menu is made with tea as an ingredient. In 2017, Lisa launched a sister business called Eat More Tea, which focuses on using tea as an ingredient, offering tea-based cooking spice blends, candies, gelato, and more.

In 2022, TeaHaus expanded again to offer a full bar menu with tea-infused cocktails, partnering with small breweries and distilleries to make tea-infused beer and spirits. Her tea bar and lounge has become an important part of Ann Arbor, providing a community meet-up space as well as a great place to learn, shop, and enjoy. Heavily invested in the community, Lisa supplies weekly free meals at the local shelter kitchen; spearheads and participates in community events; and donates her time, knowledge, and tea.

Lisa continues to consult for tea shops, tea companies, and even government agencies in tea-growing regions. Education remains the focus of her tea obsession. Lisa's husband, Marc, and two boys, Tim and Andrew, have come to enjoy tea and know that "I'm almost done" means a couple more hours.

Jill **Rheinheimer** is a lifelong tea drinker who became totally enmeshed in the intricacies of tea when she joined the TeaHaus family, where she draws on her deep background in scientific research and written communication to make tea-related research and history accessible to a general audience.

She began her career in cell biology labs, which immersed her in the research world that included scientific experiments, electron microscopy, photography, and writing. She then moved into archaeology and anthropology as editor and publisher of scholarly monographs. In this one-person role, she brought book manuscripts through the editing, design, typesetting, publishing, and marketing process, doing research, website development, photo editing, and more along the way. Throughout her life, Jill has simultaneously both volunteered and freelanced as editor, writer, researcher, photo editor, and book designer. Besides co-authoring scientific journal articles, she has written for *World Tea News*.

Jill brings a love for research and photography, attention to detail, and deep appreciation for the world of tea to her research-based blog, It's More Than Tea (ItsMoreThanTea.wordpress.com) and to her work at TeaHaus in Ann Arbor, Michigan. Like Lisa, Jill focuses on education, believing that insight into the vibrant world of tea can enrich a person's personal tea journey while heightening awareness of the tea industry and its challenges, including recognition of the many people who make our favorite brew possible.

Jill lives in Ann Arbor with her husband, Terry, who cheerfully supports the family tea obsession, and tea-loving daughter Alissa. Her mother, who lives nearby, always has the kettle on. Tea aficionado-daughter Kristin and her husband, Andrew (who recently discovered that he actually likes iron goddess oolong), introduced their first daughter to tea at an early age. Adorable two-year-old Maya is currently an avid fan of both smooth strawberry dream, a honeybush blend, and her newborn sister, Kaylee. The family's frequent get-togethers are accompanied by lengthy deliberations over tea, teapot, and teacup choice.

Contributing author **Phil Attee** generously wrote the Tea Mixology chapter and collaborated with Lisa to develop tea cocktail recipes for both this book and for the TeaHaus Tea Bar and Lounge.

With a professional background working in biology and chemistry labs, Phil chose to pursue a career with a little more spirit. . . . literally. He trained for several years in the art and science of distillation and cocktail making. He is currently the national sales manager and blending consultant for Mammoth Distilling in northern Michigan. His newest project, The Formulary, is a bitters and herbal liqueur company that features a handful of spirits infused with various teas. Phil currently resides on a small farm in rural southern Michigan with his lovely wife, Mallory, and their menagerie of plants and animals.

Dedication

To our families — both at home and in the Haus — and to tea drinkers everywhere.

Authors' Acknowledgments

First and foremost, we want to thank our families for not getting frustrated when we were only half listening so we could "get this chapter done."

Thank you to our amazing customers and staff, both past and present (you know who you are); to our friends, who continually encouraged us, reminded us of what parts they would most like to see in this book, and kept us sane; and to Chief! Many thanks also to Ty for agreeing to read along; to our in-home barista, Marc, who made us the best coffees (shhhhhh) while we wrote on the patio; and to Acar, for yelling at us and getting us on track. Also, thank you to Peter and the rest of the Bilakos family, the best landlords *ever!* We miss you, Olga.

A very special thanks to Phil Attee for his contribution to this book. His knowledge of chemistry, blending, and mixing is beyond amazing. Talking — and tasting — tea, booze, and food with Phil is always a great adventure! A shout-out to Natalie Marble for sharing some great recipes. She is one of the best chefs we know — and is an even more amazing person. Thanks also to Ren and Taka in Japan for letting us share their photos. (We can't wait to visit you and your gardens again someday.)

A special thank you to Jennifer Yee for seeking us out and giving us this opportunity, and to the Wiley team for bringing this project to fruition.

Publisher's Acknowledgments

Senior Acquisitions Editor: Jennifer Yee
Development Editor: Linda Brandon
Copy Editor: Kelly D. Henthorne

Production Editor: Tamilmani Varadharaj
Cover Image: © dream79/Adobe Stock Photos